# A BOWL FOR A COIN

# A BOWL FOR A COIN

## *A Commodity History of Japanese Tea*

William Wayne Farris

University of Hawai'i Press
HONOLULU

Paperback edition 2021

Printed in the United States of America

26 25 24 23 22 21 6 5 4 3 2 1

Library of Congress Cataloging-in-Publication Data

Names: Farris, William Wayne, author.
Title: A bowl for a coin: a commodity history of Japanese tea / William Wayne Farris.
Description: Honolulu: University of Hawai'i Press, [2019] | Includes bibliographical references and index.
Identifiers: LCCN 2018040370 | ISBN 9780824876609 (cloth; alk. paper)
Subjects: LCSH: Tea—Japan—History. | Tea trade—Japan—History.
Classification: LCC HD9198.J32 F37 2019 | DDC 338.1/73720952—dc23
LC record available at https://lccn.loc.gov/2018040370

ISBN 978-0-8248-8991-3 (pbk.)

University of Hawai'i Press books are printed on acid-free paper and meet the guidelines for permanence and durability of the Council on Library Resources.

Cover art: Tea peddlers around 1400. Source: "A Bowl for a Coin (ippuku issen)," Shichijūichi ban shokunin utaawase emaki (artist unknown). TNM Image Archives.

*To my beloved brother Al, his wife Sarah, and their family*

# Contents

*Acknowledgments* ix

Introduction
1

CHAPTER ONE
The Prehistory of Japan's Tea Industry, 750–1300
7

CHAPTER TWO
Tea Becomes a Beverage for a Wider Market, 1300–1600
34

CHAPTER THREE
Tea Triumphs during the Edo Period, 1600–1868
73

CHAPTER FOUR
Modern Tea: From Triumph to Uncertainty
125

**Conclusion**
167

*Notes* 177

*List of Characters* 203

*Bibliography* 209

*Index* 219

# Acknowledgments

I would like to thank the Japan–US Educational/Fulbright Commission for funding a nine-month research stay in Tokyo and Kyoto during 2010–2011. I am especially grateful to Hongō Kazuto for serving as my adviser at the Historiographical Institute of Tokyo University. Satō Yūki, a PhD candidate from Tokyo University, served as my tutor as we read the difficult tea documents of the medieval and early modern periods. Special thanks go to Hashimoto Motoko for guiding me on a tour of Yoshida tea farm/factory/shop in Uji. I would also like to express my gratitude to Iwama Machiko, Nagai Susumu, Kodomari Shigehiro, Oka Atsushi, Nonaka Yasushi, Abe Kiyoko, Kimura Shigemitsu, Nakane Fukuji, Sakamoto Hiroshi, Murai Shōsuke, Takahashi Tadahiko, Tsutsui Kōichi, Sawamura Shin'ichi, Nakamura Shūya, Tajima Isao, and Fujii Jōji for help in various aspects of my work.

In 2014, the History Department and the College of Humanities at the University of Hawai'i at Mānoa and the Northeast Asia Committee of the Association for Asian Studies funded me for a two-month research period at the Research Center for the Study of Japanese Culture (*Nichibunken*) outside of Kyoto. Thanks also go to Kiki Leinch for arranging a visit to the Uji tea company Marukyū Koyamaen during that summer of 2014. Harald Fuess, then of Heidelberg University, gave me some helpful pointers on commodity history.

I would like to admit the great debts I owe to Eric Rath of the University of Kansas and Rebecca Corbett, then a postdoctoral fellow at Stanford University, for the advice and references that they gave me for this study of tea during the Edo and modern periods of Japanese history. I would also like to thank Peter Hoffenberg of the University of Hawai'i at Mānoa for discussing endlessly various aspects of modern economic history and major league baseball.

I am also grateful to two anonymous readers for their trenchant comments on the manuscript and to my editor, Stephanie Chun at the University of Hawai'i Press, for her guidance.

My deepest gratitude goes to my wife, Carol Brewer, who has supported my research and writing in ways too numerous to list. She has been a constant companion and good conversationalist, while coming up with questions that never cease to bedevil me.

This book is dedicated to my brother Al and his family for everything that they have done to see the Farris family through some difficult times.

Any mistakes, of course, are the responsibility of the author.

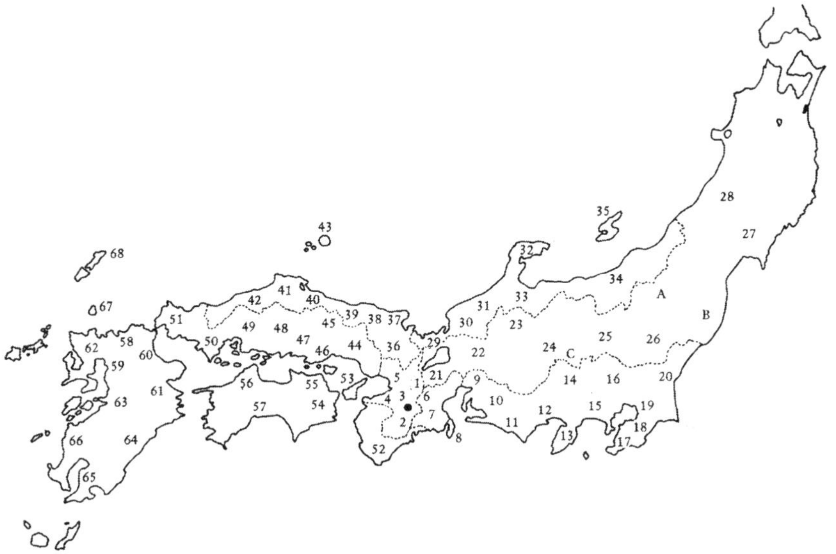


*Map 1.* Provinces and circuits of traditional Japan. From William Wayne Farris, *Population, Disease, and Land in Early Japan, 645–900* (Cambridge, MA: Harvard University, Council on East Asian Studies, 1985), pp. xvii–xix.

*Key:*

**Kinai**
1. Yamashiro
2. Yamato
3. Kawachi
4. Izumi
5. Settsu

**Tōkaidō**
6. Iga
7. Ise
8. Shima
9. Owari
10. Mikawa
11. Tōtōmi
12. Suruga
13. Izu
14. Kai
15. Sagami
16. Musashi
17. Awa
18. Kazusa
19. Shimōsa
20. Hitachi

**Tōsandō**
21. Ōmi
22. Mino
23. Hida
24. Shinano
25. Kōzuke
26. Shimotsuke
27. Mutsu
28. Dewa

**Hokurikudō**
29. Wakasa
30. Echizen
31. Kaga
32. Noto
33. Etchū
34. Echigo
35. Sado

**San'indō**
36. Tanba
37. Tango
38. Tajima
39. Inaba
40. Hōki
41. Izumo
42. Iwami
43. Oki

**San'yōdō**
44. Harima
45. Mimasaka
46. Bizen
47. Bitchū
48. Bingo
49. Aki
50. Suō
51. Nagato

**Nankaidō**
52. Kii
53. Awaji
54. Awa
55. Sanuki
56. Iyo
57. Tosa

**Saikaidō**
58. Chikuzen
59. Chikugo
60. Buzen
61. Bungo
62. Hizen
63. Higo
64. Hyūga
65. Ōsumi
66. Satsuma

**Islands**
67. Iki
68. Tsushima

A. Iwashiro
B. Iwaki
C. Suwa

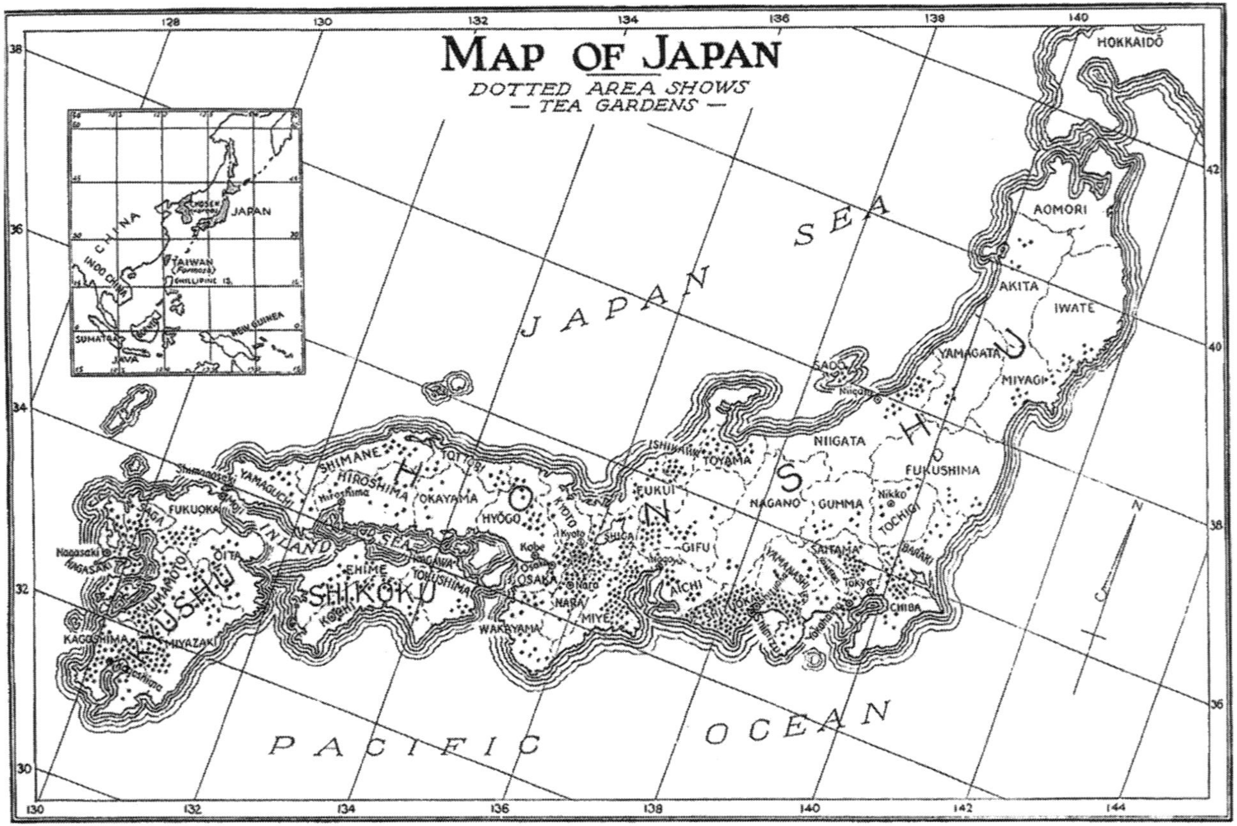


*Map 2.* Prefectures of modern Japan. From *Nihon cha bunka taizen*, in William Ukers, *All about Tea* (Tokyo: Chisen shokan, 2006), p. 41.

# A BOWL FOR A COIN

# Introduction

In September 2010, I was preparing to order a meal at a restaurant called The Gold of Africa in downtown Cape Town, South Africa. The waitress was dressed in appropriately African garb, and the menu listed specialties from Morocco, Kenya, and Egypt as well as South Africa. As I glanced at the drinks list, however, a most unexpected item caught my eye—Japanese green tea. About six months later, I was in St. Louis, Missouri, to care for my ageing parents. My brother, who had just rescued me from Lambert Airfield, took me for brunch to a greasy spoon called Goody Goody, known for serving the best omelets and hash browns in the area. Once again, while reviewing the beverage menu, I was surprised to find Japanese green tea listed.

It seemed astounding to me that these two restaurants, separated by thousands of miles and a greater cultural divide, had arrived at the decision to serve a drink from a country at least as far away as The Gold of Africa and Goody Goody were from each other. The worldwide appeal and availability of Japanese green tea were clearly evident, but I began to wonder what had made that possible. How had the Japanese come to produce, distribute, and consume tea, and why?

To be sure, historians have authored many excellent and insightful books on the Japanese tea ceremony (called *chanoyu* or *sadō*) and related arts.[1] Typically, these studies begin with a general discussion of the early history of tea during the Heian (794–1185) and Kamakura (1185–1333) periods and then shift into a conventional chronology that follows the development of *chanoyu* during the fifteenth and sixteenth centuries. Often these books either conclude the narrative at that point or touch only briefly on the tea ceremony in later centuries.[2] These works have blazed a wide trail for those interested in the ritualized practice of tea in Japan, but they left me as a social and economic historian with more questions than answers.

If tea had been around in Japan for more than a thousand years, then somebody must have pursued the farming of it. By what methods was tea first grown in Japan? What important changes occurred in the methods of cultivation as farmers learned more about the plant? What were the lives of tea cultivators like? Considerations of farming techniques and development are vital for a full comprehension of the origins and eventual popularity of Japanese green tea.

As I quickly discovered, there is much more to producing a bowl of tea than merely growing the plant. Concerning the processes by which the plucked leaves were converted into a palatable drink, I first asked: What were the forms of tea consumed during ancient times? When and why did powdered tea (*matcha*) become a type of tea imbibed in Japan? I soon found out that, historically, innumerable varieties of tea had been prepared in the archipelago, and they easily eclipsed *matcha* in both quantity and popularity.

Cultivating the plant and processing its leaves may yield a bowl of tea, but it does not guarantee that consumers' thirsts will be quenched. So I investigated the ways in which tea was exchanged and marketed as a commodity throughout Japanese history. For the Buddhist monks and aristocrats who were the first eager consumers of Japanese tea, usually as a medicine, the commodity first had to change hands from producers to drinkers. In what form did this exchange take place: as gifts, taxation, trade, or some combination of all three? When and how were the first brand names for tea created? What were the lives of tea merchants like? Japanese tea was shipped abroad to Europe from a surprisingly early date, and the modern export trade transformed production and consumption in the archipelago.

Finally and more broadly, I wanted to know how tea made its imprint on Japanese civilization. Although one would never know it today, tea is not native to the Japanese islands. What important ritual, political, and medicinal functions did it serve? How have these functions changed over the centuries? The custom of tea drinking has affected and been represented in Japanese literature and the arts beginning with the first poetry and scroll paintings. From art forms as diverse as prints, plays, advertisements, and Edo-period verse to the radio, newspaper, and television commercials of the modern era—all have featured tea. Examining the cultural meanings of tea in Japan rounds out the picture of this beverage.

Historians interested in the full story of modern Japanese green tea should therefore recognize the need to address these four interrelated aspects—the farming, processing, distribution, and various social and cultural functions of tea—because they supply the broader context within which *chanoyu* was created. Teasing out and describing these threads over nearly thirteen hundred years reveals a far more significant role played by the beverage in Japan's economy, society, politics, and culture than heretofore recognized. Despite its origins as a cultural item from Tang China enjoyed by only a handful of people, Japanese tea spread gradually but surely to become an important part of the historical record. Several centuries later, by the early 1400s, many commoners were enjoying tea, cultivation was more intensive, the market came to the fore as a means of exchanging the beverage, and most notably, the tea plant originally imported from China lost its exotic appeal and became nativized to Japan. City folk would have been familiar with the cries of street tea peddlers. "A bowl for a coin (*ippuku issen*)!" they would shout, hoping to entice potential customers to try their particular concoctions. Tea went on to become a daily fact of life for all the inhabitants of the archipelago. For this reason, it serves as a lens through which to view the development of Japanese society over the ages.

A history of Japanese tea may encompass many local points of production and chronology, but it also highlights at least three historical themes with more universal application. First, I have already mentioned that tea was served early on as a medicine. By the Tokugawa period (1600–1868), the beverage was being drunk by much of the population. Did the widespread consumption of tea, the preparation of which included boiling water, have effects on the health and longevity of the archipelago's population? Did it also stimulate people to work harder in an ongoing "industrious revolution"? Tea may have played a central but little noted role in Japan's economic and social transformation from a land of peasants to one of office and factory workers in the nineteenth and twentieth centuries.[3]

The second and third themes are interrelated and concern the economic development of modern society since the Industrial Revolution, circa 1750. During the 1950s and 1960s economists wondered why certain regions of the globe industrialized while most did not. It seemed like a simple problem of money and technology, so economically advanced countries spent large sums of money trying to force-feed industrialization upon so-called backward countries. Unsurprisingly, these attempts failed. In recent decades, economic historians have realized that the process of industrialization is much more complex than simply parachuting in advanced technologies. At the very least, there are two crucial prerequisites: (1) the development of a productive agriculture that yields a surplus; and

(2) the creation of classes of people with extra cash to spend on commodities in an evolving consumer society. Of course today, as humans face a looming environmental crisis, citizens may not necessarily view these twin accoutrements of modern society as unalloyed "goods," but they are undeniable factors in the evolution of the contemporary world nonetheless.

The history of tea in Japan speaks to issues of agricultural development and the rise of consumer society for what is often called a "late developer" but looks increasingly like an early one. First, the history of tea cultivation serves as an example of how Japanese farming intensified and matured over the centuries. It is no accident that by 1850 tea production was so sophisticated that it could help to bankroll Japan's industrialization. Second, as many have noted, tea is a commodity with a mildly addictive property. An examination of the growth of demand for the beverage over thirteen hundred years reveals important points about how peasants became consumers and their numbers multiplied until they embraced all of Japanese society.[4]

The overwhelming preponderance of tea currently produced in Japan is "steeped" tea (*sencha*) for home consumption.[5] Japanese continue to drink green tea for its good taste and as part of their highly varied contemporary diet. As modern consumers outside Japan have learned to enjoy Japanese foods and become obsessed with health concerns, Japanese green tea has come to enjoy a niche market and a worldwide reputation for good taste and purported effectiveness in fighting cancer, heart disease, diabetes, and Alzheimer's.[6] It is a tribute to the modern Japanese green-tea industry that its product saturates the domestic market and reaches places as diverse as Cape Town and St. Louis.

Today in Japan, green tea is so common that restaurant patrons are almost never charged for repeated servings. It is served at birth, marriage, and death ceremonies. People of all social classes enjoy the beverage, although not always in the same way. It carries medicinal, ritualistic, religious, economic, social, and political meanings. The history of green tea takes the reader to the heart of Japanese society and culture and underscores themes that appear again and again in the Japanese and global past.

Tea, or *Camellia sinensis,* is a dark-green shrub with leaves of an elliptical shape. Shoots are soft, while older leaves are leathery and may be serrated. The tea plant has white flowers about an inch in diameter with five to seven white petals and containing stamens and a pistil that allow the plant to reproduce freely in the proper climate and soil conditions. The shrub may grow as high as forty-five feet but is usually much shorter. The tea plant is native to southwest China and/or northeast India, where the climate is subtropical with lush vegetation. There mists fill the air and rainfall is plentiful.

Successful cultivation of the tea plant requires three environmental conditions: relative warmth, plentiful rainfall, and the right kind of soil.[7] The ideal temperature for growing tea ranges from thirteen to seventeen degrees centigrade and should never fall below minus ten. The tea plant needs lots of rain—more than 15,000 millimeters per year. Soil should be relatively fertile and porous; good drainage is necessary and heavy clay soils will not do. For much of its history the plant was grown on mountain soils in Japan.

Traditionally, the propagation of the tea plant begins with the appearance of the blossom in November. It is important to note that the cultivar is not self-pollinating, that is, the stamen and pistil of the same plant cannot reproduce. With the help of bees, butterflies, and birds, the flowers will yield hard, full seed packets within a year. Normally, human intervention is necessary for the maximum number of tea plants to reproduce, but under the right conditions some tea shrubs may make seed packets on their own. Whether sprouted from seeds or cuttings, as is the case today, tea bushes never yield a harvest right away. Typically, it takes about seven years for a new bush to make an average crop.

There are about as many ways to prepare and drink tea as one can imagine. It has been made into blocks, ground, steeped, and combined with rice, butter, yogurt, jam, and many other foods. Black teas commonly consumed in Europe and the United States differ from Japanese green tea only in their mode of preparation, being oxygenated to reduce the bitter taste. This processing permits manufacturers to produce their black teas on large plantations and in factories on a scale unimaginable for Japanese green tea.

Tea is different from most other beverages in that it naturally contains caffeine and catechins. Caffeine stimulates the nervous system, inhibiting sleep and rejuvenating a tired body. It strengthens the heart, encourages blood circulation through frequent urination, and makes the body's metabolism more efficient. According to the Mayo Clinic, coffee contains anywhere from 95 to 200 mg of caffeine per eight-ounce serving. By comparison, tea has less: black tea has 14 to 61 mg in the same serving, while green tea holds 24 to 40 mg, again in an eight-ounce serving. It takes about 100 mg of caffeine a day to lead to addiction, so while coffee drinkers frequently become psychologically addicted to their beverage, such a state is rarer with tea. That is not to say that repeated servings of strong tea may not lead to addictive behavior, and perhaps even hallucinations.

The antioxidant tannin in tea has been proven to strengthen the body's immune system and fight off bacteria and viruses. Habituation to tea's caffeine, however, was likely the initial reason for the popularity of the beverage. How the residents of the islands became such avid consumers of green tea is a story that begins near the dawn of Japanese civilization.

CHAPTER ONE

# The Prehistory of Japan's Tea Industry, 750–1300

When tea was introduced for the first time to Japan around 750, a tiny aristocracy ruled over about 6.5 million inhabitants. Buddhism was becoming increasingly predominant as a belief system within this tiny elite, and to explain and implement Buddhist rituals the court ordained monks and nuns. Compared to these political and religious elites, however, the great mass of the population lived a hard life and existed from hand to mouth. Japanese society resembled a rigid pyramid with a small, pointed tip where the elites enjoyed lives of great opulence while most barely survived.

The nature of Japanese society profoundly affected the way in which tea was received and propagated in the islands. Since most commoners had to struggle to survive, they did not take cultivation of the less than nourishing product too seriously nor was it very widespread. Cultivators might farm tea for a while and then abandon cultivation for another more stable and promising life. When it came to processing the leaves, the kinds of tea available were few in number and the beverage itself looked and tasted nothing at all like Japanese green tea does today. Again, because the number of consumers was severely limited, they usually knew each other and exchanged tea leaves almost exclusively as a gift. There was no need for a market. Finally, in a time when life expectancy even for the elite did not exceed thirty, the primary function of tea was as a medicine to cure ailments of various types. Aristocrats and the clergy seized upon this function and devised rituals stressing the beverage's supposed health effects. They wrote tracts and poetry about drinking tea. By 1300, the size of the tea-drinking elite had expanded somewhat, but these essential characteristics remained the same. Indeed, tea retained its role in gift giving and as a medicine into the present.

## THE ORIGINS OF TEA IN JAPAN

As noted in the introduction, southwestern China was likely one region where tea flourished. It remained a product primarily of south China during the Latter Han and Northern and Southern Dynasties (25–589 CE), where it was popular with Daoists and reclusive poets, among others.[1] By the 700s, however, it had grown in popularity to encompass north China, too. The scholar Lu Yu (733–803) composed *The Classic of Tea* (*Chajing*) around 760 and described a society that had gone mad for the beverage. Even prior to Lu Yu, "tea had become an integral part in the lives of Buddhist monks," who cultivated, drank, and offered tea to visitors and the imperial court.[2] By the 760s, migrants headed for south China to work in a flourishing tea industry. As Victor Mair and Ehrling Hoh have written, "the drink spread to every nook of the land and stratum of society."[3]

Both Korea, where the Kingdom of Silla held sway, and the Japanese court, where Sinophilic leaders such as Fujiwara no Nakamaro (706–764) dominated politics, looked to China for the latest in elite culture. More important, Buddhist monks traveled regularly to China and were familiar with customs there. Each court sent embassies to China to pay tribute items and receive courtly accoutrements frequently during the 700s. The elites of both Silla and Japan could easily have known of the Chinese addiction to tea and fallen prey to the same habit at this time. And yet Japanese wooden tablets and paper documents listing the Chinese character (*t'u*) that may mean tea measure the herb in units that cannot possibly have been utilized for the plant or beverage.[4]

Recently, though, biology and archaeology have provided the most convincing evidence to date that visitors carried tea to Japan earlier than previously thought. Japanese and Chinese molecular biologists have examined tea specimens throughout East Asia and have found that all tea in Japan originated in south China and came in waves as the archipelago's most famous invasive species. The first and most venerable comprised a tea strain with a long pistil that entered both Korea and Japan from south China at about the same time, probably several decades prior to 800. For those with knowledge of the close relationship between the peoples and cultures of the ancient Korean peninsula and Japanese islands, this revelation should come as no surprise.[5] Korean elite tea culture possibly dates back as early as the late seventh century.[6]

Archaeologists in Japan have uncovered additional valuable evidence.[7] Shards of light-green porcelain vessels, many of them tea bowls, have come to light from the foundation of Sūfukuji, the temple where an early ninth-century sovereign is known to have imbibed his tea, as well as the Yamashiro provincial headquarters. More important, archaeologists have found them at Kōfukuji, the famous temple at the Chinese-style capital Nara, dating to the late Nara period (710–794). A site thought to be a detached palace or temple has revealed these treasures for the 730s or 740s. *The Ordinances of Engi* also refer to tea bowls manufactured in Owari Province, one of the production centers where shards have been recovered.[8] The Chinese Yue ware that served as the model for these tea bowls has come to light at numerous sites throughout Japan for the eighth century. To be sure, tea bowls may be used for many purposes, but the most reasonable hypothesis is that Buddhist monks and court aristocrats in Japan were familiar with tea drinking during its heyday in China in the mid-eighth century.

Scholars will probably never know just who was responsible for the introduction of tea to Japan. One expert has surmised that two little-known monks who spent the years from 750 through 778 in Tang China may have been the first to carry tea seeds from China to Nara.[9] They lived at Daianji in Nara; a list of the possessions from that temple shows items that could have been used for tea drinking. Moreover, Daianji was a center of East Asian culture, with many Tang monks residing there including disciples of the famed Chinese cleric Jianzhen (Ganjin, 688–763). Dōji (?–740), another Daianji priest, wrote odes referring to "fragrant water." Monks at this temple may well have been the first to grow the tea plant in Japan, given that cultivation of *Camellia sinensis* in Nara prefecture is probably the oldest in the entire archipelago.[10] Yet court annalists tell a tale of more heroic origins.

## TEA DURING THE NINTH CENTURY: CULTIVATION AND MODES OF EXCHANGE

In the first verifiable written records, tea seemingly makes a dramatic appearance in Japan.[11] Texts link the introduction of tea to two of the most famous men in Japanese history: the Buddhist monks Saichō (767–822) and Kūkai (774–835). To elaborate, it is generally known that each cleric was the founder of a famous school of esoteric Buddhism, Tendai and Shingon, respectively. These sects offered great solace to wealthy Japanese aristocrats in search of the ritual trappings of salvation. To learn about these sects, each cleric went to Tang China in 804; Saichō returned in 805/6, then

Kūkai in 806/10. At the party for Saichō's departure, there was a reference to "drinking tea"; eight years after sailing back to Japan, Kūkai wrote in 814 that he was "learning Indian writing while sitting and drinking tea." Both men had frequent experiences drinking the habit-forming herb while in China and are presumed to have carried tea seeds back to Japan with them.

As if to prove this point, in 815, Saichō sent ten "pounds" (*kin*, about 600 grams) of tea to the monk Taihan, a Kūkai disciple. That year was an important one for tea in Japan. The beverage was apparently quite popular at the court of the current "Heavenly Sovereign" (or emperor) Saga, as there are repeated allusions to tea in Japanese poetry of the time. In that same year, Saga went to Sūfukuji over the mountains from Heian, and the monk Yōchū, who had himself spent thirty years in Tang China, demonstrated his prowess by boiling up some tea leaves for the enjoyment of the weary travelers. Within two months, Saga had ordered eight provinces in or near the Kinai (the Kyoto-Osaka-Nara region), including Yamato and Yamashiro where the capitals Nara and Heian stood, to plant tea and present it as a tribute-tax item. The narrative thus gains the stamp of imperial approval.

There are, however, problems with attributing the origins of tea to these two men. First, all of those traditions date from long after the early 800s, as late as the sixteenth century. Second, neither Saichō nor Kūkai returned to Japan in a season appropriate for the planting of tea. Third, unless the men brought back with them plentiful amounts of seed, they could never have produced enough tea by 815 to quench the thirsts of Saga and his court. Knowledge of the plant's reproductive processes cast substantial doubt on the conventional tale of tea's origins.

Rather than attributing the beginnings of tea in Japan to either of these two clerics, it makes more sense to posit that the cultivar was already being grown and consumed in the islands by the early 800s. In other words, the insight that tea cultivation in Japan probably dates to the second half of the Nara period is essential. By the time the two monks had returned from China, modern scientific and archaeological testimony shows that tea had likely been farmed and consumed in Japan for over half a century.

Consider Saichō's generous gift to Taihan in 815. Most narratives simply assume that Saichō had the tea available from his trip to China, but it had been eleven years since the Tendai prelate had returned from the Asian continent. The tea could not have been left over from his time in China because it would have gone bad in the meantime. It might have been a gift sent from Chinese monks in 815, but there is no record of such a gift, and besides, the amount would have been too large to pass rigorous inspection tests of continental goods conducted at court.

In my view, all the tea-drinking activities of Saga's court make sense only if tea was already a daily fact of life for the elite in the early ninth century. The nature of tea cultivation supports such an inference. As noted in my introduction, after planting tea seeds, it typically requires eight years before tea shrubs are capable of producing palatable tea. Is it reasonable to believe that Saichō and/or Kūkai and/or Yōchū could have brought enough seeds with them in 805/806 to supply Saga and his court fully by 815, just eight or nine years later? Although it is not completely beyond the realm of possibility, the long maturation of tea bushes suggests that none of these monks who traveled to China could have brought back the seeds for Saga's tea with them. The truth is more likely that Japan's elites were used to consuming tea because the plant was already being grown in several places around the capital by that time.

All the tea consumed at the Saga court was therefore farmed in Japan, even possibly at Daianji, where Saichō had a disciple. Sad to say, there is no credible evidence that either prelate ever carried seeds to Japan. There are many traditions that attribute the origin of tea in Japan to Saichō and even Kūkai, but they have no basis in ninth-century sources. The attempt to tie the importation of tea to these famous figures is analogous to similar urges in Japanese tea history to link origins to well-known historical persons.

The tale of Saichō and Kūkai raises the question of the earliest cultivation methods in Japan. How does one interpret the order to establish tea fields in all those provinces in 815? Was the order ever carried out? The answer can never be known for sure, because there are no further references to the command or to tea-farming methods for this era. Yet some historical evidence suggests a more optimistic view of the implementation of Saga's order. First, at least one of the provincial governors charged with planting tea, Fujiwara no Fuyutsugu, was a frequent drinker of the beverage.[12] Then, too, there was a tea plot located within the imperial residential grounds.[13] Inspired by the example of Yōchū and his apparent tea-making skills acquired after thirty years in China, Saga may well have issued and implemented his command.

Let us assume that tea seeds were planted in 815 and eventually germinated into seedlings. What happened to the resulting bushes? Such a question carries the argument into the realm of speculation about ancient Japanese cultivation methods, but if informed by knowledge of the reproduction of the tea plant, then such speculation can be insightful. First, if the court's tea plants germinated and the seedlings were cared for by conscientious farmers, then naturally the resulting shrubs were likely productive, but there are no further references indicating that this was so.

What if the tea seeds were planted, the surviving plants tended for a while and then abandoned, a fate that frequently befell rice and other fields? As noted earlier, left on their own, tea flowers are not self-pollinating, that is, the stamen and pistil of the same plant cannot produce seeds. Butterflies, bees, and birds must fly from plant to plant to pollinate the flowers, yielding hard pouches of tea seeds. Without human intervention, the rate of successful pollination is not very high, but if Saga ordered enough seeds planted and they yielded bushes, then undoubtedly some would have produced seed pouches, while others might have died. Whatever seed pouches there were would have fallen to the ground, where they may or may not have germinated. Interestingly, animals such as boars, deer, and monkeys are known to assist in the growth process by eating the seed pouches. These animals then carry potential tea plants inside them until they defecate the undigested seeds, fertilized and ready to germinate.

To summarize this discussion: the tea seeds ordered for planting in 815 may have had a widely varying fate because tea farming in ancient Japan was likely so spotty and simple. From seed to full-grown shrub, minimal care with no fertilizer was the rule. Some attempted tea plots undoubtedly failed and disappeared; some produced seedlings, and then bushes, and grew to large dimensions; and others yielded offspring that traveled a considerable distance before becoming productive. To my mind, there is no reason to assume that the dearth of historical sources means the failure of all the plants. The first cultivation methods for tea during the Nara and Heian periods were rude and exemplified the extensive farming so characteristic of early Japan.

Despite the hit-or-miss nature of ancient tea farming, the beverage soon acquired a limited and slowly expanding appeal for Japan's civil and religious elites. A major reason for tea's popularity among ruling cliques in Japan and greater East Asia lay in a second characteristic of early Japanese tea: its utility as a gift, the primary way that the leaves changed hands during this century.[14] The example of Saichō's gift to Taihan has already been cited, but Saichō also gave tea directly to Kūkai, perhaps from a tea field on Mount Hiei.[15] Yōchū, who was a central figure among Saichō, Kūkai, and Saga, donated tea to Saga on more than one occasion; Saga appreciated the beverage for its addictive ability to transport him to "the world of spirits and immortals." It is also notable that Yōchū had close ties to the East Asian state of Parhae, where he acted as an intermediary, granting gifts of gold and possibly tea.[16]

Japanese clerics probably learned the custom of bestowing tea upon thirsty guests from their hosts in Tang China. There is no doubt that during his thirty years in the empire Yōchū frequented temples with Kūkai where the hard work of sutra transcription was taking place. There the pair took tea repeatedly to fight the fatigue that set in during their labors. These Tang temples also carried out ceremonies in which tea played a prominent role. Other clerics, aristocrats, and members of Saga's family also participated in the exchanges.[17]

The story of the Tang priest Yi-kong and his travails in Japan help show how the Chinese, Japanese, and Koreans eventually came to participate in such a tea gift-giving network.[18] The Chinese Zen monk Yi-kong spent the years 849–852 at Tōji in the capital at Heian, where he was close to the Japanese imperial family, especially the Empress Dowager Tachibana Kachiko, teaching her about the virtues of Zen. While he was living in Japan, he naturally grew homesick and corresponded frequently with the Chinese trader Xu Gong-you and his financier brother Gong-zhi. Eventually, the trader brothers decided to send Yi-kong and his servant some presents, including incense, tea, a white tea bowl, and a variety of other porcelains. Since the Xu brothers were from south China, they were giving Yi-kong what amounted to local specialties.

The Heian court, however, had a regulation about commodities shipped to Japan from abroad. Merchants had to stop at Dazaifu in northern Kyushu and off-load their goods for inspection. In doing this, the Heian court was adhering to a law that dictated that individuals could not trade with foreigners without first giving the Japanese government what amounted to confiscatory powers. While no one knows for sure where the contraband ended up, it seems likely that the most coveted goods found their way into the hands of Japanese courtiers. And that is exactly what apparently happened to the goods bound for Yi-kong. They were locked in storage at the guesthouse (*kōrokan*) at Dazaifu and later transported to the capital, where they were auctioned off to thirsty aristocrats. Yi-kong may have seen some of his gift, but most of the goods fell into other hands.

The story of Yi-kong emphasizes at least three important points. First, the gift-giving network extended from south China to Japan, and probably to Silla and Parhae in northeastern Asia too. Second, tea was an essential good cementing together donors and recipients, who were usually Buddhist monks. Third, the Heian court and its aristocrats had developed a healthy taste for tea from China, and apparently their demands outran supply.

The story of Yi-kong and his tea involved primarily Chinese, but the tea network crossed borders and helped knit the diverse East Asian Buddhist community together. For example, not long before Yi-kong spent his time in Heian, the Japanese Tendai master Ennin resided in China for nearly a decade (838–847) in search of the Buddhist law. During his stay, Ennin proved to be a real tea addict, imbibing thirty-four times on the record.[19] He drank not only the brick tea that Lu Yu boasted of, but two types of leaf tea. Ennin undoubtedly had first developed a taste for the beverage while on Mount Hiei, where Saichō and so many other monks had garnered their tea leaves. Then again, between 853 and 858, the Japanese monk Enchin followed the same path to China, where he climbed Mount Tientai and examined the tea shrubs there. Enchin was also a correspondent with the Chinese monk Chang-ya, especially when it came to tea matters.

Although Buddhist monks were the primary drinkers of tea during the ninth and early tenth centuries, Sinified aristocrats could also fall under the sway of the tea habit. Sugawara no Michizane (845–903), the famed courtier banished by a Fujiwara plot at the end of his life, probably imbibed the beverage throughout his adulthood.[20] He wrote Chinese poetry referring to tea both during his tenure as governor of Sanuki and while he resided at Heian, where he undoubtedly received many gifts. In 894, he received samples of the plant from a garden in China. After his banishment to Dazaifu he wrote another poem on spring tea in northern Kyushu. His wife, children, disciples, and colleagues enjoyed tea as well.

Michizane's story is also a testament to the gradual spread of tea cultivation in Japan. When Sugawara was a child growing up in Heian, monks cultivated the plant at various temples throughout the Kinai, such as Daianji, Enryakuji, Tōkōji, and Anshōji.[21] Moreover, while historians cannot be certain how effectively Emperor Saga's order was implemented in 815, provinces in the Kinai—as well as Tanba, Harima, and Ōmi—were supposed to deliver the herb as a tribute item. As noted above, Sugawara served as the governor of Sanuki, where apparently a field supervised by the provincial headquarters yielded tea. Sanuki was also the home province of Kūkai and Ennin, both longtime tea drinkers. Finally, Michizane wrote more poetry about tea when he was banished to Dazaifu in northern Kyushu. A major port of call for Chinese merchantmen and eventually home to a sizable immigrant Chinese community, northern Kyushu may also have been evolving into a center of cultivation. Farming methods may have been simple, but Japan's soil, climate, and topography were certainly conducive to the diffusion of the tea plant to new regions.

## TEA, THE BEST MEDICINE

Farmed in a few regions with little attention and simple techniques and exchanged almost exclusively as a personal gift, tea merited only a small place in Nara and Heian society. The obstacle that restricted the leaf's appeal was not simply the farming methods, but went to the heart of the way that tea was processed during these centuries. It had big clumps and tasted quite bitter. The willingness of the elite to imbibe that brown concoction was related to its presumed health benefits. Nothing illustrates both the rude method of processing and tea's supposed medicinal qualities better than a court ritual involving this unsavory beverage.

In 737, Japan was in the throes of the worst smallpox epidemic in quite some time. Among the palliatives announced at court was the recitation of the *Sutra of Great Wisdom* (*Dai hannya-kyō*) by specially cleansed monks from Daianji.[22] It was apparently believed that by calling upon the name of the Buddha using this particular sacred text, the terrible, death-dealing crisis would abate. The year 737 was only the third time that the *Dai hannya-kyō* had been recited at court following a calamity, and it was certainly the most notable, followed as it was by the placing of that sutra in provincial temples (*kokubunji*) and nunneries (*kokubun niji*) around the country. The actions of Emperor Shōmu (r. 724–749) helped cement the place of this sacred text in court ceremonies for warding off or ameliorating calamities of all sorts.[23]

The problem was, of course, that famines, epidemics, and other disasters were nearly annual events in ancient Japan. By the mid-ninth century at the latest, the seasonal recitation of sutras (*ki no midokkyō*), especially the *Sutra of Great Wisdom,* had become common features of court life. According to *The Ordinances of Engi,* compiled in 925 but reflecting practices of earlier times, the recitation of the *Daihannya-kyō* had been instituted twice a year, in the spring and fall, to take place in the Throne Room (*daigokuden*) of the Imperial Palace.[24] The entire aristocratic class was required to be present; statues of Vairocana Buddha were situated in the flower-laden room and incense filled the air. Eventually, the ceremony was fixed for a propitious day in the second and again in the eighth months, with one hundred monks in attendance to read the auspicious sutra. This elaborate ritual was supposed to have taken four days. Court records describe this rite both in 859 and in 877, as it was already a biennial event by that time.

*The Record of the Western Palace* (*Saikyūki*) also conveys essential facts about this ceremony to ward off disasters. It dictated, for example, that monks should be nominated from elite temples, including Enryakuji, Tōdaiji, Kōfukuji, Tōji, Saiji, and other important Buddhist centers. Most important, *Saikyūki* noted that the court chamberlain (*kurōdo*) requested from the Bureau of Medicine (*ten'yaku-ryō*) payment for the picking and preparation of tea, along with other items such as a Chinese medicine, dried ginger (*kankyō*), a sweetener made from the boiled, dried skins of the persimmon (*chinpi*), and earthenware bowls. According to another source, middle-ranking courtiers served the tea, mixed with the other ingredients, to the sutra-reading monks as gifts for their labors in front of the emperor.[25]

*The Record of the Western Palace* is important for two other reasons. First, it describes how the Chamberlain's Office (*kurōdo dokoro*) received provisions and payment for the picking and processing of the tea. It is quite likely that, since the recitation was a court ritual, the tea was picked from the plot within the Imperial Palace. Second, the large number of officials with backgrounds in medicine is striking. Doctors and pharmacists played a prominent role, and recall that the request for the ingredients went to the Bureau of Medicine. It was as if the tea and those in charge of it could cure the ills of the state.[26]

The various court handbooks on ritual describe in great detail the actions to be undertaken by each of the participants, but the nature of the tea is only generally clear. One expert believes that the Japanese of the eighth century consumed tea as a kind of soup or gruel.[27] Tastes may have changed later, for a fragment from an ordinance for the Chamberlain's Office writes that the tea for this court ritual was a kind of "steeped" (*senjicha*) beverage; some scholars apparently believe that this term refers to leaf tea dried or roasted in a rudimentary manner.[28]

Another stronger possibility is that it was brick tea (*dancha; kokeicha; heicha*). In his *Classic of Tea,* Lu Yu had described in some detail how brick tea was prepared, and it took quite a bit of effort. After the tea leaves had been picked on the appropriate day in early spring, they were then steamed, pounded in a mortar with a pestle, formed into round bricks with holes in the middle, dried, and then tied together and sealed against the elements. When the drinker wanted to imbibe, he undertook the hard work of grinding the brick on a druggist's mortar (*yakken;* figure 1).

Figure 1. Druggist's mortar. From Shaanxi Sheng kaogu yanjiuyuan, *Famen si kaogu fajue baogao* (Beijing: Wenwu chubanshe, 2007), p. 62.

Why use a druggist's mortar? The answer is that, until the mid-1200s, that was the only implement available to grind tea. In other words, the conventional tea grinder (*chausu*), made of stone with striations to crush dried leaves into a fine powder, had not yet been invented in China (1073) or imported to the Japanese islands (around 1250). Lu Yu described the druggist's mortar, and the term may also appear in a Japanese encyclopedia of the mid-tenth century.[29]

The employment of the druggist's mortar has important implications for the uses to which tea was put and how it tasted and looked. This druggist's grinder is molded from metal and looks like a wheel on an axle turning in a metal trough. Experimenters working at the tea company Itoen have found that the druggist's grinder produces granules much larger than powdered tea ground on a stone grinder, and that the taste is bitter and the color of the tea brown. In a word, the tea consumed as brick or leaf tea ground on the druggist's wheel would have been quite pungent and rather unpalatable to modern tastes.[30] It is small wonder that the monks had sweetener, ginger, and other herbs put into their beverages.

Why would these monks, not to mention highly placed civil aristocrats and even the emperor, have chosen to imbibe such a concoction? This question goes right to the heart of the reason that the ruling elite utilized tea so widely at this time: it was considered good medicine. That is undoubtedly a major reason that the court served tea to the monks performing sutra recitation. A rite to heal the court and the country required the main participants to have excellent health. It is no accident that tea appears in the court's first two books of medicine.[31] Even during the mid-tenth century, courtiers knew that a bowl of tea was a good remedy for a hangover.[32]

An anecdote about Fujiwara no Michinaga, the most powerful courtier between 995 and 1024, serves to highlight the expected health benefits of tea. First, Michinaga was an avid fan of the beverage; his diary records four occasions on which the leader received tea utensils, including once from a Chinese.[33] When his child's house burned down, he was apparently distraught at the loss of all the possessions, including tea bowls. Second, as is well known, Michinaga suffered from diabetes. His relative and confidant Fujiwara no Sanesuke records that for several days in 1016 Michinaga "was always drinking cold water, . . . but that his mouth was still dry and he had no strength." Doctors prescribed various remedies, but before Michinaga tried them, "from today he imbibed tea once and two or three times arose to go into the other room, but it was always to drink more water."[34] The point of the story is not that Michinaga's attempted use of tea seemingly did not work, although it might have helped had he tried more libations, but that he *expected* the tea to have a regenerative effect on his body.

A later story from *Tales of Times Now Past* (*Konjaku monogatari*) equally suggests the close tie between tea and medicine. One day the chief of the Bureau of Medicine spied a finely dressed woman in a carriage, but when he asked who she was, there was no answer. The woman left the carriage only to reveal white thighs with a swelling on them. The chief dedicated himself day and night to curing the condition in hope of winning her hand. Eventually, the woman recovered from her condition, and then the chief ground some medicine and put it in a "tea bowl" (*chawan*), stirring the concoction with feathers. In the end, the woman left the chief, so even his medical skills were not enough to make her his own. Yet the chief's use of a tea bowl and grinder for the medicine shows once again the close connection between medicine, tea, and the metal grinder during the ancient period.[35]

The seasonal recitation of *The Sutra of Great Wisdom* continued until the thirteenth century, and is noted in aristocratic diaries at least fifteen times from 982 through 1110. This ceremony functioned to ameliorate the effects of the numerous plagues, famines, droughts, floods, earthquakes, and other disasters that afflicted both the court and the common people. The prominent role played by the earliest bitter tea in the rite also suggests the medicinal value attributed to this herb, as well as its part in a gift economy. Buddhist monks were the center of the economy for tea, as they grew, processed, and drank tea somewhat more widely beginning in the tenth century.

## THE SLOW SPREAD OF TEA AND ITS CULTURAL CACHET DURING THE HEIAN PERIOD

In spite of all the considerable problems—spotty farming, processing methods that produced a bitter soup, and exchanges limited to personal contacts—demand for the caffeinated drink apparently continued unabated during the eleventh and twelfth centuries. Besides the entries from Michinaga's journal, several high-ranking aristocrats write of tea. Fujiwara Yukinari (972–1027), holding the Second Rank, reveals his participation in the rite for the seasonal recitation of sutras and describes his tea bowls and possibly other unnamed utensils. Minamoto Tsuneyori (976–1039) of the Third Rank mentions unspecified tea implements and states that the ashes of the former Heavenly Sovereign GoIchijō (r. 1016–1035) were interred in a tea bowl imported from China.[36] Sanesuke (957–1046) was not shy about commenting on his tea bowls and other accoutrements, including gifts from provincial governors anxious for a lucrative appointment at court. The powerful Fujiwara leader Tadazane (1078–1162) listed more tea rituals at court. Tadazane's son Yorinaga (1120–1156) recorded in his diary that he had banquets in 1136, 1151 (twice), and 1152 (twice) where tea bowls and other items played a prominent role.[37] Even Kujō Kanezane, the leading courtier of the late twelfth century, had many tea bowls and was regularly concerned with the rite for the seasonal recitation of sutras, in which tea was distributed.

Aristocrats of more humble station were involved with the beverage too. Fujiwara Tamefusa (1049–1115) described two court rituals requiring tea and in 1107 noted the burial of the ashes of two highly placed aristocratic women in tea vessels. Other lower-ranking bureaucrats, such as Taira no Nobunori (1112–1187), Fujiwara no Tsunefusa (1142–1200), and Fujiwara no Tadachika (1131–1195), owned tea bowls and other accoutrements. Nobunori participated in the rite for the seasonal recitation of sutras at least five times and made trips to Uji.[38] During the 1180s, tea bowls and other unnamed implements were de rigueur for the great banquets (*daikyō*) thrown by Fujiwara leaders at court.[39] Nakahara Hirotoshi, another noble of modest status, possessed his own tea field.[40] Indeed, these journals suggest that many civil aristocrats owned tea utensils and that the court and its members frequently demanded tea.[41]

Civil aristocrats aired their sentiments about tea in their poetry, suggesting how those elite consumers viewed the beverage. To be sure, almost all of the poems were written in Chinese, and not in the more familiar Japanese *waka* form, but that should not be surprising given that tea was originally imported from China and had strong associations with Chinese culture. Between 814 and 1205, no less than twenty compilations included sixty-three poems referring to tea, its utensils, tea fields, or some other aspect of tea culture.[42] Consider this verse from the early ninth century by tea connoisseur Fujiwara no Fuyutsugu:

> To avoid the summer heat I have come to an Imperial Palace.
> At a lake pavilion there is a bundle of fishing poles.
> The green of the willows lining the banks turns dark at dusk.
> The sound of the pines bending on the water's edge turns the day's heat cool.
> Writing poetry and pounding fragrant tea—neither is to be disdained.[43]

Or these lines from this mid-eleventh century poem, noted previously:

> There is a hall in Aoumi District in Mikawa Province
> Called The Temple Where Medicine Is King.
> Gyōki the bodhisattva founded it in olden days.
> Though his saintly remains are old,
> The scenery is simply fresh.

In front of it is water of lapis lazuli;
In back there is a grove dyed in yellow.
There is a grass hall and a miscanthus hut.
There is a bell tower.
There is a tea field and a medicine garden.[44]

Or this poem from 1135:

The mountains are quiet
And there is little human society.

The smoke from the tea boiler disappears
And the kitchen help sleeps.
The sun sinks behind the crags of pine
And the crane alights on the moor.[45]

Poetry, like the entries in aristocratic diaries, suggests that tea remained popular among the civil elite throughout the Heian period. Associations with nature and the hermit life suffuse this poetry, written in Chinese. References to Gyōki and the place in Mikawa help to nativize what must have been an exotic, alien habit for most nobles.

While civil aristocrats imbibed tea readily enough, Buddhist monks and nuns who lived in large complexes were the most frequent drinkers of the beverage. Associations with Buddhism and famous clerics were an important aspect of the cultural meaning of Heian tea. At Enryakuji, the famous chief monk Ryōgen wrote a twenty-six-point opinion piece in which three clauses dealt specifically with tea. The first noted Ryōgen's "surprise at the thickness of the tea smoke" and criticized monks for paying more attention to food and tea than to the required lectures. The second and third admonished monks who just "boiled (tea) and begged." In addition, Ninnaji, which harbored imperial offspring and imported fine porcelains from China, as well as Tōji and Onjōji, were justly famous for their tea.[46]

More than ever, tea was a common feature of the world that bound Buddhist clerics together from all over East Asia. Jōjin (1011–1081) was one of the most famous Japanese monks to go to the Asian mainland. At the advanced age of sixty-two, Jōjin left northern Kyushu for Song China and stayed there for the rest of his life. He kept a detailed diary in which he mentioned tea in 221 passages.[47] A great many entries note Jōjin's participation in banquets or other occasions at which he drank tea, including while boating. The number of drinkers might even be in the hundreds and included Indians as well as Chinese. On one occasion, he imbibed tea with eight other Japanese monks. When asked what was needed in Japan, he replied incense and tea bowls. He sent tea back to Japan with returning monks on several occasions. Jōjin showed interest in the processing of tea as well, noting the wages of Chinese tea workers. While at these gatherings, he consumed both brick and leaf tea. His experiences are testimony to the role of tea as a lubricant in the social relations of monks from all over Asia.[48]

By the twelfth century, monks cultivated and processed tea widely in temples throughout the capital region. Major Buddhist complexes such as Enryakuji, Tōji, Kōfukuji, Tōdaiji, Onjōji, Ninnaji, and Mount Kōya had their own tea fields. Even smaller branch temples like Jōshōji in Kyoto and Genkōji in Yoshino raised their own tea for local consumption.[49] According to the record for Jōshōji, the temple even had a shop where it may have bought tea when demand outran supply and sold the herb when production went to excess. Poetry written around 1205 even mentions "a person who sold tea."[50] Anrakuji, a small temple in northern Kyushu near the ruins of Dazaifu, was another production center located far from Kyoto.[51] As quoted in the poem above, temples as distant from the capital as Mikawa's Yakuōji boasted a tea plot.[52]

To be sure, none of these tea fields was very large, and almost all of them were on temple grounds. By comparison with later medieval and early modern Japan, production was still for a small elite class of consumers, usually Buddhist clerics. They were both donors and recipients in the gift economy that bound courtiers in Japan to Chinese traders and to the religious community throughout East Asia. There were signs that the gift economy was just beginning to change, however, as the mention of tea sellers implies. In the next century, the web of gift exchange would remain mostly intact, even as the cultivation and processing of this medicinal herb would continue to spread.

## WHY YŌSAI VIEWED TEA AS "THE IMMORTAL MEDICINE"

The monk Yōsai (also known as Eisai, 1141–1215) is one of the most famous figures in Japanese history. He traveled to China in search of the Buddhist law, much like Saichō before him; the parallels between their lives are eerie. Both supposedly carried tea seeds from China that then led to a flowering of tea culture in Japan. Each is supposed to have founded a new sect of Buddhism in Japan, Saichō starting Tendai and Yōsai Rinzai Zen. Each is associated with a different type of tea: Saichō with the brick tea of the early Heian period and Yōsai as the hero who brought powdered tea (*matcha*) to Kamakura Japan. One other similarity these two men share is that their respective roles in Japanese history are largely mythological, especially when it comes to their places in the story of Japanese elite tea.[53] Both of them, especially Yōsai, mostly represented continuities with previous aspects of tea's production and cultural meaning rather than a radical new departure.

Yōsai was born in 1141 in Bitchū Province along the Inland Sea, about midway between northern Kyushu and Kyoto.[54] At the age of fourteen, he traveled to Kyoto and climbed Mount Hiei, where Enryakuji was located. There he took the tonsure and studied the teachings of Saichō's Tendai school. In 1168, he took passage on one of the many Song junks ferrying passengers to China. In China, he met the famous monk Chōgen, who would later engage in a campaign to rebuild Tōdaiji after it was incinerated during a battle in 1180. They became fast friends and together climbed Mount Tiantai. Yōsai stayed in China for only about half a year at this time before returning to Japan. One author speculates that the reason for Yōsai's brief stay was his disappointment that the temple he had visited on Mount Tiantai was no longer following Saichō's Tendai teachings but rather had turned to Zen Buddhism. Knowledge of Zen in Japan was sketchy at the time, even though Saichō had insisted on meditation as one of the elements of Tendai doctrine.

During the time that Yōsai was in China, unrest mounted in Japan, as warriors began to assert a stronger role for their class in a land of clerics and civil aristocrats. In the outcome, war enveloped much of the archipelago between 1180 and 1185 as rival leagues of fighting men tried to assert the right for their own government, eventually founded by Minamoto no Yoritomo. By 1185 at the latest, the new shogunate, charged with collecting revenues and keeping the peace, was in place in Kamakura. The wealthiest administrators, such as the Minamoto and Hōjō families living near the capital city, had their own sources of revenues. Soon Yōsai would develop a special relationship with these rough-hewn warriors.

By the time Kamakura had become a military capital, Yōsai moved his home to distant northern Kyushu. Then, in 1187, he returned to China aboard a Song trading vessel and eventually climbed Mount Tiantai for a second time. This time he devoted himself to the practice of seated meditation (*zazen*) and received a certificate for his efforts. In 1192, he sailed back home to Hirado in northern Kyushu, where he opened a small temple and built the retreat Fushun'an. Thereafter he continued his activities near the port of Hakata, and eventually he tried to spread Zen teachings in Kyoto; but the monks of Enryakuji would have none of it, and they used their influence at court to have Zen banned. He returned to Hakata.

In 1199, Yōsai sojourned all the way to Kamakura. He got on quite well with Yoritomo's widow, Hōjō Masako, and in 1200 he was permitted to found a new temple there called Jufukuji, but it was not devoted to Zen.

The new shogun Minamoto no Sanetomo also took a great liking to Yōsai, donating a large parcel of land to him; and in 1202 the monk opened Kenninji in Kyoto and required that Tendai, Shingon, and Zen be taught there. Yōsai stayed in Kyoto for some time, eventually taking over from Chōgen in the campaign to build a splendid new Tōdaiji incinerated in a battle in 1180. In 1213, he was appointed Extraordinary Chief Monk (*Gon no sōjō*). Later the next year, he returned to Kamakura to care for the ailing Sanetomo. In the second month of 1215, Yōsai passed away at Jufukuji.

Two points are notable about Yōsai's life and help to clear up his role in the history of tea at this time. First, like so many young men during the late twelfth and early thirteenth centuries, an apocalyptic time of great spiritual turmoil known as the Latter Days of the Buddhist Law (*mappō*), Yōsai clutched at the certainty of that age-old institution of Buddhism, Saichō's Enryakuji. As a monk there, he would have undoubtedly encountered tea, prepared as it always had been, and drunk his fill of it. In fact, Yōsai probably imbibed tea from his early youth. Sad to say, there is no evidence that he ever brought tea seeds with him from China.

Second, note Yōsai's close association with northern Kyushu, a region that had probably possessed small tea fields since the days of Michizane in the early tenth century. There, too, he could have had a bowl of tea whenever it pleased him. The existence of a large immigrant Chinese community in northern Kyushu only bolsters this proposition. In a well-known incident that occurred in 1151, two samurai attacked the ports of Hakata and Hakozaki and more than sixteen hundred Chinese merchant families fled.[55] The late eleventh and twelfth centuries were the heyday of the trade between Japan and Song China, with cash flowing into Japan in larger and larger quantities.[56]

According to one tradition, Yōsai was active in Imazu, a center of the Song–Japan trade, and may have founded Shōfukuji in Hakata with the support of Chinese ship captains early in the thirteenth century.[57] Yōsai may well have had a close friendship with the Song captain Zhang Guo-an.[58] Little is known of this particular friendship, but there is no doubt that Yōsai benefited greatly from his association with the immigrant Chinese community in Hakata and environs. They may well have supported him financially and provided a strong link to Song China and its Zen culture.

Understanding the geographical and social context for Yōsai's beliefs raises interesting questions about the monk and the possibility that he learned about powdered tea there. By the late eleventh century, Song Chinese had invented the tea grinder (*chausu*) to replace the druggist's mortar (*yakken*) and were making a much tastier beverage, probably something close to powdered tea (*matcha*). As noted above, there was a sizable Chinese immigrant community in Hakata by the mid-twelfth century. Although archaeologists have recovered no tea grinders from the region, they have found tea bowls (*katsuyū tenmoku*) appropriate for imbibing this tea from soil layers in Hakata dating to the end of the eleventh century.[59] Perhaps these Chinese immigrants had tea grinders and were drinking *matcha* too.

Did Yōsai learn about powdered tea from his Chinese friends in northern Kyushu and drink it for the first time with these immigrants? Did he popularize the practice of imbibing powdered green tea after learning about that habit from the Song Chinese? Once again, as noted previously, scholars enter the realm of speculation.[60] Fortunately, however, there is a decisive answer to these questions as viewed through Yōsai's own handiwork.

What, then, was Yōsai's true role in the history of tea? Two achievements, one innovative and the other conservative, signify his contribution. First, note his close relationship with the warrior class and their capital, Kamakura. Yōsai received both political and economic support from Hōjō Masako and her son the shogun Sanetomo. Early in 1214, he advised his patron Sanetomo to drink tea: "The shogun was a little sick and people were running around. . . . It was probably the result of Sanetomo having been drunk the night before. The chief monk was in charge of arranging the protection of the various Buddhas, removing evil, and *giving him medicine.* When he heard of Sanetomo's state, he said that he had some good *medicine,* and called for a cup of *tea* from his temple."[61] Acting as a medical adviser to Sanetomo, the monk administered tea to the shogun after a night of drunken revelry. This story suggests that, despite the use of tea by monks and civil aristocrats for hundreds of years, warriors were as yet unaware of the healing properties of the caffeinated drink. Credit should go to Yōsai for being one of the first people to introduce tea to the samurai class, an addiction that would last until the collapse of the last martial government in 1868.[62]

In the same passage, the Zen monk also bestowed a gift on the warrior leader: "He also presented a one-chapter book to the ailing shogun. It praised the efficacy of tea. The shogun was quite pleased. Last month, in a moment away from seated meditation, [the chief monk] had written this book, at least so he said."[63] Yōsai's second contribution to the history of tea was his writing, later entitled *Drink Tea and Prolong Your Life* (*Kissa yōjō ki*).[64] This work tells its readers a great deal about how the author viewed the production and function of tea. In this respect, Yōsai was conservative, following the age-old cultural interpretation of the beverage as a medicine. The reasons that he viewed tea as a cure for various ailments were intimately bound up with how tea was farmed and processed during his lifetime. As it turned out, the Zen monk's tea was not so very different from that of centuries past when the concoction was part of the seasonal recitation of sutras.

There is much to be learned from this abbreviated text.[65] In his introduction, Yōsai lays out his case for tea as medicine. The very first sentence reads: "Tea is an immortal medicine (*sen'yaku*) that, during this degenerate age (*matsudai*), prolongs life and is a marvelous method for extending human relationships." He then notes that "ever since olden days this country [Japan] and others in every case regarded it highly." He argues that simply because the current age is one of spiritual uncertainty there is no reason to discard the drink. Yōsai saw his role as a defender of the beverage during the upheaval of the Latter Days of the Buddhist Law.

Next, the author moves to a detailed discussion of just how, according to the precepts of Chinese medicine, tea prolonged life. Here he lays out his thinking about the importance of the heart among the five vital organs of the body (liver, lungs, heart, spleen, and kidneys). These five organs should be harmonized by eating foods with different tastes; the taste that benefited the heart was bitter. In particular, the diet of the Japanese was deficient in bitter-tasting foods, and therefore tea was just the drink to supply the needed antidote. This theory of the five organs corresponding to five tastes was drawn from Chinese thought and esoteric (Shingon) Buddhism.[66]

After a brief exposition on the various terms for tea and the appearance of its flower, Yōsai then quotes numerous Chinese texts to support his belief in the efficacy of tea as a medicine. He writes that tea can help overcome drowsiness, "the root of ten thousand sicknesses." He recommends tea as a cure for numerous other illnesses, including depression, indigestion, fevers, weak urination, various sores and poxes, and hangovers. In composing this detailed defense of tea as a medicine, Yōsai was, of course, not breaking new ground but rather harking back to a tradition in Japan that had been central ever since the introduction of that libation during the Nara period.

In the final portion of the first and original chapter, the monk discusses the method for processing tea that he had observed in China. After quoting Lu Yu's *Classic of Tea* and a later Song book, Yōsai explains that workers have plucked tea during the early spring since the Tang dynasty. During the Song dynasty, they also picked the leaves during the early spring from a tea field within the Imperial Residence. Then, "during the first through third months, they assembled lower orders of people who entered the tea field. Their speech was loud and they ran hither and yon to the end of the day."[67] This passage suggests that Yōsai actually witnessed the picking of tea, maybe not at the Imperial Residence, but in other parts of China. He did, however, know the value of such tea: "a thousand strings of cash."

Just a few lines later, Yōsai describes how tea was processed in Song China. He wrote that

> in the morning they pick it, then steam and dry it. . . . If you dry the tea on a shelf, then put down some paper. Without scorching the paper, encourage the fire to come in for drying. . . . Without sleeping for the whole night, finish drying the tea leaves.
>
> Then put them in a good jar and seal it with bamboo leaves. Even though years pass, the tea will not go bad.[68]

In this brief passage, Yōsai was relating to his readers the best practice for processing and preserving tea as he had seen it done in Song China. The crucial point is how simple this "best practice" was for processing the herb.[69] Just pluck the tender shoots in the early spring and then steam and dry the leaves. There is no mention of forming bricks as described by Lu Yu in his *Classic of Tea.* According to *Drink Tea and Prolong Your Life,* the final product was leaf tea. How must the drinker prepare his tea? This question goes right to the heart of whether Yōsai knew of powdered green tea.

On this point Yōsai's little book is just as valuable for its omissions as for its contents. Since his first chapter was what he presented to the shogun Sanetomo, readers of *Drink Tea and Prolong Your Life* will note that there is no mention of how to grind the tea. Indeed, based upon his reading of the later second chapter about the consumption of mulberry leaves, one authority has argued that Yōsai still used the druggist's mortar, popular during preceding centuries.[70] Another possibility is that Yōsai merely boiled up the leaves and drank that concoction.

Nowhere in his little book did Yōsai explain how to drink tea. There is no mention of a whisk, probably in use initially during the Song period. Instead, tea drinkers used a spoon to ladle out the rough tea flakes. Whether it was the method for planting tea, processing it, or grinding the tea leaves, each seems to have been the same one popular earlier during the Heian age. The consumer could make no powdered tea, but merely the same types of tea beverage consumed previously, as he had no new technologies or implements.[71]

As was the case for Saichō, the role of Yōsai in the history of tea should not be ignored, but neither should it be exaggerated. Although he innovated when he introduced tea to the warrior class of Kamakura, in all other respects the monk was deeply conservative. Tea was of use exclusively as a medicine. The processing of the tea leaves, still accomplished with the aid of the druggist's mortar, undoubtedly yielded the same bitter brown liquid that Buddhist monks and civil aristocrats had been imbibing for four hundred and fifty years. In the elite Japanese society of 1200, tea held a minor and restricted but curious place.

## INCIPIENT CHANGES IN TEA DURING THE 1200s

Despite its popularity during the 1600s, scholars of the medieval era (1185–1600) roundly ignored Yōsai's *Drink Tea and Prolong Your Life.* Rather than marking off a new era in the history of tea, the book served to summarize things as they had already evolved. During the thirteenth century in particular, the state of tea remained very much as it had always been: part of a gift economy and ritual life among the Buddhist clergy.[72]

Buddhist institutions were the main setting in which ceremonies involving tea occurred. A religious ritual of 1202 refers to the intoning of sutras and the drinking of tea at Tōdaiji.[73] In 1225, on the thirteenth anniversary of the death of Jōkei, a cleric of the Hossō sect, Buddhist prelates recited sutras and utilized tea.[74] In 1270, appropriately enough, a tea bowl was involved in a Mount Kōya ritual (*mieiku*) honoring the memory of Kūkai.[75] In 1290, medicine, tea, and tea bowls appeared in a funeral ceremony for the monk Eison (1201–1290), associated with the venerable traditions of centuries-old sects such as Shingon and Ritsu.[76] Inventories of several temples mention tea implements, usually bowls, including Tōji, Mount Kōya, Daigoji just outside of Kyoto, and Daijiji in northern Kyushu. In the case of Daijiji, the list includes some five hundred tea vessels used for serving the drink.[77]

Retired emperors, holding the reins of power at court during much of the epoch 1100–1300, were closely involved in the world of tea. In 1215, when a ceremony (*gyakushū*) took place to assure GoToba his heavenly reward before his death, his consort Kamegiku presented him with various types of Chinese medicine, some of it in tea bowls.[78] In 1256, Retired Emperor GoSaga sponsored a ceremony (*hokuto goshūhō*) to pray for his own good health and that of the entire realm; Buddhist monks were instructed to "steep tea" (*cha o senzu beshi*).[79]

One theme runs throughout these Buddhist rites: none involve Zen. Rather, the older sects of the Nara and early Heian periods are prominent. There is a saying that "Zen and tea are one," but such a notion does not fit the period before 1300. Rather, the esoteric schools of Buddhism played a much more important role in the initial popularity of tea among Buddhist clerics and their institutions.[80] The critical role played by the clergy of the older sects in promoting the use of tea through their rituals is yet another continuity with the preceding period.

Conservatism defined the role of tea for the 1200s. At the same time, there were a few faint signs of what would later become crucial harbingers of change in a tea world that had been nearly static for more than five hundred years. Three stand out: the appearance of the first tea "brand name," the growing participation of the warrior class as tea aficionados, and the conversion of tea gifts into taxes and commercial items. These changes were signs that tea was becoming a beverage with much broader appeal. Naturally enough, all the innovations came through the most frequent imbibers of tea, Buddhist clerics.

Myōe (1173–1232), the founder of a temple lying in the hills north of Kyoto, started cultivating the tea that would soon be known as the first "brand" in the land. Like Yōsai, with whom he is almost always associated, the myth of Myōe has obscured his true role in the history of Japanese tea. Accordingly, Myōe is supposed to have gone to China and brought back tea seeds, or struck up a friendship with Yōsai, from whom he received seeds. In fact, neither of these stories is true. While Myōe did give and receive tea, he did so, like many other Buddhist clergy, as part of a larger gift economy.[81]

Myōe's life reads like a novel written during the tumultuous twelfth century. Born to warrior (Taira) parents in Kii Province, he was orphaned at the age of eight. It fell to his uncle, a Buddhist prelate at a temple in the hills to the north of Kyoto, to raise him. At sixteen, Myōe took the tonsure at Tōdaiji, which was still undergoing rebuilding after the disaster of 1180. There he studied the precepts of one of the oldest sects in Japan, the Kegon school, as well as other doctrines of esoteric Buddhism, especially Shingon.

While still in his youth, he fell ill and returned to his native Kii Province. There he practiced seated meditation and refined his understanding of Kegon principles. He planned a trip to India, which was never realized. In 1206, Retired Emperor GoToba donated to the monk land to the north of Kyoto at Toganoo, and Myōe proceeded to rebuild the burned-out temple Kōzanji on the site. Myōe was active in the same religious debates as Yōsai during this age of spiritual turmoil called the Latter Days of the Buddhist Law. For his part, Myōe advocated a return to the strict rules that had previously governed the clergy as a remedy for the ills of the day. He is also famous for writing about sexually charged dreams in which he had intercourse with a bodhisattva. He died during a widespread famine in

1232, still trying to enforce the time-honored precepts of Kegon and esoteric Buddhism.

In the first missive below, written between 1210 and 1226, Myōe reports receiving and returning tea seeds from his teacher:

> O Tsuru Zen Master, my deepest appreciation . . . Since the tea seeds that you spoke of from before have not yet ripened completely, even though it is just a little I present these to you.
> To [a monk] From Myōe[82]

In this second letter, written around 1230, Myōe prepares for a meeting with an unknown noble called Lord Hyōe no jō

> O Lord Hyōe no jō, you will be honoring my humble living quarters with a visit. . . . When you arrive . . . , I'll give you some tea. . . .
> To Hyōe no jō From Myōe[83]

These two letters confirm that Myōe received tea seeds while in residence at Kōzanji and that he was eventually successful in cultivating tea at the temple. To be sure, it is likely that there had already been tea fields at Kōzanji before the fire that destroyed the temple, but Myōe took great pains to rejuvenate those fields. Remember that the temples were located in the northern Kyoto hills at a place called Toganoo. Shaded from the effects of the sun, Toganoo tea seemed sweeter than the others grown in open areas. Eventually the tea from those fields at Toganoo would become renowned as the most delicious in all Japan and represent the first tea "brand." Even in the highly restricted tea world of the early 1200s, consumers searched for the beverage with the best reputation. Of course, applying a brand name to a commodity is one step toward a market for discerning consumers.

A second notable departure from tradition was the ferrying of tea leaves from the Kinai to Kamakura to slake the thirsts of parched warriors. According to *The Record of a Journey to the Kanto and Back* (*Kantō ōgenki*), the Saidaiji monk Eison (1201–1290) received an invitation from the leader of the Kamakura *bakufu* to make the long journey from Nara to the warrior capital in 1262. Nine times along the way, Eison prepared, drank, and offered to others the tea that he had brought along with him from the fields of Saidaiji. Once in Kamakura, he participated in Buddhist ceremonies involving tea. His journey undoubtedly helped to spread the custom of tea drinking eastward to the warrior capital during the mid-thirteenth century.[84]

At the time of his arduous journey, Eison was sixty-one years old. It is hard to imagine the old cleric making the long trek, even with the aid of his followers. For this reason, it is likely that Eison himself partook of the tea to relieve the exhaustion arising from his trip and to help his body stand up to the rigors of so many days on the road. Eison's expedition to Kamakura not only served to spread the news of the healthful beverage eastward to the warrior city but also reinforced the idea that tea was a potent medicine in those Latter Days of the Buddhist Law.[85]

At about the same time, the otherwise unknown cleric Son'ei played an even greater role in acquiring the beverage for the military residents of Kamakura. Son'ei, who lived during the mid-thirteenth century in Kamakura, is strongly associated with tea and the gift economy. Around 1249, he wrote to the clerics of Kōfukuji in Nara:

> Among the tea harvests of recent years, this year's tea was especially superior in quality. The monks of my entire temple [in Kamakura] were happy. They came and looked on from all directions, and because they all desired to drink some, in just three or four months it was all used up.
>
> Next year prepare for this eventuality and take six measures (*rokuto*) to hand and please let us receive your beneficence. . . . [S]elect some workers for this purpose so that they can take some tea and bring it here from Nara.[86]

Besides providing insight into the donation of tea among Buddhist clerics in Nara and Kamakura, the cited document gives an impression of wider cultivation of tea in Japan. It also supports the proposition that the drinking of tea was becoming a growing enterprise, driven by the demand of drinkers for more and more of the habituating caffeinated beverage.

Just five years later, in 1254, Son'ei reveals how the tea was moved from Nara to Kamakura: "Also, take one bushel (*ikkoku*) of tea, and as in previous years send it to Kenninji as soon as possible. When you do so, next seventh month entrust it to [the samurai] on guard duty (*ōban*) and at his convenience take and send it down here [to Kamakura]."[87] In this case, a large amount of tea (one bushel) was to be sent to the temple Kenninji in Kyoto from Kōfukuji and shipped by means of a warrior returning from Kyoto to Kamakura on guard duty. This route of shipment seems to have been customary; a samurai was used as the courier. Apparently, the clergy of Kamakura were leading the warriors down the path of habituation to their drug.

Later in 1254, Son'ei brushed another letter showing two more important points about the cultivation of the herb in Nara and its presentation to the thirsty fighting men of Kamakura:

> This autumn, the [warrior] land steward (*jitō*) of both Tomi and Yata Estates will come to Kamakura. I wish that he would be entrusted with some mountain tea (*yamacha*) for us.
>
> From Son'ei To Gonren[88]

First, the term "mountain tea" provides a clue about tea farming, suggesting that the herb was grown deep in the mountains of Nara. Perhaps it spread there naturally as part of a slash-and-burn farming regime. Second, the tea was being shipped from two revenue-producing farms (Tomi and Yata Estates) located in Yamato, the home province of Nara. To elaborate, estates (*shōen*) such as these two had begun appearing as early as 1050. Cultivators paid various dues in kind to landlords residing both within the estate and in the capital at Kyoto. Apparently, Tomi and Yata Estates produced tea as part of a tax mechanism. In other words, what was once a gift was slowly becoming a routine obligation. As in so many other cases from the ensuing centuries, however, tea was a near tax, not quite the same as a government-mandated labor duty or rice impost.

Indications that tea was becoming a tax suggest that there was an incipient change in the gift economy by the late 1100s.[89] As early as 1191, tea served as revenue sent from northern Kyushu to Kyoto.[90] Recall that a poem of 1205 mentioned "a person selling tea." Tea was no longer simply a gift exchanged among friends in a tiny elite; instead, impersonal mechanisms were arising to facilitate the shipment of the habit-forming leaves. Like the invention of the Toganoo brand name and the wider inclusion of wealthy warriors among the consumers, the evolution of exchange mechanisms was a change pointing toward the future.

Tea's new status as a near tax or a commercial item was probably an outgrowth of its original place as a gift item. The transition from gift to tax or trade commodity was easily effected. When a temple or individual had too little or too much of the herb, then the would-be consumer might turn to trade. Furthermore, when gift obligations became routine, it was easy to turn tea into a tax item. Japan's economy was changing and along with it the restricted appeal of tea to a narrow elite. At this stage, however, because tea was still predominantly an elite beverage, donating tea as a gift was still by far the most common form of exchange.

The shipments of tea cited above all turned out well, as the recipients praised their patrons. Such was not always the case, however: "Yesterday I thought to speak to you at my convenience, but I forgot. I received some bad tea (*waroki cha*). Even though it was bad, I ought to . . . receive a lot more [good tea]. I'll have a person go over there for that purpose."[91]

The mention of "bad tea" in this letter, written by an unknown monk in Kamakura, suggests that the beverage was becoming plentiful enough for consumers to distinguish among the varying qualities of tea. By the late 1200s, members of Japan's political elite had been transformed into a tea-mad ruling class.

In contemporary Japan, green tea is a beverage enjoyed by millions in a thriving consumer society. Cultivated and processed according to the most scientific methods, the drink is proudly displayed in stores and vending machines around the nation. Television and other media promote the purchase and consumption of Japanese green tea throughout the islands and around the world by appealing to the residents of the archipelago to be real "Japanese," or to drink the beverage to improve the quality and length of their lives.

The tea produced in small plots here and there in Japan between 750 and 1300 betrayed almost nothing of this modern character. Cultivated rudely within a few patches in the archipelago, the Japanese herb of this era was processed in just a few ways that yielded a bitter brown concoction. Drinkers of the beverage, usually familiar with each other, exchanged their leaves almost exclusively as a gift. Because the plant had been introduced from China, the tiny elite of civil aristocrats, Buddhist clerics, and later high-ranking warriors associated the herb with the exotic land of its origins and the hermits, poets, and adepts there who were famous for their cultural exploits. The elite that composed much less than 1 percent of the population used Japanese tea mostly as a medicine in rituals designated by the government and Buddhist monasteries.

The period lasting from the introduction of *Camellia sinensis* around 750 until the late 1200s constitutes the prehistory of the modern Japanese green tea. Although it is easy to dismiss that period as having little relevance for modern consumers, it is interesting to note that tea retains its ancient function as a medicine and is still the object of gift giving throughout Japan today. The medicinal effects of tea may have even contributed somewhat to the health of those who imbibed it, a precursor to the "industrious revolution" that occurred centuries later. Even the simple agricultural techniques employed during tea's prehistory contributed to the wisdom of later generations of farmers who cultivated more and better tea. Gift giving evolved into the routine of taxation and the mechanism of the market.

By 1200, the signs of change were inchoate but unmistakable. Some evidence, scant to be sure, suggests that a few individuals and institutions were becoming involved in the trading of the herb, a new form of economic transfer. Then, too, by the second half of the twelfth century at the latest, some gift relationships were routine enough to be transformed into a near tax. During the thirteenth century, the habit of tea drinking was spreading to the elite samurai who guarded Kyoto and had a chance to imbibe there. They carried the tea that supplied Kamakura, the next great center of production and consumption in a new age.

CHAPTER TWO

# Tea Becomes a Beverage for a Wider Market, 1300–1600

Between 1300 and 1600, Japanese society underwent a thoroughgoing transformation. The population of the archipelago nearly trebled to seventeen million or more. To support greater numbers, agriculture stabilized and intensified, farmers became much more productive, and rural life took place in compact villages where peasants made their own rules about water and commons rights and the policing of crime. As cultivation of rice and other crops became more productive, many people dwelling in large cities chose other occupations as merchants or artisans. In a word, the economy became much more specialized and Japanese society more complex.

In politics, warriors battled their way to become the dominant elite, overwhelming civil aristocrats and religious institutions. Samurai took control of the polity during two prolonged but sporadic periods of conflict: the Wars of the Northern and Southern Dynasties, lasting from 1333 to 1392; and the Warring States Era, covering over a century of bloodshed from 1467 to 1590. From 1560 to 1600, three powerful leaders—Oda Nobunaga, Toyotomi Hideyoshi, and Tokugawa Ieyasu—helped to bring a greater degree of peace and unity to the archipelago than it had ever known.

The Iberians with their muskets and Catholicism arrived from Europe and remained for about a century, from 1543 to 1639. Naturally, they became involved in politics and the wars, but their most lasting impact may have been as commentators on Japanese culture and society. The Dutch came and were allowed to stay, serving as a window on European and world affairs. In matters of culture, the appeal of China waned after a while. Buddhist worship and artistic representation began to adopt more native forms, expressed in oral war tales, Noh drama, the tea ceremony, and gigantic castles.

Tea played its own role in and was profoundly affected by this three-hundred-year transformation. Cultivation of the plant not only continued its geographical diffusion but was increasingly practiced by peasants seeking to pay their taxes or trade for a profit. Once commoners began to deal with tea in these ways, they also became ready customers for a swig of the caffeinated beverage. As tea spread downward through the social pyramid and outward geographically, changes in cultivation and processing methods inevitably ensued. As those innovations took place, aesthetes from old and new elites found the improved beverage to be the proper object of new literary and art forms, symbolized most readily by the tea ceremony (*chanoyu*). By 1600, Japan could be described as having a true tea industry, and the islands were well on their way to becoming a major center of tea production and consumption in East Asia and the world.

## THE TRANSITION FROM A BITTER MEDICINE TO A HABIT-FORMING BEVERAGE DURING THE 1300s

In 1219, the shogunal Minamoto line that had done so much to support Yōsai in his advocacy of tea died out. The Kyoto court under Retired Emperor GoToba challenged the right of Kamakura to govern and attempted to destroy the shogunate during the Jōkyū War of 1221. Under the able leadership of Yoritomo's widow's family, however, the armies of Kamakura vanquished GoToba's motley force and emerged from the conflict even stronger. The new leadership of the shogunate (the Hōjō) managed to secure an imperial prince to serve as its titular head while they held the real power as regents in Kamakura. The Hōjō replaced recalcitrant samurai on the land with their own men, simultaneously increasing warriors' incomes and security of tenure as on-site landlords. Most important for the story of tea, the Hōjō also opened a new office at Rokuhara in Kyoto to keep an eye on the wily courtiers.

For most of the thirteenth century, Kyoto and Kamakura ruled the archipelago jointly as a dyarchy, with the court dominant in western Japan and the shogunate ruling over eastern and northern Honshu. Beginning with the Mongol invasions of 1274 and 1281, however, political power shifted dramatically to the warriors. Kyoto remained a cultural, economic, and social center, but Kamakura also grew to be a large metropolis of seventy thousand or so. Its warriors, now guaranteed a job and an income that they constantly fought to raise, began to covet the finer things in life, including tea. The story of Son'ei and his shipments of tea from Nara to

Kamakura, described in chapter 1, is a good example of the growing popularity of tea in the warrior capital by the 1250s.

Like many warrior families of the Kamakura age, the Hōjō split into contending branches, one of which was later called the Kanezawa Hōjō.[1] In 1285, the leader of the Kanezawa Hōjō (Akitoki) was implicated in a struggle for power within the shogunate, and because his faction was destroyed, Akitoki took the tonsure and retired from politics to the safety of lands the Kanezawa Hōjō held in Shimōsa Province near Kamakura. Eight years later, in 1293, Akitoki was reinstated and served in various important posts in the samurai government until his death in 1301. His family also returned to prominence, with one son receiving ordination at Onjōji in Kyoto and the others learning the Confucian classics at the family school located near modern Yokohama and named, appropriately enough, the Kanezawa Library (Kanezawa bunko). The family temple, called Shōmyōji, was also on the library grounds, having been founded in 1267 as a Ritsu center. The Ritsu sect dated back to the 700s, and Shōmyōji's affiliation immediately gave it strong connections to the old capital at Nara and, in particular, a temple there (Saidaiji).

The heir to the Kanezawa lands and status was named Sadaaki, born in 1278. As his father returned to politics, Sadaaki acceded to largely ceremonial posts at the Kyoto court, as befitted his bloodline. In 1296, he reached the coveted Fifth Court Rank, symbolic of aristocratic standing, and continued to occupy court positions such as Captain of the Right and then Left Imperial Guards. In 1302, just a year after his father's death and his own assumption of family leadership, Sadaaki took up residence in Kyoto while serving as a high official in the Rokuhara Office. His tenure there was to last until 1308 and he was reappointed during 1310–1314. Sadaaki was a capable administrator and also produced several offspring, one of whom, Sadayuki, served in the Rokuhara Office from 1324 to 1330 while his father was still alive and active in politics. In 1333, Sadaaki and the rest of the Hōjō were annihilated during the collapse of the Kamakura shogunate.

Not simply literate but also highly learned, Sadaaki brushed numerous letters and other documents during his lifetime. His missives, along with those of many other warriors and clerics, were then preserved after his death in the family library at Kanezawa. Fortunately for historians of tea, Sadaaki was a habitual consumer of the beverage and frequently wrote about his experiences with the drink in his 642 extant letters. The entire collection of about seven thousand documents comprises one of the most fascinating and illuminating sources on tea for any era.[2] Most important, these letters and other records chronicle the history of tea just as it was undergoing the critical transformation from a bitter medicine utilized in political and religious ceremonies to a more palatable beverage, an object of business and pleasure to be enjoyed by many more individuals.

The Kanezawa compilation tells historians about numerous aspects of tea production, processing, exchange, and consumption during the first third of the fourteenth century.[3] Essentially, the Kanezawa collection mentions three types of tea: leaf tea (*hacha*), brick tea (*kokeicha*), and tea ground from leaves or bricks (*matcha*). A letter from the monk Tan'ei notes the loan of three small bags (*tsutsumi*) of leaf tea; another letter from another cleric states that he "wishes to send one bag of ground tea (*suricha*)" to each of two samurai officials.[4] Brick tea appears less frequently, but in another letter a monk describes what could only have been brick tea being transported by a warrior.[5]

Although most of the correspondents were consumers, the Kanezawa collection adds much to the sketchy picture of tea cultivation heretofore available. At least on the tea fields within the precincts of Shōmyōji, the Kanezawa family temple, monks seem to have done both their own planting and picking.[6] Harvests varied considerably from year to year; the best tea was new or "early tea," picked in the third month (early April). The weather did not always cooperate during the cold thirteenth and early fourteenth centuries, however, leading one monk to comment on the tardiness of the tea harvest in one particular year.[7] A Shōmyōji monk warns that in one year "new tea was plentiful here and there" and that the temple should "investigate its profits" before selling.[8] Naturally, new tea also fetched the highest price.[9]

In the best years, tea lasted until the winter. The collection records a present of tea given during the tenth month.[10] In especially plentiful seasons, cultivators were able to "pluck all the way up to the fifth picking" (*gobancha*).[11] One record states that yields were four *kin* (2,400 grams) for the first picking (*ichibancha*), two *kin* (1,200 grams) for the second (*nibancha*), one *kin* (600 grams) for the third (*sanbancha*), and one *kin* for the lowest grade (*hikutsu*).[12] Not all harvests were so successful, however, as the documents also speak of tea to be thrown away (*sutecha*), and tea with a bad color.[13] Consumers considered both the color and the odor of the tea to be of prime importance in their evaluation of the leaves before drinking.[14]

Generally speaking, tea fields were small, usually less than .3 of an acre.[15] In one document, the fence around a tea patch needed repair, and Shōmyōji may have employed as many as twenty-eight workers to get the job done.[16] Shōmyōji's reputation for growing delicious tea must have been great, because a cleric requested a "few seeds" from Sadaaki to farm tea on a mountain in Kamakura.[17] The same monk planted and cultivated Kamakura tea as far away as Kumidadera in Izumi Province.[18]

In fact, the impression that these documents give is of the continuous spread of tea cultivation throughout the Kanto and beyond. One common type of tea was "country tea" (*inaka cha*), easily available but of low quality.[19] Such a term implies that numerous rural areas grew and consumed their own tea. The words "mountain tea" appear frequently, too, and suggest the diffusion of the plant to new areas. In one letter, for example, the aforementioned Tan'ei presented some of this tea to a samurai.[20] Sadaaki also gave mountain tea as gifts.[21] The patches of "mountain tea" likely went in and out of cultivation rather often, as they were tended in a swidden style, if at all. "Mountain tea" also referred to plots that had come into being as tended fields reproduced naturally, and the seeds were spread to new regions.

Once the tea had been harvested, it needed to be processed. In its basic steps, processing was about the same as it was described by Yōsai in *Drink Tea and Prolong Your Life*. In other words, the plucked tea leaves were steamed, dried, and then ground. The tea bowl of choice was the black Chinese *tenmoku;* Shōmyōji had lots of these utensils.[22] There were also scoops (*hishaku*) and tubular containers made of bamboo.

A crucial change that was to have long-term consequences took place in the grinding of the leaves and bricks during the second half of the thirteenth century, however. Stone tea grinders (*chausu*), invented in China in the late eleventh century, were imported into Japan and replaced the druggist's wheel as the utensil of choice (figure 2).[23] The result was a much finer granule of tea that tasted sweeter. Kanezawa Sadaaki helped to finance at least three trade missions to China; in 1307, he dispatched a Shōmyōji monk to China, where he bought one of the new tea grinders. Once the monks at Shōmyōji had a model of the new grinder from China, they began to carve some on their own. By 1309 or 1310, Sadaaki was sending his family's tea to Shōmyōji to have it ground there, as requested in the following letter from Sadaaki to Shōmyōji's head monk Ken'a:

> I (Sadaaki) present the three bags (*tsutsumi*) of leaf tea (*cha no ha*) that I received from [a monk]. . . . If you would grind these so that I could consume the tea, I would be very happy.
>
> From Sadaaki Respectfully to the Head of Shōmyōji 3/29[24]

The Kanezawa collection is filled with such requests from warriors and others to have their tea ground at Shōmyōji.[25]

The improvement that came with the advent of the stone grinder from China around 1250 constitutes a major turning point in the history of tea

Figure 2. Tea grinder. From Uji shi rekishi shiryōkan, ed., *Rokucha no jidai* (Uji: Uji shi rekishi shiryōkan, 1999), p. 10.

production and consumption in Japan. Ground tea no longer looked brown, but the more familiar bright-green. The taste became sweeter, and tea became a beverage for enjoyment as much as for good health. The tea parties of this era are unthinkable without the advance heralded by the arrival of the tea grinders. Grinders were also used for noodles, and so tea parties came to include a light snack of boiled fare. Eventually, the stone grinder would lay the foundation for tea to become an art form during the fifteenth and sixteenth centuries.

Along with the new, improved grinder came a second advance: the tea whisk.[26] Also a Chinese invention, it probably dated to the Song period and was imported into Japan at the same time as the grinder. Sadaaki requested a tea whisk from Ken'a at Shōmyōji:

> Tomorrow if [a messenger] could bring one tea whisk, I would be so very happy.
>
> From Sadaaki To the Head [Ken'a] 2/26[27]

The use of the whisk also turned out to enhance the color, odor, and taste of tea. Taken together, the stone tea grinder and the bamboo whisk marked a new stage in the processing of tea as it moved from bitter medicine to a sweeter, party beverage.

Once processed, the tea had to be preserved for future use. Most newly processed tea or tea sent as presents was encased in bags (*tsutsumi*), also an innovation. These bags held only a little tea and in turn were often placed inside tea boxes (*chabako*), as in the following example: "I present one box (*hako*) containing twenty tea bags for tax purposes (*shotō*)." [28]

The term "box" appears frequently in the Kanezawa collection, signaling the growing role of tea taxes in Shōmyōji's economy. When tea was sent from afar, the operative unit was also the tea box, counted with the Japanese term *gō*.[29] Finally, some tea was preserved in jars (*tsubo*). Tea was also wrapped in paper and sent in buckets, but the preservative power of these containers is very much in doubt.

The transformation of tea into a tasty beverage was the most important change for the future history of Japanese tea. Appropriately enough for a commodity now in greater demand, it is on the topic of tea exchange that the Kanezawa documents may be most informative. Both Sadaaki and his family temple, Shōmyōji, found themselves at the intersection of a maze of tea flows.[30] As for the tea that Sadaaki and his family consumed, none came from Kanezawa landholdings; apparently they did not produce tea. The family's consumption included tea that the Kanezawa household expended in ceremonies, parties, and everyday drinking, a percentage that was given as gifts, and a portion that was sent to Shōmyōji from other places. The tea that the Kanezawa received included that collected from the tea fields of Shōmyōji and its branch temples, tea received as gifts from others, and tea delivered to the family from Kyoto.

A few generalizations about this maze of flows seem apparent. The tea that went back and forth between the Kanezawa family and its temple was of considerable volume, but because each side delivered its tea only as it was needed, overall there was little difference in the total amount exchanged. Then too, the Kanezawa family was a powerful member of Kamakura society and therefore undoubtedly gave many more presents than they received. Even with the ceremonial, party, and daily uses, Sadaaki and his family were responsible for a much greater overall movement of tea in one direction or another than they actually consumed. Finally, because Sadaaki could always send to Shōmyōji for more tea leaves, the family never seems to have run short.

Teasing out these tea flows in detail requires quite a bit of detective work. To begin with, there was the annual flow of tea to Shōmyōji from its properties and branch temples. One of the properties, located in Musashi Province, was called Segasaki in Mutsuura Estate, where many fields sent tea to the temple.[31] The temple also received tea as a tax from Akaiwa, a low-lying swampy area situated in Shimo Kawabe Estate in Shimōsa Province.[32] Branch temples in the Kanto also sent tea to Shōmyōji, including Tōzenji at Tsuchihashi and Eikōji at Migatani, both places in Shimōsa.[33]

As residents of a major temple in the Kanto, it is not surprising that the clerics of Shōmyōji collected tea from lands located there. What is most intriguing is the flow of tea connecting the temple and the Kanezawa to the Kinai. As a member of the Ritsu sect, Shōmyōji had a close relationship with Saidaiji in Nara. Saidaiji possessed many tea fields, and it would not be surprising if some of that tea found its way to the Kanto.[34] Ninshō (1217–1303), a Saidaiji cleric, is reputed to have planted hundreds of tea seeds when he founded Gokurakuji, another Ritsu temple in Kamakura.[35]

Yet Kyoto was the main external source for Shōmyōji's and the Kanezawa's tea. Early on, Sadaaki commented in a letter that the beverage was "becoming more and more popular" in the city.[36] For example, while Sadaaki was serving in the Rokuhara Office in Kyoto, he wrote to Ken'a at Shōmyōji that he was sending one "bucket" to the monk.[37] No one knows how Sadaaki came by this tea in Kyoto, but on another occasion the tea came to Kamakura via a Kanezawa holy place in Kyoto called the Taishi dō.[38] Moreover, because one of Sadaaki's sons was serving there, the temple Ninnaji—long a producer of fine tea—sent a large amount of its product to the Kanto.[39] Sadaaki was even able to get his hands on a box of tea (*chabako*) from distant Iga Province.[40]

The most prized tea "brand" at this time came from Toganoo, where Myōe had rejuvenated the fields of Kōzanji around 1200. When Shōmyōji conducted a ritual reading of the *Lotus Sutra,* Sadaaki sent especially fine tea from Toganoo. Undoubtedly his political connections helped him secure this brand of tea. In fact, Toganoo tea was transported to Kamakura on more than one occasion.[41] Toganoo is mentioned twelve times in the Kanezawa collection; it was so popular that warriors serving in Kyoto often found that there was not enough to go around.[42] There were many housemen and guards serving under Sadaaki (and later his son Sadayuki) in Kyoto, and they seemed to have been used to ferry the tea from the Kinai to Kamakura.[43]

Why was the Toganoo brand so highly prized? A visit to the region helps provide an insight. Kōzanji is situated deep in the mountain recesses north of Kyoto, and today a canopy of trees shelters the fields. These trees provide protection against the sun and retard the process of photosynthesis. Tea produced in these shady areas such as Toganoo tends to be sweeter and less bitter. Taken together with the use of the stone grinder and the bamboo whisk, the natural roof for the Toganoo tea fields made for a truly delicious beverage. The tree canopy presaged another advance that would occur two centuries later: the roof-over method of cultivation, described later. Toganoo tea was preferred for a reason, and again the trend was toward a sweeter, more delectable form of the beverage. In 1326, the tea from Toganoo was mentioned as one of several "brand names" (*shōgan*).[44]

Besides taxation and trade, gift giving was still a common form of exchange. For example, when Sadaaki assumed a high position in the shogun's residence in 1330, he gave out many gifts, including tea.[45] It was customary for Sadaaki to give gifts of tea at the end of the year.[46] The most common time of the year to make presents of tea, however, was during the third month, when the new tea had just been picked and processed.[47] In 1332, Sadaaki gave a box (*hako*) and three different types of tea to the monks of Shōmyōji through Ken'a, his most faithful correspondent.[48] The monks of Shōmyōji also participated in the gift-giving network, as when the temple gave leaf tea to an important official.[49]

Consumption of tea took three basic forms: as a medicine, in ceremonies, and in parties. In line with the new popularity gained by tea due to its improved texture and taste, tea is mentioned only rarely as a medicine. In one case, a cleric recommends that a fellow monk who is taking the waters to heal an ailment drink tea too.[50] In another, an unnamed cleric asks for "tea as a medicine" to help in a battle with boils.[51]

In keeping with a long tradition, the ceremonial use of tea was common. When there was a birth in the Kanezawa family or on the third anniversary of his father Akitoki's death, tea was consumed.[52] One document describes a variety of tea utensils employed in the coming of age ceremony for Hōjō Takatoki in 1309.[53] The Kanezawa also frequently provided tea to Shōmyōji and other Buddhist institutions for ceremonial purposes. The reading of the *Lotus Sutra* has already been noted as a ritual requiring tea; Sadaaki gave Ken'a three bags of tea for use in a great tea bowl (*dai chawan*) for the summer ritual when the ancestors were venerated (*urabon*).[54] Rites honoring Buddhist patriarchs such as Kūkai could not have proceeded without the necessary amount of tea.[55]

The Kanezawa collection reveals that Shōmyōji was a major consumer of the beverage, essentially in four ways.[56] First, Ken'a, the chief monk throughout most of Sadaaki's active life, used the beverage for a variety of events befitting his position. These would include some of the rituals already mentioned. Second, he also gave presents to the branch temple Gokurakuji in Kamakura and to the Kanezawa family, although he received more presents than he gave. Third, the many monks who dwelt within the precincts of Shōmyōji also drank tea daily. Finally, tea was utilized to provide financial support to the temple both through its production and in other business dealings. In a document dated to 1317, an individual asks for the purchase of five *kin* (3,000 grams) of tea, three *kin* at one price and two at another.[57] This type of transaction undoubtedly helped to fill Shōmyōji's coffers.

Tea gatherings were the newest form of consumption, coming on the scene as the quality of tea improved in step with technological breakthroughs. Sadaaki was a main figure in the tea parties of the early fourteenth century, whether they were held in Kyoto or Kamakura. No one knows how Sadaaki came by his affinity for tea, but it is likely that he began imbibing the drink at an early age. Even before he was appointed to the Rokuhara Office in 1302, Sadaaki had ample opportunity to consume tea at his homes in the Kanto. One was located in Kamakura near the Tsurugaoka Hachiman Shrine and was for official business, and the second was situated on the Kanezane ancestral lands, to which Sadaaki retired. In Kamakura, his home included a room (*kaisho*) for greeting and entertaining guests. Tea was served there. In Kanezawa, Sadaaki apparently held frequent tea gatherings (*chakai*): "If I could receive even a little of the best new tea (*shincha*) from the temple, I would be happy. Because people who like tea come and enter [into our house], I must always prepare for them."[58] This particular record dates from 1317, after Sadaaki had returned from his appointments in Kyoto, but it is likely that his wealthy and politically powerful family prepared for tea gatherings often. The documents even refer to a storehouse for charcoal for use in tea parties.

Moreover, it is clear that "the temple" to which Sadaaki was referring was Shōmyōji, just over the mountains from his ancestral Kanezawa estate and lands. As noted earlier, this temple had tea fields within its precincts and produced the herb from several of its proprietary lands, so there is every reason to believe that Sadaaki was exposed to tea at a young age, even while still a resident of the Kanto. On another occasion, Sadaaki mentioned wisteria viewing, for which he requested "two or three kinds of new tea" from Shōmyōji.[59]

The tea parties as revealed in the Kanezawa collection suggest themes apparent in gatherings of later times. At the typical party, friends such as Ken'a prepared not only tea but also noodles, Chinese dumplings, or teacakes for a light snack. Chinese poems were written and exchanged among the guests. The room had its full complement of Chinese goods (*karamono*), brought from China in one of the ships traveling there under Sadaaki's auspices. Sources imply that Ken'a, an avid Zen monk, had enjoyed these parties with Sadaaki's father and some of his housemen.

Sadaaki refrained from writing Chinese poetry; he mostly enjoyed the tea and ceremonial activities.[60]

Tea parties such as those noted symbolize the transformation that tea was just beginning to undergo at the end of the Kamakura period. Acquired through trade and taxation as well as gift giving, tea had become an object of individual pleasure seeking, although it still retained its medicinal purposes. As stone tea grinders and bamboo whisks became more common, they had made this newest function for the beverage possible. The cultivation methods at Toganoo also spread to new areas. As more care was taken in the farming of tea, Toganoo became Japan's first brand name for the beverage. This transformation in the taste and ultimately in the function of tea would hasten its spread to other social classes, who cultivated, processed, and consumed tea in an increasingly mass market.

## THE GRADUAL EXPANSION OF THE TEA MARKET DURING THE MID- AND LATE 1300s

With the destruction of the Kamakura shogunate in 1333, Japan entered a long era of sporadic civil strife and disunity. After a brief period of rule in the Kenmu Restoration of 1333–1336, Ex-emperor GoDaigo squared off against the Ashikaga family in internecine combat engulfing Kyoto between 1336 and 1338. GoDaigo established his headquarters in Yoshino, south of Kyoto in Yamato Province, and Ashikaga Takauji captured another branch of the imperial family to create the Muromachi shogunate seated in Kyoto. From 1339 through 1350, hostilities became regionalized in eastern Honshu, Kyushu, and Yamato. Then widespread violence erupted again within the leadership of the Ashikaga family during 1350–1355. After 1355, the two courts fought mostly in western Honshu, Kyushu, and Yamato. Warfare decreased noticeably after 1363, but violence erupted now and again until 1394, by which time the Ashikaga had managed to unify the imperial line under their control.

The effect of these wars and campaigns was to accelerate the trend toward political and economic regionalism. The new Muromachi shogunate reigned in conjunction with about thirty-seven local leaders known as constable lords (*shugo daimyo*), each of whom controlled about one to three provinces in a rather tenuous grasp. Usually these daimyo were the most powerful family within their bailiwick, but there were other samurai bands and religious institutions that held considerable properties and economic interests within the daimyo's jurisdiction. During the fourteenth century, with violence widespread, Japan became a mosaic of political and economic blocs.

The habit-forming beverage, now sweeter and tastier than ever, prospered within this decentralized context. Beginning around 1350, a budding tea industry began to emerge. Different regions of Japan competed against each other with their own unique brands of tea:

> Of the famous tea mountains of our dynasty, Toganoo is the best. Ninnaji, Daigoji, Uji, Hamuro [in Yamato], Hannyaji [in Yamato], and Kannōji [in Tanba]: these are next. In addition, Muroo in Yamato, Yashima in Iga, Kawai in Ise, Kiyomi in Suruga, and Kawagoe in Musashi—all these are specially mentioned throughout the realm. The famous places at Ninnaji and Yamato and Iga compare to the tea fields here and there just like agate to trash. Then, too, Toganoo compares to Ninnaji and Daigoji like gold to lead.[61]

This quotation, taken from a source completed during the mid-fourteenth century, lists the most famous tea production centers in Japan. While the most delicious tea apparently still came from Yamato and Yamashiro, it is notable that tea drinkers could also find the tasty beverage in Tanba, Iga, Ise, Suruga, and Musashi.

These named places may have been the best, but tea patches were also located "here and there" throughout the realm. Other records dating to the period 1340–1400 describe fields in Saidaiji and Hamuro in Yamato, Yamashina (2), Uji (2), and Saga in Yamashiro, Kii (3), Settsu (3), Tanba (3), Izumi (2), Mino and Shimōsa (3).[62] By the 1350s, tea was being cultivated, processed, and consumed widely throughout the Kinai, central Honshu, and the Kanto plain. As one writer of the 1300s put it, "new tea flows unexpectedly throughout the world."[63] Outstanding brand-name centers of tea had multiplied with the shift to a more regional political and economic structure, and would become an essential ingredient in the rise of a consumer society much later.

With many different brands competing against one another, tea was on its way to becoming big business, as is implied in this incident dated to the first half of the fourteenth century:

> Every year we collect ten *kin* [6,000 grams] of your Akaiwa tea, don't we? This year, too, we collected ten *kin*, and according to various rumors at this time, mysterious "evil bands" (*akutō*) rose up on the roads. We took great precautions and found a guide. Because of this, we did not lose a great deal [of tea]. In the end, the road guide desired two *kin* [about 1,200 grams], and since we said that we would give up that much, we have been grievously admonished in various ways. Despite this, because we have brought [the tea] with no incident, we present to you eight *kin* [about 4,800 grams].[64]

This tea was probably due to Shōmyōji annually as a tax, but during the period of violence accompanying the fall of Kamakura and the wars between GoDaigo and the Ashikaga, outlaws on the road made transporting the valuable cargo dangerous. In this case, the brigands lost out when the carriers engaged a guide who knew the value of the cargo that he was bringing to the temple. What he did with his portion of the tea is not known, but his ready acceptance of one-fifth of this freight as payment for delivery suggests that tea was a valuable market commodity. The temple's admonition of the haulers also shows that tea was an irreplaceable item for the clergy.

There are other indications of the increasing value being assigned to tea. During the wars between the Northern and Southern Dynasties, tea from Tōzenji in Migatani is listed right along with rice provisions, implying that the beverage was procured for troops.[65] Perhaps troops carrying tea provisions spread the beverage to new areas. Most notably, tea fields increasingly appear in land documents, particularly deeds of commendation to temples and other Buddhist institutions in memory of a believer. The very first describes a donation to Mount Kōya in 1341; later sacral gifts include a Hamuro field (18 x 33 meters) in Yamato to Rinsenji in 1354; two Settsu patches to Tada Shrine in 1363 and again in 1366; a Tanba field given to the provincial Gokurakuji in 1368; a Saga patch donated to Rinsenji in 1368; an inheritance of a tea plot in Kumano, enacted in 1382; two fields listed near Kyoto in 1389 and 1391; another commendation of .1 acre to Tada Shrine in 1393; and finally, two gifts to Kumidadera in Izumi Province in 1393 and 1394. Usually these gifts include information about other dry fields in the vicinity; the local landscape seems to have been a mixture of small farming patches used for various purposes. The growing value attached to these fields undoubtedly implies improving cultivation methods for tea patches, a trend evident in other types of dry and irrigated agriculture at this time too. Just as clearly as tea itself was now a marketable commodity with a cash value, the lands that produced the bush had acquired considerable economic value for their owners.[66]

By the end of the fourteenth century, the first prices for tea become available.[67] In a tax document dated to 1382 for Akaiwa in Shimo Kawabe Estate, property of Shōmyōji, one *kin* (600 grams) is listed as bringing 300 copper coins.[68] Altogether, between 1355 and 1402, prices for tea appear twelve times—five for Kyoto, thrice for Kanezawa, and once each for Kamakura, Ninnaji, and Harima. Because the amount of tea sold is not always specified, it is possible to make only a few generalizations from these prices, except that Kyoto tea was for sale for between 28.5 and 32 copper coins per *kin*, while tea in Kamakura cost 172.2 coins. One batch of what must have been especially fine tea from Ninnaji cost 300 coins per *kin* in 1384. Therefore, tea seems to have been plentiful and cheap in and around the Muromachi capital, while the beverage came at a much dearer price in areas farther away from the city. Still, it is significant that by the late 1300s a market for tea extended from Kyoto to Kamakura.

All kinds of individuals and institutions were involved in the fourteenth-century tea market. Historians have uncovered a more detailed picture of the major role that tea continued to play in the economy of Buddhist temples, especially the aforementioned Shōmyōji. During one year in the 1340s, tea fetched more than thirteen strings of cash, and Shōmyōji utilized the proceeds to buy rice, beans, and perilla oil.[69] A document from about the same period states that the tea harvest from a previous year was worth 6.8 strings of cash, and that after the temple paid tea gatherers 3.45 strings for their work, the remainder was to be allotted toward the expenses of the institution.[70] In 1354, Shōmyōji paid out at least 900 copper coins to tea pickers on some of its far-flung lands.[71] References to tea workers suggest that the industry was moving toward a higher level of complexity and organization, as the population increased, laborers were more plentiful and thus cheaper, agronomic techniques grew more productive, social units turned more numerous and cohesive, and commercial relations became more monetized and efficient.

Specifically, overcoming the labor bottleneck was an important improvement for tea, with the large workforce required for plucking and processing. Unsurprisingly, tea dealers provide the first information about the condition of their employees beginning in the mid-fourteenth century.[72] Such workers as pickers and roasters must have been in demand, because in 1350 the head of Gion Shrine quarreled with Enryakuji on Mount Hiei about some "borrowed" tea pickers from the shrine. The shrine wanted Enryakuji to grant the laborers freedom from their normal obligation to work fields in Yamashiro producing for Kōrakuji, a temple located in the Kyoto vicinity. Perhaps there was some confusion on the matter, because, in a letter dated to 3/29, another lower Gion official lamented that laborers had not yet even begun to pick the tea for Kōrakuji. He applied to begin plucking on 4/1, probably to receive Gion's workers back in a hurry. He also recorded the gift of one bag of tea from Enryakuji, possibly from the fields of Kōrakuji. The shrine head, however, sent a letter on 3/29 expressing his pleasure at learning that his workers had indeed been freed from their labors because the leaves had not yet sprouted in great quantity at Kōrakuji. On the same day, Gion Shrine noted that it had received two more bags of tea—three in total—all from the fields of Kōrakuji controlled by Enryakuji.

On 2/23/1352, correspondence from Gion Shrine reveals more about the nature of the workforce. It mentions a tea patch apparently at issue during 3/6 and 3/7/1352. To be more specific, lowly shrine workers called *rincha* were scheduled to begin processing tea on 3/6, even as other female laborers known as a *miyagomori* were busy plucking leaves. Two roasters produced two *kin* (1,200 grams), or about twenty bags of what was probably powdered tea on that day. On 3/7/1352, both types of workers continued the tea picking and used one roaster to make thirty *ryō* of tea, a smaller amount. Thus at Gion Shrine, the plucking and roasting of the tea leaves fell to lowly female attendants, even though they did not produce too much of the beverage.[73] On 4/28, the Head of Gion Shrine made a present of low-quality leftover tea leaves, "even though the shape [of the leaves] was poor."[74]

Three years later on 12/20/1355, Suda Hachiman Shrine in Kii Province tried to prohibit abuse of its workforce.[75] A record of three articles was sent from a locally powerful warrior also serving as the shrine head to six shrine attendants, prohibiting certain behaviors. In the first article, attendants overseeing tea picking are accused of forcing the laborers (*waranbe*) to do the tea plucking without pay, a practice the head condemned. In the second, attendants were warned against having the workers pick, not only the attendants' own tea, but also that of their sons-in-law. In the third article, the head of the shrine writes that because the attendants were not providing much remuneration to the tea gatherers, they were going hungry. Moreover, when the attendants did not need workers they took collateral from them anyway, a breach of conduct roundly disapproved. It is difficult to determine how widespread these labor abuses may have been at other centers such as the aforementioned Gion Shrine, but this record certainly emphasizes the lowly status accorded to tea workers. Those laborers toiled in poor conditions during the Tokugawa and modern eras in Japan too, and today often make great exertions in such circumstances in India and Sri Lanka.

During the latter half of the fourteenth century in Japan, tea appears to have been rapidly becoming a commercial commodity. Multiple brand names were well known, even as improved cultivation spread to new areas. Tea was so valuable to Buddhist clerics that the commodity played a significant role in financing their institutions' activities. Lands producing the plant gained in value until tea patches appeared in numerous kinds of economic transactions. What prices are available for the beverage indicate that a tea-trading network encompassed the region from Kyoto to Kamakura. The first information on tea organizations show the widespread employment of tea gatherers and processing agents, individuals of lowly status sometimes suffering abuse. All these facts point to the distant future of the delicious beverage for a modern industrial and consumer society. That modernity, however, was a long, long way off in the 1300s.

## TRADITIONAL CHARACTERISTICS OF FOURTEENTH-CENTURY TEA

Even during this transitional epoch, tea retained many of its more conservative aspects. Gift giving was a most common means of exchanging tea leaves. Not all tea suddenly became the green powdered variety; in fact, beverage types multiplied as the knowledge of tea processing became more widespread. Court functionaries resisted buying and selling tea on the market and instead did preparations on their own, or had their servants do them. Most important, for the leading intellectuals of the period tea retained its associations with China and Buddhism as an exotic and foreign drink.

For example, on 12/1/1343, the head (*shamu shikkō*) of the very same Gion Shrine that had its own labor force to pick tea expressed gratitude for a gift of one bag (*tsutsumi*) from distant Mino Province. He then stated that next year there would be a tea picking at the imperial palace (*gosho*), suggesting that those patches originating in the Heian period were still productive.[76] In the lean year of 1350, Gion bought some leaves from the Yamashina district of Kyoto. In 1351, Gion Shrine purchased more "fresh leaves" from the same place.[77]

No one knows for sure what the officials at Gion Shrine did with the tea leaves they had accumulated. On 3/23/1350, however, an attendant at Gion put to work two tea roasters (*hoiro;* figure 3) and dried 1.65 *koku* of oxidized black tea (*kuronicha*) and 1.42 *kin* of toasted tea (*aburicha*), possibly for sale.[78] What types of tea were *kuronicha* and *aburicha?* Although it is clear that these two products were not powdered green tea, it is difficult to tell exactly what they may have been.[79] The former appears to have been some type of oxidized black tea, perhaps akin to what is known in Japan today as *batabatacha.* The latter is still consumed in China today; tea leaves are roasted but not ground and then placed in hot water for drinking. It may well have been what later came to be known as stir-roasted tea (*kamairicha*). The exact process remains unclear, but it is important to note that residents of the Japanese islands consumed an increasing variety of teas.[80] *Matcha* hardly took the islands by storm.

The diary of Nakahara Moromori, a low-level legal expert employed by the court, reveals that some people resisted the commodification of their favorite drink. During the wars that beset the region, minor officials

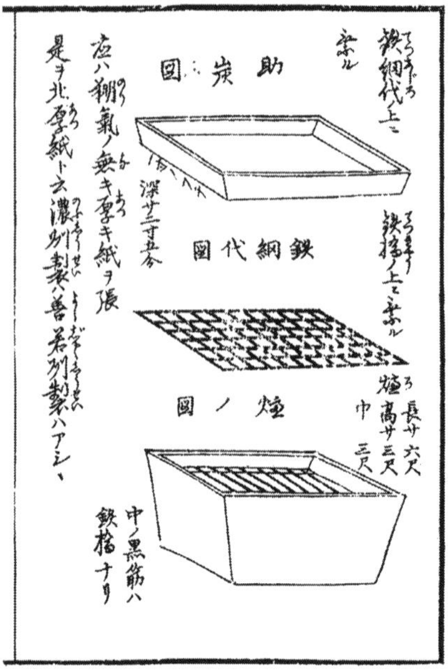


Figure 3. Tea roaster of the 1500s. From *Nihon nōsho zenshū 47: Seicha zukai* (Tokyo: Nōsan gyoson bunka kyōkai, 1997), p. 218.

such as Nakahara probably suffered a decline in income. Rather than buying tea in the Kyoto market, they continued their age-old practice of gift giving by searching out tea plots within the city and doing the work of picking and processing themselves.

In entries ranging from 1339 through 1367, Nakahara jotted down his experiences with tea.[81] On 8/1/1339, a ceremonial day (*hassaku*) when gifts were exchanged, Nakahara gave and received several types of tea from acquaintances in the bureaucracy.[82] On 5/11/1340, Nakahara processed tea from a patch at Ume no kōji, located within Kyoto.[83] There were probably several places within urban Kyoto where tea bushes flourished. On 4/6/1345, Nakahara processed tea from a place known as the "granary" (*gokusōin*), situated in the western part of the city, and gave the product as a gift to an official in the retired emperor's household.[84] Given the date, the tea must have been the first of the season. Later on 4/3/1365, after processing tea leaves, Nakahara reported that the group had just over four *kin* (2,400 grams), which they entrusted to their servants to bring home.[85] Occasionally, Nakahara dispatched some underlings (*aozamurai; kabu*) to do the plucking, but an official usually processed the leaves. On 4/24/1367, Nakahara accepted nine bags (*tsutsumi*) from faraway Iga Province.[86] Even in Kyoto, the market for tea was limited at this time.

Finally, consider the cultural image of tea in the 1300s. Zen clerics were, of course, the leading intellectuals of their time. As early as the late thirteenth century, Zen Buddhism began flourishing in Japan and tea played a critical role in the life of Zen monasteries. Many Zen institutions adopted rules governing the drinking of tea.[87] Called the *Pure Precepts of the Great Mirror* (*Daikan shingi*), these principles were based on Chinese models and governed all aspects of the behavior of Zen monks. For example, when one entered a Zen temple for the purpose of religious practice, rules dictated that the visitor be given a bowl of powdered tea by four monks, all seated in Chinese fashion around a low table (*yotsugashira charei*). Tea was also served during various ceremonies throughout the year (such as Yōsai's birthday at Kyoto's Kenninji). *Pure Precepts* also outlined the care of tea utensils, as they were used for meals as well.[88] Zen monks even took tea with their baths in the summertime.[89]

Zen clergy produced a voluminous literature revealing some of the associations that the beverage had for them.[90] In particular, the so-called Five Mountains Poetry composed during the late Kamakura and Period of the Northern and Southern Dynasties frequently refers to tea:

**"In Gratitude for the Blessings of Tea"**

Visiting snowdrifts in the early spring,
I plan a marvelous meal.
I crush the golden powder in a grinder (*usu*).
I boil brownish-red fowl and beast in a pot.
Gathering spring waters, I use Lu Yu as my master.
Holding a small bowl, I recall Lu-tong.
The Wuyi flavor tried once,
How can it be as good as this one pouch [of tea]?

**"My Feelings on Planting Tea"**

I regret every day my black karma and every year it becomes heavier.
Taking up a hoe alone by myself, I walk across the garden in spring.
If I do not plant tea in the mountains, all will remain like this.
After my life, will there be some way that my name can be known?

**"The Pavilion for Collecting Pure Water"**

In the sky under the pavilion, the snow on the river has half cleared.
For boiling tea, first I try to collect deep clear water.
If Lu Yu tried this flavor,
Would he change his mind and make Lian and Quan the most famous places?[91]

Originating from such renowned Zen temples as Nanzenji, Kenchōji, Engakuji, Manjūji, Tōfukuji, Jufukuji, and Shōkokuji, the poems show that, at least for these religious intellectuals, tea still had strong associations with the exotic and foreign. The poetry was written in Chinese, and references to adepts like Lu Yu and Lu Tong, such scenic spots in China as

Mount Wuyi, and the springs at Lian and Quan suggest that tea reminded its fourteenth-century Zen drinkers very much of the land of its origin. Buddhism is another theme particularly apparent in the second poem; all three poems evoke a sense of reclusiveness and being alone with one's thoughts. Even after 650 years in Japan, tea was often a foreign—even mysterious—thing, to be cherished for its ability to inspire poetry, aloofness, and visions of the distant Middle Kingdom.

## THE DRAMATIC GROWTH OF A GREEN-TEA INDUSTRY, 1400–1550: CULTIVATION

During this century and a half, a synergy of the general demographic and agricultural trends noted previously encouraged tea production to grow by leaps and bounds. Historians suspect this because references to the amounts of tea to be consumed increase by ten or even one hundred times.[92] For instance, in a document from 1400 listing expenses for a pagoda, tea was given in nineteen bags for the first plucking and eighteen for the second. A diary entry for 1405 mentions twenty bags carried to Kyoto from Kii Province, and the next year an estate produced seventy bags. Amounts ranging from thirty to fifty bags were common during the early fifteenth century. Then, beginning in the 1430s, the amounts of tea given as gifts or produced on farms rose yet again, to the hundreds of *kin* (over 60 kilograms). According to the *Kanmon gyoki,* a diary kept by an imperial offspring, in 1431 the diarist received over 200 *kin* (120 kgs) of special tea (*racha*); then, in the next year, the amount was 300 *kin* (180 kgs). The year 1432 must have seen an unusually rich harvest, because another document states that Yoshioka Estate in Inaba Province produced 100 *kin* (60 kgs) in the fourth month alone. In 1441, an estate in Tōtōmi Province yielded 300 bags, while in 1442 an estate in Settsu produced 120 *kin* (72 kg). Although, of course, small amounts still appear, in general references to tea are in amounts of 30 bags or more.[93]

The diffusion of tea cultivation to virtually all the regions suited climatically for the plant is a second measure of the growth of the industry. Altogether, historians can pinpoint the location of about ninety tea fields for the era dating from Emperor Saga's order to plant in the Kinai in 815 until the end of the medieval period in 1600. Of those ninety tea patches, exactly half date from 1397 to the end of medieval times. Another thirty-two are found in historical materials originating from the preceding period discussed above (1341–1396). Clearly, the fourteenth century was a time of expansion for tea growing, and the ensuing two hundred years continued the trend to its natural limits. What is more, scholars have not yet finished culling sources for references to tea fields, and so it is likely that many fields have gone unnoted.[94]

It is not simply that there are so many more references to tea patches during the closing centuries of the medieval era. Those forty-five tea fields show a geographical distribution throughout western, central, and eastern Japan where the soil and climatic conditions are the most appropriate for the tea bush to grow. As might be expected, the Kinai and its nearby provinces garner the most references, with Yamashiro having eleven, Yamato eight, Ōmi four, Kii three, and Settsu, Wakasa, Kawachi, and Tanba one each. Proceeding outward from the capital region, western Honshu has one allusion each for Harima and Inaba, while central Honshu includes data for Mino (3), Tōtōmi (2), Iga (1), Ise (1), and Echizen (1). There is one reference each for Sanuki in Shikoku, Shimōsa in the Kanto, and for northern (Buzen) and southern Kyushu (Satsuma). Clearly, tea production had become an enterprise that flourished within many provinces south of cold northeastern Honshu. The scholar who drew up these statistics believes that many unnamed Zen temples also took up cultivation during the Muromachi period (1333–1573), especially in Kyushu.[95] Tea was so popular that merchants found profit in marketing the beverage to northeastern Honshu.[96] There is even indirect evidence that farmers were cropping tea, imported through China, to the far south in the independent kingdom of Okinawa.[97]

The increase in tea production proceeded as part of a more general social and economic transformation beginning to sweep Japan from the late thirteenth century.[98] In particular, population expansion yielded larger numbers of cheaper labor, a bottleneck that had discouraged most enterprises, especially tea production, before 1300. The improved flavor, habit-forming character, close ties to Zen, and possible use for military provisions also comprised factors particularly related to rising demand for the herb. Another specific reason for the wider diffusion of tea was the importation of a new strain from southern China.[99] As noted in chapter 1, tea seeds were first introduced to Japan and Korea from China during the middle or late eighth century, a relatively long pistil being their distinguishing feature. For Japan, scientists have also noted only the widespread diffusion of a second tea plant with a short pistil and a flower shaped differently from that of the earlier strain. Analysis puts the date of its importation into Japan at some time during the middle Muromachi age, likely the fifteenth century. This second tea variety probably came from Hangzhou in southern China, where numerous Zen temples were located. One theory would have it that when the Muromachi shogunate and the Ming dynasty initiated the tally trade in the late 1300s, Zen monks and other travelers brought seeds and perhaps even plants back from this region in southern China. This second, fifteenth-century strain of tea plant spread rapidly throughout Japan, possibly because it was hardier or tasted better. Under these circumstances, it is little wonder that tea cultivation spread quickly and widely in Japan during this era.

Tea could also be grown in small, marginal areas where other crops could not, and the leaves were harvested in the spring before rice was transplanted. Careful study has allowed scholars to develop a typology for the various tea fields of this era.[100] First, there were those true tea fields (*honbatake*) planted as unirrigated dry fields. Bushes were located in one spot and measured in the same units (*chō.tan.bu*) utilized for rice paddies, although they seem to have covered only a small area. Often pine trees were dispersed among the tea bushes to provide cover from the sun and produce a sweeter tea. Because these were dry fields, it was not unusual for peasants to crop wheat, soybeans, and even untaxed products such as chestnuts or persimmons among the tea plants too. In modern agronomy, scholars distinguish between those often rather sizable fields devoted exclusively to tea cultivation and those where other crops are mixed in, but during the medieval period such a distinction did not exist.

Second, there were those tea patches farmed in the mountains (*yamacha*). It is important to remember that the first tea grown in Japan was associated with temples such as Enryakuji and Shōmyōji, and that these temples were situated in the mountains. Toganoo was also a mountainous, tree-filled location. Examples of these hilly tea fields have appeared throughout this narrative, especially in the section concerning the Kanezawa Hōjō. As later examples, in 1451 Mount Happō in Yamato Province produced tea, and in 1508 Mount Daigo near Kyoto was recorded as the source of mountain tea. Among the mountain fields, many must have been cropped in swidden style.[101] Mountain tea patches were also mixed with groves and commons near villages. Even today, farmers in Yamanashi prefecture grow tea bushes intermingled with trees and prepare the beverage for consumption there in the wooded mountains.

Third, cultivators tended tea bushes in their household plots. As tea increasingly became a tax item from estates (*shōen*), on-site landlords grew tea fields near the offices of the estate. Two examples exist for the fourteenth century: in 1354 at Sumida Estate in Kii Province, and in 1382 for land controlled by an official of Ise Shrine. Later, in 1553, a local magnate of Suruga Province possessed near his residence a tea field allotted exclusively for his own use.

The fourth type of tea patch was perhaps the most noteworthy, as it was located on the raised boundaries (*aze; kuro; mama*) between rice paddies (*keihan chaen*). As rice farming spread and became more stable after 1300, cultivators looked for second crops to grow on the raised dividers between wet-rice paddies, including beans and tea. As one may imagine, often rice paddies were situated on the flat extensions molded from mountains; the boundaries among the paddies might be steep and curved. Apparently, these paths were well suited to tea cultivation. The scholar who has described this type of tea patch in greatest detail has found examples from 1397, 1425, 1539, 1559, and 1575.[102]

Such cases reveal much about tea cultivation and the land rights associated with them at this time. In 1397, a document of commendation indicates that a tea field was included along with eight *tan* of rice paddy; a subunit of Tōdaiji simply farmed and harvested the tea without regard for the entity collecting the rice tax. In 1425, a document of commendation indicates that tea bushes occupied the long, slim raised dividers between rice paddies in Ōmi Province. According to the record, the tea patch was small but located on the southern exposure of the house where it would receive more sunlight.

At first, the paddy and tea field were considered a unit, but as tea bushes began to produce more, the tea and rice lands fell under differing jurisdictions. In 1547, this complex set of rights led to a dispute (*sōron*) about the tea field's status as a set with the rice paddy, with one side asserting their oneness and another protesting that they were separate. In the outcome, the Muromachi shogunate decided that the two were indeed different lands under separate jurisdictions, implying the increasing productivity and value of tea patches.

Because of the complexity of tax and land tenure arrangements, all sorts of agreements were written. In 1539, Upper Kamo Shrine loaned the product from tea bushes situated on twenty-four paddy boundaries in Yamashiro Province to an aristocrat for ten years. In this manner, the unnamed civil aristocrat undoubtedly came into possession of tea for both drinking and gift giving. In 1559, a peasant associated with Ise Shrine sold one of these "boundary tea fields" together with other dry fields, but in other cases the two might be auctioned off to different owners. In 1575, a "boundary tea patch" shown in maps for Yamashiro Province was among the lands commended to a minor local Buddhist temple by the Mibu family, a middle-ranked aristocratic family. The agreement allowed the temple to cultivate and harvest the tea in return for 10 coins paid to the Mibu family annually. The beverage was then used during a reading of the *Lotus Sutra* for the funeral services of farmers in a nearby village. The "boundary tea field" played a crucial role in the spread of tea cultivation throughout the southwestern two-thirds of the archipelago and was part of the transformation in agriculture that took place during the latter half of the medieval age.

Early on, landlords directly managed, cultivated, and harvested the tea in most patches, no matter what kind they might have been. In 1450, on Mount Happō the tea bushes were regularly cleaned with more than fifty laborers, and in the fourth month Kōfukuji used twenty-seven people to pluck tea leaves.[103] The Mibu family had servants pluck and process their tea in 1478.[104] Another aristocratic family called the Konoe allotted 200 coins to maintain a tea field in Yamashiro Province, while the aristocratic Yamashina family planted tea bushes in 1480.[105]

Tea fields located within estates were usually associated with a small temple (*jian*) that served the residents. These small temples might also be located within the estate official compound. Apparently, all the equipment for tea processing—a stone tea grinder, a roaster (*hoiro*)—was available on these tea farms, and historical materials typically show that cleaning of the estate tea patches commenced in the second month.[106] Tea picking then followed during the third and fourth months, utilizing as many as fifty workers. Thereafter processing took place, much as it had since the mid-thirteenth century.

Also during the 1400s, however, some peasants living in communal settlements (*sō*) began taking control of their own tea fields. At Suganoura and Imabori Villages in Ōmi Province, for example, the members controlled and managed their own tea fields. The same also held true for the bushes already noted in the 1575 example, while in Ise Province peasants bought and sold dry fields that included tea bushes. During the 1500s, many peasant communities took over direct management of tea fields in return for paying rent or taxes. At Wachi Estate in Tanba Province, for instance, the landlord collected 400 coins per year from numerous small tea fields. By the Warring States period (1467–1590), small but stable tea fields had spread to innumerable peasant villages, with the tea being collected as a tax or sold on the market. Tea production had reached a new high by 1550, thanks to more intensive cultivation methods that engaged many sectors of the population.

## THE CONTINUING MATURATION OF A MEDIEVAL TEA INDUSTRY, 1400–1550: EXCHANGE, MARKETING, AND CONSUMPTION

With production at an all-time high, more and more tea changed hands. Three modes predominated: gift giving, land taxation, and buying and selling on the market. Even during the fifteenth and sixteenth centuries, gift giving still represented an important form of exchange; over a third of the references to tea shipments in one compendium of sources portray the commodity as a gift.[107] Of these references, almost all involve donations to civil aristocrats; apparently these customs continued despite the straitened circumstances in which many families found themselves during these centuries. Presents to Buddhist institutions occur occasionally, but most temples either grew their own bushes or found other ways to obtain the tea that they needed. The rest of the time warriors were the donors or recipients of tea gifts. The Muromachi shogunate maintained its own tea patches for the purpose of donating tea to various persons and groups.[108] Gifts were doled out as thank offerings, funeral presents, seasonal gifts, and congratulations upon the assumption of an important governmental post. The elites also gave tea gifts for an audience (especially with the emperor), and for the safe delivery of a child. Usually the gifts were in small quantities of a few bags or so. Toganoo tea was popular as a gift denoting special respect or meaning: "[T]he annual tea from Toganoo has arrived. Please convey my thanks and happiness. Hirohashi Morimitsu"[109]A prominent civil aristocrat, Hirohashi was clearly pleased with the regular gift from the "sweet fields" of Toganoo.

These gifts were so frequent among the elites because tea continued to play a multifaceted ritualistic function. Among warriors, there were rites involving tea for the shogun Ashikaga Yoshinori (1394–1441) on several occasions.[110] The Muromachi shogunate utilized large amounts of tea for ceremonies conducted on 2/24 of each year.[111] The Irobe, a samurai family living in Echigo Province during the Warring States period, conducted New Year's rituals during 1/8–1/15 in which they doled out the herb in large amounts. This samurai family also used tea for other festivals and possessed tea shops.[112] In overseas relations, Muromachi emissaries to Korea expected and received tea for their visits during the 1400s.[113] In 1420, Korean ambassador to the Muromachi shogunate Sŏng Hui-gyŏng spent half a day at the Zen temple Myōrakuji, admiring the green grass and imbibing stir-roasted steeped tea (*kamairicha; tōcha*) popular by that time in both Ming China and Chosŏn Korea.[114] Civil aristocrats and Buddhist clerics continued to drink and make offerings of tea in rituals, as described throughout this book.[115]

It is symbolic of the age and the increasing productivity of tea fields that most references in which the plant changed hands between 1396 and 1514 encompassed taxation from estates. About 40 percent of the time exchanges during the fifteenth and sixteenth centuries involved a tax item.[116] With the exception of an estate in Tōtōmi Province in 1441 that provided 300 *kin* (180 kgs) to a temple, all the tea-producing estates were located in the Kinai or nearby provinces. Most recipients were temples, including Kōfukuji, Tōji, Enryakuji, and Tōdaiji. Civil aristocrats also received small amounts of tax tea from local farms. In only one case was a warrior (*shugo daimyo*) the beneficiary, and then apparently for his help in collecting the tax.

The tea tax was usually collected in kind and shipped to the big cities of Nara and Kyoto. By the 1400s, some peasant villages had a freestanding teahouse (*chaya*) where merchants or other estate representatives gathered the tea tax for shipment to the city.[117] Amounts were usually small, especially payments to civil aristocrats. Examples include the Yamashiro estate that delivered 30 *kin* to Kōfukuji and an Echizen farm that sent twenty bags of tea to Nara. Large amounts ranging from 60 to 180 kgs also appear however. Some tax collectors preferred cash to the commodity.

As one might expect from the collection of the tea tax in cash, buying and selling the beverage on the market was a growing method for obtaining tea. Altogether there are nine references to the marketing of this item between 1405 and 1506, about 22 percent of the total number of tea exchanges.[118] With one exception for Kōfukuji, these exchanges involved civil aristocrats buying or selling tea on the market. For example, a civil aristocrat sold 3.5 *kin* of tea in 1405 to pay his workers.[119] When Kōfukuji bought in Nara, it bought in quantity (35 *kin*), at prices varying from 12 coins per unit to 80 coins per *kin*.[120]

The Yamashina family of civil aristocrats appears in over half the references to the buying and selling of tea. In fact, the diary of the Yamashina family provides an excellent example of the ways in which the typical aristocratic household might expect to come by its tea. One entry for 1468 reads:

Point: [On 5/7] there were four *kin* from Noguchi. The Otowa hut produced 50 bags. Thus Noguchi Hyōe's fee for serving as a middleman [in this tax] is secretly calculated as 100 *hiki* 6 coins.
Point: [On 5/10] Noguchi Hyōe's purchase of tea in the amount of five *kin* arrived. We allotted 150 coins per unit.
Point: [On 5/13] Noguchi's tea was two *kin* at 120 coins per unit. Also, one *kin* of tea tax came.
Point: [On 5/14] two bags of Fushimi tea were sent.[121]

According to this short passage, the Yamashina received tea as a gift (from Fushimi), as a tax item (from Otowa hut and elsewhere), and through buying on the market. So one family took advantage of all three methods to obtain its tea, a mixture of methods likely employed by civil aristocrats, temples, shrines, and warrior families alike.

Finally, sources on the price of tea for the fifteenth and sixteenth centuries are much more plentiful and informative than ever before.[122] Between

1413 and 1567 there were 178 records of transactions in which prices were listed, far more than during the fourteenth century. Of these deals, over one hundred took place in Kyoto. It is not always possible to determine the unit price for the transaction, but apparently tea commonly sold for as little as 2–6 coins for a drink, although Uji tea fetched a far higher price (500 coins). Other centers of the tea business included Nara, with over twenty transactions, and Kanezawa, Hyōgo/Nishinomiya, and Kamakura with eight each. Although scholars cannot be certain about all these markets, the price of the beverage did not vary nearly as much from place to place as it had during the 1300s. In Nara, it was possible to buy tea for as little as 11 coins; in Kanezawa, 15 coins was the going price. Notably, transactions also apparently took place at tea-producing estates; both Niimi Estate in Bitchū Province and Kuze Estate in Yamashiro were scenes of market activity. Altogether, these data suggest that tea production had expanded greatly ever since the early 1300s and that the result was a vigorous market in tea that enveloped much of the archipelago.

There are other signs that tea was a growing business. Between 1408 and 1530, the transfer, donation, and sale of tea fields occurred eighteen times, at least according to one list of sources.[123] Most strikingly, this total includes only two transfers, two commendations, one dispute over a tea patch, and one use of a tea field as collateral. In other words, two-thirds of the references are to the sale of tea plots. For example, in 1455, one Tarōbō sold a tea patch located within the precincts of Kumano Shrine in Kii Province:

> On the sale of a tea field:
>
> Concerning the above, out of necessity, I sell the above place for one string of cash. From next year through the year of the rat, for the next twelve years only, I sell [the tea field]. When the twelve years are over, it should be returned in its original state. Thus the sale is attested to as in this deed.
>
> Kyōtoku 4/4/23 (1455)[124]

In this particular case, the sale was only temporary, but usually the patches were permanently alienated. Particularly between 1449 and 1530, documents in which tea plots are bought or sold predominate, and over half the cases involve tea fields at Uji. Notably, in 1524 and 1530, the Kanbayashi, a family that came to control the production in Uji during the Edo period, was beginning to accumulate parcels in Uji as the reputation of Uji tea soared during the sixteenth century.

Although much of the buying and selling of tea was free on the market, there are indications that some institutions where the demand for tea was especially high created their own merchant organizations (*chaza*).

In particular, Kōfukuji sponsored its own association of tea merchants to operate in Nara. In return for this monopoly privilege, the merchants promised to pay a fee and keep the temple well supplied with its favorite beverage. In 1459, for example, an aristocratic diary attests to a dispute that erupted between the head of the temple and one of its constituent clerical groups known as the *roppō shū*.[125] The dispute was over the imposition of a tax (*kuji*) on shipments of tea within Nara, but the document reveals neither how the dispute was resolved nor anything about the composition of the merchant organization. In 1488, the same source again mentions the tea traders when the head of the organization donated the profits for that year for a festival.[126]

Kōfukuji's tea business in Nara ran into a problem in 1513 in the form of a recalcitrant samurai.[127] Apparently, under normal circumstances the temple collected a tax (*shibachairi kuji*) on merchants selling tea in Nara. In 1513, however, the warrior Hashimoto Kanbenosuke "without reason" held up the shipments and then collected the tax normally due to the temple. According to the complaint, Kōfukuji usually sent permits to these businesspersons at the entrances to Nara and allowed them to trade. Despite that, the warrior robbed the merchants of their permits to do business in Nara and tried to force his own permits on the traders. For instance, the temple complained that the merchants Shōjirōmaru and Yashichi had fees imposed on them as high as 500 coins for their tea shops (*chaya*). According to one scholar, this "Shibacha" was an inferior grade of tea produced locally and then collected at the village level, where a designated merchant then transported the commodity to Nara.[128] In Nara at least, greedy warriors wanted their slice of the increasingly lucrative tea trade.

By the early 1400s at the latest, merchants also made a living by running tea shops throughout Kyoto and Nara.[129] To explain, during the second half of the thirteenth century, clerics set up "hospitality stations" (*settai sho*) at road intersections.[130] Originally affiliated with religious institutions, these hospitality stations served free food and drink to prelates making pilgrimages to sacred sites. Usually, the operators were residents of the local temples or shrines; Zen institutions were especially prominent. Because they were designed to give comfort to and bolster the health of wayfaring monks and pilgrims, running these hospitality stations was considered a proper function of the temples and shrines, and they set aside the harvest from certain fields to maintain them. At first, the stations served food and beverages other than tea. According to the *Jizō bosatsu reigenki-e*, a pictorial source produced during the mid-fourteenth century, however, local monks began serving tea along the roads in western Japan at around 1350.[131] In this scroll there are shelves and a stone tea grinder in the back of the shop, along with a whisk, black-lacquered round teacups, a *tenmoku* tea bowl, and green-and-white porcelain tea bowls. The male server is dressed as a monk. Tea maintains its Buddhist meaning, but in this instance, there is little connotation of the foreign or exotic. The beverage is well on its way to becoming native to the archipelago.

By the late fourteenth century, these "hospitality stations" had become for-profit tea shops aiming to attract the general populace. Records from as early as 1380 indicate that a merchant had established a tea shop near Kenninji, while one from 1395 suggests a going concern related to Gion Shrine. Kitano Shrine had a tea shop as well. The best-known example hails from Tōji in 1403:

> I respectfully request:
>
> The following points as a salesperson of tea: one cup for one copper in front of the Southern Great Gate [of Tōji]
>
> Point: As originally stipulated, I will be allowed to dwell along the southern bank of the river, and even though it is only for a short time, I should not live near the foundation stones under the Gate.
> Point: I will never place my tea-making implements in the rooms of temple servants (*miya no tsukai*) of Chinju Hachiman Shrine for even a short time.
> Point: I will never take fire into the buildings of the temple.
> Point: I will never collect water from the well on the premises.
>
> Concerning these points, if I vary from even one of them, I should be expelled right away from the temple precincts. Respectfully submitted.
> [Signatures] Ōei 10/4 (1403)

Tōji's fears about the fire used to brew the tea turned out to be well-founded, as the very next year, in 1404, the tea seller was tempted by the crowds gathering around the temple and started a fire on the grounds of Tōji. As a result, the temple banned all tea shops from its premises.[132] A law of 1411 repeats many of these points, but also proscribes the "assembling of women for selling tea." Apparently, the use of young beauties to lure customers into the tea shops began well before the Edo period.[133]

Despite such setbacks, tea shops apparently continued to spring up around Kyoto and Nara, and even in the countryside throughout the 1400s. In 1443, Sin Suk-ju served as an ambassador to Muromachi Kyoto: "People are happy when they drink tea. Some set up tea shops (*chajŏm*) along the roads and sell tea. A wayfarer pays out a coin and drinks a bowl."[134] Historians know much about these tea shops because they are portrayed so frequently in pictorial sources of the fifteenth and sixteenth centuries.[135] Tea scenes are set in common Japanese surroundings.

According to these scrolls and screens, tea shops were of two kinds. First, there were small huts built temporarily on the premises of shrines and temples for pilgrims and festival goers. Second, there were more permanent shops that had a roof of thatch or shingles and an earthen floor with the boiler in a corner and a table where the tea was served. Merchants who had their own more or less permanent shops might belong to an organization such as those of Kōfukuji (*zauri*) or might be independent (*miseuri*). Those who worked out of temporary huts often carried their tea-making implements on their backs as peddlers (*furiuri;* figure 4).[136] As they made their rounds, they shouted to passersby to try a bowl, as is attested to in a poem written in 1380 by a Zen monk:

> Opening the window, I hear it:
> A voice selling tea.[137]

There is no mistaking the religious meaning of many of these tea shops especially the temporary ones.[138] They are portrayed at the festivals of Gion Shrine, at good-fortune rites (*setsubun kai*), at ceremonies to ward off hungry ghosts (*segaki*), and at gatherings where living things were

Figure 4. Street tea peddler. *Tsukinami fūzoku zu* (artist unknown). TNM Image Archives.

released into the wild (*hōjō-e*). Tea shops also operated during fund-raising campaigns (*kanjin*) and pilgrimages. Apparently doling out a swig of tea was related to the health benefits of the beverage, as it was intended to guard the wellness of the various participants. Even though tea shops aided in all these religious functions, as they did business for cash, the shrine or temple in question usually collected dues from the tea merchants. Low-level shrine residents, such as those mentioned in connection with the processing of tea at Gion Shrine (*rincha* and *miyagomori*) or those noted in the 1403 document (*miya no tsukai*), often pitched in to brew and dole out the tea. According to the Jesuit Luis Frois, many workers were female. Most traders could not afford a stone grinder, and so the religious institution allowed them to use theirs.

For the most part, the tea provided to the general populace is assumed to have been powdered tea (*matcha*), as may be inferred from the use of a stone grinder. Evidence from short comedic skits (*kyōgen*), however, suggests that the tea was of low quality (*hikusu*).[139] Then, too, there were peddlers selling a variety of "steeped" tea (*senjicha*) with dried ginger or persimmon seeds added as a medicine. The operator simply boiled up the concoction consisting of processed tea leaves and the additives and ladled it into cups. The comedic skit "Something Steeped" (*senjimono*) portrays just this sort of merchant saying, "Every year I have a seat at the Gion Festival for my tea shop and sell this kind of steeped stuff (*senjimono*)."[140] Some tea was probably simply steeped tea of a common variety (*bancha*) that included twigs and stalks, while there was also whipped tea, made by boiling the leaves of the tea and then stirring them into froth with a whisk. Because the leaves were often dried in the sun, some degree of oxidation may have taken place.

Although the saying "a bowl for a coin" has made its way into history books and was mentioned in the 1403 document cited above, the actual price of a bowl of this common tea is a matter of some debate. Based upon documents of practice, one authority believes price to have ranged from three to thirteen coins.[141] Evidence from the Korean envoy cited as well as a comedic skit suggest that a bowl of low-grade tea cost indeed only one coin.[142] In any case, such a low price for a bowl of tea reinforces the idea that a new tea strain entered Japan from China and helped lead to the spread of cultivation and tea sales.

For the commoner population that imbibed tea at these shops, however, the peddlers and sellers must have put on quite a show. Usually the merchants are portrayed with an inferior-grade Chinese porcelain in the palm of the left hand and a tea whisk poised to whip the liquid in the right. For most commoners, it must have been a rare treat to see a porcelain bowl from China. Tea procedures (*temae*) for the later "Way of Tea" may have got their start from these traders, who arranged the utensils in a rational way in a small space and prepared the tea with great acumen before a group of drinkers, only to receive the bowl back and clean it for the next guest. Cleanliness, skill, artistry, and hospitality were the watchwords to attract more clients and help them pass the time quickly.[143] The role of these merchants and peddlers in naturalizing the Chinese import for a populace resident in the Japanese archipelago cannot be overstated.

Urban tea shops prospered so long as the Muromachi shogunate (1333–1573) was able to guarantee peace in Kyoto. In the Ōnin War (1467–1477) that so devastated the city, however, many of the tea shops there were destroyed by fire. A 1495 shogunate source, for example, condemns an evil band (*akutō*) for pillaging the tea shop at Gion Shrine during the night.[144] During the general mayhem of the Warring States period (1467–1590), many tea shops became havens for criminals, and gambling and other illegal activities took place there. Yet even then tea shops flourished in certain areas of the burned-out city. According to the pictorial source the *Uesugi bon rakuchū rakugai zu byōbu,* these houses continued to serve tea in front of the Southern Gate of Gion Shrine and the entrances to Kiyomizudera, Kitano Shrine, and some other places.[145] Even Tōji gave another permit for a tea shop during the Ōnin War.[146]

Finally, although the most detailed written and pictorial sources concern cities such as Nara and Kyoto, there are indications that, beginning in the 1400s, tea shops developed in some peasant villages too.[147] The most well-known example is Imabori Village in Ōmi Province. Such tea shops not only served the local populace but also functioned as a collection point for the tea tax headed to Kyoto. The case of the "Shiba cha" produced for Kōfukuji and already noted also suggests the consumption of tea by villagers around Nara. A collection from 1518 (the *Kankinshū*) contains the following songs that suggest tea production and consumption at the local level:

> I'm late gathering the water for tea. Please let me go . . .
> Like the young leaves of new tea, I pluck and am plucked . . .
> That young girl is like a tea jar.[148]

The villages that produced and consumed tea usually did so in connection with religious rites, as well as employing tea during negotiations with the lord of an estate or a marauding band of warriors. Some of these rites included festivals surrounding the start and the end of the year, various shrine festivals, and the rite for the return of dead (*obon*). A song for a dance (*obon odori*) from 1539 shows that the consumption of tea was popular among the residents of Kyoto:

> Since the shop owner is absent,
> Let us call together those nearby
> And have a big laugh
> As people talk and drink lots of tea.[149]

The wealthiest peasants may even have possessed a stone grinder to make powdered tea.[150]

The drink appeared in daily life at all levels of society. Documents show, for example, that the peasants at Tara Estate in Wakasa Province possessed numerous vessels for tea.[151] At Kusado Sengen, the site of a medieval town excavated by archaeologists, one wooden tablet spoke of tea contests conducted by the locals, suggesting that the custom filtered down to merchants in areas rather distant from Kyoto.[152] Tea and its various implements appeared commonly among the possessions of the small temple located at Imabori Village for use in assemblies of the members of this corporate settlement.[153] Ethnographic and some historical studies suggest that tea was consumed by common folk during all the important occasions in life—in birth rituals, by newlyweds, and especially by bereaved folks when a close relative passed away.[154] By the Warring States period, commoners also learned to combine the pleasures of a bath with tea.[155]

Other points suggest that the production and exchange of tea had reached levels never attained in Japan before, and that the maturation of the tea industry during the fifteenth and sixteenth centuries led to widespread popular consumption. First, as early as 1405, common workers received a dole of the beverage as part of their reimbursement.[156] Second, in 1419, laborers who ferried goods to Tōji from the port of Hyōgo were also allotted tea to drink as part of their payment.[157] Third, in 1446, the tea producer Uji Saburōemon doled out tea in the amount of forty coins to guests on a trip.[158] Finally, according to the *Daijōin jisha zōjiki,* in 1485 the travelers aboard a ship to China also received thirty-days-worth of tea for their long journey.[159] Taken together, these sources indicate that labor bosses, tea merchants, and ship captains all viewed the regular drinking of tea as part of everyday life.

As the numbers of consumers increased, there was a health advantage too. No matter how inferior the grade or exactly how the tea was prepared, merchants provided a major benefit by boiling the water. This action undoubtedly killed off parasites and bacteria in the water and helped to improve the well-being of the people who consumed it. It is little wonder that the population level in Japan made significant gains from the time that tea became a drink consumed by so many.[160]

The greatly expanded area cultivated in tea and the demand for more of the stimulative, habit-forming beverage were probably interrelated in complex ways. In the introduction, I raised the question of whether Japan had experienced an "industrious revolution." In general, the term refers to gradual improvements in the labor force, as it became capable of harder, more prolonged, and more efficient labor. As will be discussed in more detail in chapter 3 and the conclusion, leisure time was reduced and producers began to focus on marketable goods. Although for Japan this idea has been most frequently applied to the ensuing Edo period (1600–1868), the transformation of the farming economy, the rise of the market, and the popularity of tea all predate 1600. Were the unintended health and physiological effects of a bowl of tea already responsible to some degree for the transformation sweeping Japan during 1300–1600?

Viewing the evidence for the period 1300 through 1600, I would argue that at least some regions in central and western Japan had already entered what economist Penelope Francks has called a "virtuous circle."[161] Francks distinguishes two economic linkages operating in the "virtuous circle," one of which is demand-pull: namely, as people consume more and more of a processed good, it increases demand for production. Expanded production in turn may generate greater incomes that may be used to consume, if the tea was sold on the market. Assuming that some goodly proportion of the tea was marketed, then Francks' "linkage" seems to explain quite well what happened to the tea industry, a type of commercialized agriculture, during the latter medieval age. A better-tasting stimulative drink created greater and greater demand, in turn encouraging peasants to produce more, whether for sale or home use. And properties of the beverage helped to give rise to harder and more efficient labor on the farm. I will expand on this argument in much greater detail in the next chapter.

During the period 1400–1550, the tea industry in Japan began to mature. Cultivators grew tea widely throughout all the regions on the archipelago where the plant could be farmed. It was still exchanged as a gift, but more and more as a tax item from peasant farms and on the market by hustling entrepreneurs. Tea shops promising a "cup for a coin" sprang up in Kyoto and Nara and in many peasant villages where cultivators consumed the tea left over after tax shipment. The drinking of tea marked important rites of passage, not simply for the elite as it had probably always done, but increasingly for a thirsty commoner population. There were still more advancements before the production of tea entered a new age.

## URESHINO AND UJI: IMPORTANT NEW DEVELOPMENTS OF THE LATE SIXTEENTH CENTURY

At the end of the medieval period during the 1500s, two important innovations in the production of tea arose in Japan from two different groups of farmers living at two very different locations: Ureshino and Uji. These changes had nothing to do with each other; one took place in a heretofore unremarkable area of northern Kyushu and the other at the age-old center of Uji. The first technological breakthrough came as a result of the efforts of immigrant Chinese, while the second was an innovation developed by Japanese tea farmers.

Consider first the developments in northern Kyushu at Ureshino.[162] Earlier in chapter 1, I noted that in the twelfth century northern Kyushu had a large immigrant community of Chinese, who may have helped introduce the residents of the archipelago to Song-style powdered tea. To be sure, this community went through many fluctuations during the next several centuries as the Japanese court's relations with those in charge of China first worsened with the Mongol invasions of 1274 and 1281 and then improved when the Han Chinese Ming dynasty (1368–1644) opened tributary relations with the Muromachi *bakufu* during the late fourteenth, fifteenth, and sixteenth centuries. Travel and trade among Muromachi Japan, Ming China, and Chosŏn Korea were brisk and their implications for tea have been noted at different points in this chapter.

During the mid-1400s, Ming Chinese potters emigrated to Ureshino and other spots in northern Kyushu, where they opened kilns. In Ming China, a type of stir-roasted tea (later called *tōcha,* or "Tang tea" in Japan) was all the rage, and naturally the immigrants wanted to drink their favorite variety. They planted patches and processed their own brand, new to Japan. Later, between 1506 and 1511, Hong Lin-min, a Ming subject, moved to Ureshino from Nanjing, bringing with him a metallic cooking vessel (*tōgama*) in which to stir-roast tea (figure 5). Later, the kilns declined and the immigrant Chinese scattered to other parts of Japan, but not before introducing the beverage for which Ureshino would eventually become famous.[163] This Chinese-style tea was also called *kamairicha,* or stir-roasted tea.

This kind of tea processing was complex but yielded a cheap, steeped beverage. First, the producer took the pot, which was about 70 centimeters in diameter and about 40 centimeters deep, and tipped it at a forty-degree angle. Then, after a fire was lit under the pot, the processor stir-roasted about three or four kilograms of fresh tea leaves for about ten minutes until the bright-green color had faded. The product was then moved to a

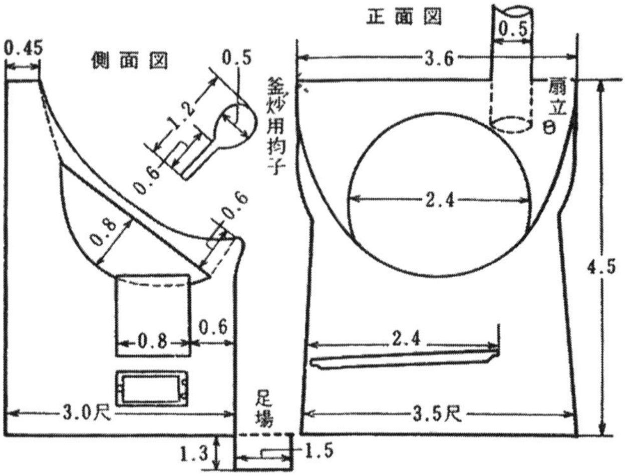


Figure 5. Stir-roasting pot. From Ōishi Sadao, *Nihon chagyō hattatsu shi* (Tokyo: Nōsan gyoson bunka kyōkai, 2004), p. 233.

rope mat and rolled (*momu*). This method of rolling or crumpling the good tea leaves was employed to make cracks on the surface of the leaves and allow their constituent juices to soak more readily into the drink.[164] As the water began to come out of the leaves, they were once again put in the pot and stir-roasted. This step was repeated six or seven times for high-grade tea, but only three or four for inferior batches. Checking the degree of dryness, the processor then roasted superior teas over charcoal and dried inferior ones in the sun. Then both types were put in the shade and finally stir-roasted one last time in the pot. This whole process took ten hours, and one male could usually make about 9.4 kilograms of stir-roasted tea in a day. The product was then steeped (or boiled) to make "Tang tea" (*tōcha*), yielding a subdued yellow-gray to gray-white tea, with a fine fragrance minus the puckery, astringent taste.

Although at least one other similar method developed in south central Kyushu along the Higo-Hyūga border in the 1500s, soon the flat areas around Ureshino became home to tea fields and Japanese cultivators that specialized in this type of tea. It became popular throughout Kyushu, in much of Shikoku, and in sectors of western Honshu. Once again, a tea that was imbibed daily in China—this time Ming China—had crossed the ocean with immigrants and become part of the repertoire of teas available in Japan. Its popularity would increase greatly during the ensuing Tokugawa era, but at this juncture the story serves to remind us that there are many varieties of delicious teas in the islands besides the much ballyhooed powdered green kind.

The second innovation at Uji initially involved the cultivation of what would become powdered green tea, but eventually it had implications far beyond that single variety. As noted earlier in this chapter, Toganoo had justly come to enjoy a reputation for producing the finest tea in the land. Monks, warriors, and civil aristocrats all enjoyed this tea from the time that Myōe had rejuvenated the bushes there around 1200. Famously, it had even been listed as the best in the realm around 1350. Presumably, it continued to be held in high regard for much of the Muromachi period. By 1383, however, Uji tea was ranked alone as the second-best tea in all of Japan, behind that of Toganoo. Around 1460, some elite tastes appeared to be changing again: "Uji [tea] during this age has recently been the favorite brand [of the shogun]. Even though it has been said that Toganoo [tea] has declined [in favor], just as in the saying, its reputation has not changed. Should it not also be highly regarded and not forgotten?"[165] The shogun in question was Ashikaga Yoshimasa, who was a tea connoisseur of the first order. Beginning with Yoshimasa and his followers (*dōbōshū*), Uji tea had come to share the top spot with its more venerable rival, Toganoo tea.

After 1460, Uji took a long, complicated path to a new status as the place where the best powdered tea in all of Japan could be found.[166] From the age of Yoshimasa (1460s), Uji tea appeared more frequently in the sources as a gift and in trade, as often as Toganoo. Another source suggests that the court sent messengers to both Toganoo and Uji to collect samples. Previously, these justly famous fields had sent tea to both warriors and courtiers. Even in 1493, Toganoo tea was expensive, fetching 500 coins per *kin* (600 grams). It was still used in rituals such as those at the Zen temple Daitokuji.

Three factors account for Uji's eventual preeminence as a source of powdered tea in Japan. First, throughout the 1500s, a dispute over ownership of the tea fields erupted among the clerics at Kōzanji, the temple that managed the tea patches at Toganoo. Apparently, the monk in charge of the Toganoo fields loaned them to a cleric at Ninnaji, but then promptly died in 1517 without leaving any written records of the transaction. This failure to leave written notice of the loan led to a dispute between the two sides, resolved by the Muromachi shogunate. Once again in 1561, however, the dispute came to the fore, causing great confusion in the production and exchange of the famous tea. Toganoo fields never recovered the top spot.[167]

While producers at Toganoo were struggling, those at Uji found increasing favor with the ruling elite of Japan over the late fifteenth and sixteenth centuries. A second cause for Uji's rise encompasses the interplay of several factors of consumption and production at the same time.[168] Consumption famously derived from the development of tea as an art form in distant Kyoto and Sakai under luminaries such as Murata Jukō, Takeno Jōō, and Sen Rikyū. Elite demand for the best-tasting powdered tea increased greatly.

Production improved in Uji under several different wealthy families such as the Hori, the Mori, and eventually the Kanbayashi. These families were not simply collectors of adjoining tea patches and careful cultivators, but also involved themselves in moneylending and other local businesses. To condense the story to its essentials, in the competition among these families, the Kanbayashi, who had moved to Uji from Tanba, proved the most politically astute, as they chose affiliation with first Toyotomi Hideyoshi and then Tokugawa Ieyasu, the eventual victors of the Warring States period. By 1590, the reward for managing tea fields in Uji was four times as great for the Kanbayashi as for the Mori, partially because the Mori had received benefits from Hideyoshi's rivals and incurred his ire. The Kanbayashi managed Uji for the Tokugawa shogunate until its collapse in 1868.

Third, once owners had control of adjoining fields, they developed better techniques for farming and processing tea. The most famous and effective new invention was called the "roof-over method" (*ōishita saibai*), in which enterprising planters built an all-encompassing roof made of grass, straw, or reeds to block out deleterious weather elements (figure 6). Of course, this technique limited damage due to insects or the mists or frosts of spring. An added advantage was that the "roof" (today often black plastic sheeting) blocked out the sun, thereby inhibiting photosynthesis and yielding a sweeter tea. Historians do not know exactly when the "roof-over" method was developed, but João Rodrigues, a Portuguese Jesuit visitor to Japan during the sixteenth century, wrote of it in 1587:

> This famous and celebrated tea comes from a small tree or rather bush. . . . Its new leaves, which are used in the drink, are extremely soft, tender and delicate, and a slight frost may easily make them wither away. So much damage can be done in this way that in the town of Uji, where the best tea is grown, all the vineyards and fields in which tea is cultivated are covered over with wooden frames bearing mats made of corn stalks or rice straw. They are thus protected from damage by frost from February onwards until the end of March when the new leaf begins to bud.[169]

By the end of the 1500s, Uji tea "stood alone" (*mujō*) as the leading brand in all Japan. In fact, Uji tea was so popular that tea producers in other regions tried to copy Uji's brand name, but apparently not its flavor.[170]

Figure 6. Inside view of the roof-over mode of cultivation. Photo by author.

Beginning in the late 1400s, tea reached the status of a high art under the three masters of the "cold and withered"—Murata Jukō, Takeno Jōō, and Sen Rikyū. Undoubtedly, a large degree of credit goes to these men for the creation of this art form, which symbolizes Japanese culture to many. It is well to remember, however, that the art was as much a product of the economic and technological developments that preceded these three savants. The invention and importation of the whisk and the stone grinder, and eventually the roof-over method of cultivation, were necessary preconditions for the creation of the "Way of Tea" (*sadō*).[171] In other words, tea the commodity long preceded and made way for tea the art form.

The period from 1300 through 1600 witnessed a veritable transformation in the world of tea, as the industry began to "lift off" from its modest beginnings. Each of the three themes highlighted in the introduction—agricultural development, the rise of a consumer society, and the creation of an eager workforce—took its first major steps during these three centuries. Tea agriculture expanded to more and more new areas until the plant was being raised in numerous regions south of a line drawn through the northern Kanto, the natural climatic limit for tea growing in Japan. Productivity must have increased appreciably, as indicated by the large amounts of tea marketed and consumed and the economic value associated with even the smallest tea plots. Farming intensified as the plant was cultivated in dry fields, household plots, mountain patches, and on the borders of other fields, especially rice paddies.

The circle of consumers expanded to include numerous commoners who either raised their own tea or bought on the market. Tea shops opened in major cities such as Kyoto and Nara, but also in several peasant settlements. There thirsty customers could buy a "bowl for a coin," or perhaps a little more. To be sure, gift giving was still a major form of exchange, but the popularity of tea taxes and markets hinted at the growing commodification of the beverage. By 1600, new brands of tea were available for a populace with an increasingly discerning palate.

As commoners streamed to buy and consume their favorite nonalcoholic beverage, the health advantages inherent in a hot-water drink made themselves felt. The populace became healthier, and more "industrious." The signs of this development are visible in the dramatic increase in population and economic activity. The changes occurring in agriculture, commerce, consumption, health, and labor were synergistic, and it is impossible to designate one ultimate cause.

At the same time, even in 1600, modernity was a long way off. Agriculture was much more intense, to be sure, but the ubiquity of mountain patches suggests that many plots were located in less than ideal places with poor soils. Commoners may have visited tea shops and consumed tea as never before, but the advent of even a nascent consumer society was still two hundred years away. The workforce may have been healthier and more easily stimulated, but life expectancy was as yet no higher than thirty. The ensuing Edo era would bring all three trends much nearer to fruition and place Japan on the doorstep of its modern transformation.

CHAPTER THREE

# Tea Triumphs during the Edo Period, 1600–1868

In 1603, Tokugawa Ieyasu climbed to the pinnacle of the political world as the first shogun of a new samurai government with its capital at Edo. Although the Tokugawa shogunate was the most powerful of all Japan's central administrations to date, it was really a federation of lords ruling domains large and small, about 260 in all. For the next century until the early 1700s, Japanese society continued on the path of growth and recovery from the wars. The population reached about thirty-one million by the early eighteenth century; land under cultivation and overall farming productivity expanded immensely. Commerce and industry increased in a rapidly urbanizing Japan that included the world's largest city, Edo. A laboring proletariat was employed through specialized agencies. Culture for the elite was Confucian, but most townspeople, including the sizable urbanized samurai class, enjoyed the pleasures of red-light districts aptly named "the floating world." Art and literature took its inspiration from stories of the denizens of this urban area. Ensconced in Nagasaki harbor, the Dutch continued to trade some goods and teach willing scholars in Europe about Japan, and vice versa.

Beginning in the early 1700s, however, overall growth slowed and diversified in nature and geographical locale. Scholarly specialists seem divided as to what happened to the Japanese economy between 1710 and 1850, although all agree on many other points. The shogunate atrophied as it first tried old-fashioned reforms and then floated untethered. Overall population in Japan remained static, hovering around thirty million. Famine stalked the land, as of old. Ideologues railed against abortion and infanticide. By 1800, signs of political and social unrest were everywhere. Commoner riots multiplied and large cities shrank. Yet workers in both the agrarian and urban sectors applied greater inputs of labor, paying attention to fine details as never before. Agriculture became increasingly commercialized and rural protoindustry appeared.

Beyond those generalizations, there is much disagreement over how much, where, and what kind of growth took place. As this admittedly nonspecialist sees it, one more venerable group believes that the Japanese economy had basically reached the limits possible under that economic and technological regime during these 150 years, just as the economy of Western Europe had during the thirteenth century before the Black Death reduced the human:land ratio there. Signs of ecological degradation and social stresses appeared widely between 1710 and 1850. Commodore Perry's sudden unannounced appearance in 1853 eventually removed the shogunate and other barriers to growth and gave way to Japan's European-style industrial revolution.

Another camp of scholars, beginning with Thomas Smith in 1959 and becoming even more dominant recently, stresses that growth, either greater or lesser depending on one's perspective, continued unabated during 1710–1850 and provided Japan with its first native sources of industrialization through commercialized farming and rural protoindustry. As Japan's population was static, the growth was per capita and thus "modern" in nature. In particular, industrial and commercial dynamism characteristic of urban Japan in the 1600s appeared increasingly in the countryside for a limited elite. The arrival of American ships in 1853 was essentially a political event; the economic ramifications were not felt until after 1900. The 1800s mostly show signs of continuity rather than a sudden break in the middle.

What can the story of tea contribute to this ongoing debate? In this chapter I shall argue, at a high level of generality to be sure, that three interrelated phenomena are apparent when one focuses on tea for the hothouse environment that was Tokugawa society, even during 1710–1850. First, farming intensified and improved much more as tea production spread to new areas in all of the islands outside of Hokkaido. Second, labor required for the farming and processing of tea became more efficient and meticulous as the effects of "industrious revolution"—launched around 1350—multiplied many times by the 1800s. Third, people from far and wide participated in a nascent consumer society by the early 1800s, to a large degree revolving around that age-old but ever-changing beverage called Japanese tea.

## THE EXPANSION OF TEA INTO NORTHERN JAPAN

During the medieval era, tea production had spread to nearly all the areas in Japan that were geographically and climatically suited to it. This fact meant that the plant was likely not cultivated or processed north of an east–west line running through the northern Kanto plain to modern Niigata. In other words, northeastern Japan was left out of the picture. As noted in chapter 2, one record indicates that traders from "the northern provinces" (*kitakuni*) were involved in some tea commerce, but in general there is very little evidence of this trade until the late 1500s.

The incorporation of northern Honshu into Japan's tea-drinking world was one of the major accomplishments of the Edo age. This expansion of Japan's tea culture occurred in two waves. During the 1600s, merchants shipped truly huge amounts of tea to the residents of the Tohoku, as northeastern Honshu was known. Apparently, northeasterners sampled the beverage and found it to their liking. Then, between the early 1700s and 1850, the same populace of northern Japan learned to grow their own tea, despite the hostile climate. In other words, natives of the Tohoku grew tired of trading their valuable goods for tea and carried out a form of import substitution. Just as the trade of the 1600s exemplified that booming era, the initiation and spread of tea farming in much of northeastern Japan symbolized the advances in rural industry during the "static" eighteenth and nineteenth centuries.

The widespread consumption of tea in northern Honshu started during the boom of the 1600s. The first tea trade centered on two ports on the Japan Sea: Tsuruga and Obama. In exchange for rice, soybeans, and other crops grown in the north, merchants in these two ports sent huge amounts of tea to the area. In fact, tea was the most common item shipped to the north through these two cities during the 1600s. The first record of a shipment dates to 1589 from Tsuruga, when Ise tea was moved northward. From the 1620s, Mino, Ōmi, and northern Ise tea was collected at Tsuruga to ship to points northward. By 1638 or so, Tsuruga had its own "tea town" (*chamachi*) with numerous merchant associations (*cha ton'ya*).[1] Its population soon exceeded fifteen thousand.

How much tea flowed through Tsuruga to northern Japan in the 1600s? One document recorded the amount of tea and its value in silver from 1664 through 1675 (see table 1).

During these twelve years, the least amount was 32,321 *hon* per year and the most was 38,857 *hon*.[2] Amounts in this column, however, include only the tea that was bought and sold in Tsuruga (*uricha*). In addition, for the years 1665 through 1667, large shipments of tea passed through (*tōricha*) the port, having been traded for elsewhere. This tea came from Mino, Wakasa, and Mandokoro in Ōmi, and two places in Ise. These are truly gargantuan amounts of tea, equivalent to several hundred thousand kilograms per year. Residents of northeastern Japan must have developed a thirst for the beverage during the medieval age, but had it completely

**Table 1** Tea shipments through Tsuruga, 1664–1675

| *Year* | *Amt. tea** | *Amt. silver†* | *Transshipped tea* |
|---|---|---|---|
| 1664 | 36,896 | 3,568 | |
| 1665 | 33,249 | 3,171 | 17,926 |
| 1666 | 33,403 | 3,332 | 18,681 |
| 1667 | 36,318 | 3,621 | 18,409 |
| 1668 | 35,306 | 3,257 | |
| 1669 | 33,207 | 3,003 | |
| 1670 | 37,288 | 3,471 | |
| 1671 | 32,321 | 3,253 | |
| 1672 | 38,857 | 3,820 | |
| 1673 | 37,896 | 3,020 | |
| 1674 | 34,981 | 3,552 | |
| 1675 | 34,439 | 3,053 | |

*Source: Kanbun zōki,* cited in Tsuruga shi shi hensan iinikai, ed., *Tsuruga shi shi: Shiryō hen,* vol. 5 (Tsuruga: Tsuruga shiyakusho, 1979), pp. 47–48, 100–101, and 141–142.
*Counted in *hon*
†Counted in *kan*

slaked only during the 1600s. Merchant associations profited handsomely from the trade, making usually over 3,000 *kan* of silver each year.

In 1660, there were twenty-five merchant associations handling tea (*cha ton'ya*) in Tsuruga, another twenty acting as middlemen (*cha suai*), and nine smaller dealers (*cha kouri*). Eventually, one middleman acted on behalf of the seller and another for the buyer. This system was established in an official document from 1664; it praised the middlemen for unifying the measures and weights used in sales in open negotiations. Typically, these middlemen on each side made .7 *monme* of silver for every one hundred in a deal, with two-thirds going to the domain government and one-third to the middlemen for their services (see table 2).

For example, in 1670 the middlemen's cut was 48.592.04 *kan,* with 32.394.96 *kan* going to the domain and 16.197.08 divided among eight buying middlemen for their services. Originally, there were six such middlemen, but in 1666, two years after the establishment of the system, two more buying middlemen were added, testifying to the vibrancy of the tea trade in Tsuruga.[3]

Consider the merchant Nakashima Masahisa from Mino. In 1671, he bought cotton and vegetable oil in Osaka and sold them in the Kanto and Mutsu. Then he bought silk, hemp, and other items and sold them in Nagoya and Edo, while selling the tea leaves he had purchased at Tsuruga. Soon

**Table 2** Amount of silver received by tea middlemen, 1664–1675

| *Year* | *Amount** |
|---|---|
| 1664 | 49.902.20 |
| 1665 | 44.390.57 |
| 1666 | 46.649.58 |
| 1667 | 50.696.30 |
| 1668 | 45.609.45 |
| 1669 | 42.035.67 |
| 1670 | 48.592.04 |
| 1671 | 45.541.58 |
| 1672 | 53.483.15 |
| 1673 | 42.279.20 |
| 1674 | 49.728.74 |
| 1675 | 42.747.11 |

*Source: Kanbun zōki,* cited in Tsuruga shi shi hensan iinikai, ed., *Tsuruga shi shi: Shiryō hen,* vol. 5 (Tsuruga: Tsuruga shiyakusho, 1979), pp. 47–48, 100–101, and 141–142.
*Counted in *kan*

he stopped doing business in Osaka and Edo, and in the next year of 1672 he sold steeped tea to Echigo, Dewa, and Mutsu, all provinces in northeastern Japan. He then bought rice and soybeans with his money and sold those items at Tsuruga. In 1674, he had lumber loaded onto boats at Tsugaru, Nanbu, and Matsumae domains up north and moved them to Osaka. He also sold Mino tea at Tsuruga and was responsible for transshipping tea to the north. With that money he then bought rice and beans and sold those items at Tsugaru.[4]

The "tea town" was a vibrant part of Tsuruga. By 1663, there were sixty-one buildings, including fifty homeowners, ten renters (*kashiya*), and one temple. Kaibara Ekken wrote of Tsuruga: "Because the north country is cold there is no tea and they bring lots of tea from the Kinai, Ōmi, Mino, and Owari and sell it here and send it north. When I returned home, many merchants were buying tea. The 'tea town' was large with lots of merchants and the city was prospering, with numerous merchants associations (*cha ton'ya*)."[5]

Even the satirist Ihara Saikaku wrote about the tea merchants of Tsuruga, so famous had they become:

> On the outskirts of town lived a man named Kobashi Risuke. With no wife or children to support, his only care each day was to provide a living for himself. In his approach to this he displayed considerable ingenuity.

> He had built a smart portable tea-server, and early every morning, before the town was astir, he put the contraption across his shoulders and set out for the market streets. His sleeves were strapped back with a bright ribbon, he wore formal divided skirts, tightly bound at each ankle—the picture of efficiency—and on his head he set a quaint eboshi cap. He might have passed for the god Ebisu himself. When he cried "Ebisu tea! A morning cup of Ebisu tea!" the superstitious merchants felt obliged to buy a drink for luck, even if they were not at all thirsty, and from force of habit they tossed him twelve coins for each cup. His luck never changed, day after day, and before long he had enough capital to open a retail tea shop and do business on a larger scale. Later he came to employ a great number of assistants, and he rose to be a leading merchant in the wholesale trade.[6]

As Kobashi's tactics changed, however, he ran into trouble. He dispatched assistants to other northern provinces where they bought up used tea leaves, pretending that they were needed for Kyoto dyes. He then mixed them with fresh leaves. People could taste no difference; his sales yielded huge profits. For a time at least his household prospered greatly, but heaven did not approve. Risuke went stark mad, babbling of tea dregs wherever he went.[7] Another of Saikaku's millionaires reaped what he had sown from ill-gotten gains.

Obama in Wakasa was also a lively port during the seventeenth century. With a population of a little over ten thousand, Obama was a center of the tea trade heading northward. In fact, it was Obama's largest export. In 1683, there were forty-five tea merchants and ten tea merchant associations (*cha ton'ya*) in the bustling city. Tea from Mino, Ise, Ōmi, Tanba, and Wakasa was shipped through the port. Mino tea was exchanged for lumber from the north in a new market established in Obama in 1670. In 1688 and again in 1698, middlemen organizations (*cha suai*) started operating for Mino and Tanba, respectively, suggesting a new level of the tea trade in Obama.[8]

The heyday of the tea trade through Tsuruga and Obama comprised the latter half of the seventeenth century. Then shippers discovered that it was easier and less costly to send the rice and soybeans of northeastern Japan by boat to Osaka or overland to Edo through Shinano Province, dealing a harsh blow to the tea trade from Mino, Ise, and Ōmi through Tsuruga and Obama. Both ports still did some business in tea, but it declined precipitously. In 1694, of 36,800 packhorses leaving from Tsuruga, 21,960 carried tea, but other cities such as Shiozu, Ōura, and Kaizu in the mountains were shipping almost as much. By 1709, things had gotten even worse, as tea bought and sold in Tsuruga amounted to 22,000 *hon* and tea transshipments netted 12,000.

The opening of new and more efficient avenues for the tea trade had an important unintended consequence: Tohoku peasants decided to grow and process their own tea, mostly for domestic consumption. Many northern provinces began to experiment with their own cultivation of the tea plant, spreading tea production to new areas not ideally suited to the industry. Early on, between 1691 and 1694, officials of Kaga domain listed five villages growing tea, producing nothing but a kind of steeped beverage.[9] Echigo Province developed its own tea patches during the 1720s and 1730s, and they increased steadily thereafter. In Kaga domain, the Maeda daimyo family began its own tea industry.[10] Soon other parts of northeastern Japan were following that example.

As an aid to the production of tea, various authors wrote highly detailed tracts concerning the special methods required for cultivation and processing of the plant in the cold north. For instance, in 1707, Tsuchiya Matasaburō wrote *Cultivating in Spring and Autumn* (*Kōka shunjū*), combining thirty years of Tsuchiya's own experience with tea cultivation. Tsuchiya wrote that in two districts of Kaga "there were many tea fields, but few people to prepare or trade the product," also complaining that in another two districts the tea was mainly bad but bought and sold. The author may have been referring to "black tea" (*kokucha*), perhaps partially oxidized.[11]

Tsuchiya detailed the special treatment necessary to cultivate the plant in the north: "The tea fields of Nomi district are . . . in the mountains. In the winter, tie up with string the branches laden with snow so that there will be no damage. Pluck tea in both the spring and autumn. In the spring take a little and in the autumn take much. . . . Also, when the tea bushes become large, dig around the outside and place a little horse dung or night soil there."[12] Note Tsuchiya's concern for the cold temperatures and heavy snowfall of Kaga; his attention to detail is reminiscent of many writers of the Edo period. The laying of fertilizer seems new, although by the time Tsuchiya wrote it was in general use in the rest of Japan.

In 1709, western Kaga resident Kano Koshiro gave wide-ranging advice about tilling and processing in *An Agricultural Testament* (*Nōji yuisho*). One important point read: "Using a shovel take out all the grass and dig once around the roots until you can see them. Then bury the roots again with dry earth. There is nothing better than this." Kano wanted tea farmers to remove all the grass and dig deeply around the roots, probably for protection against the harsh cold and snow. He also advocated plucking the first leaves early in the fifth month, undoubtedly because of the tardiness of spring in the north. Kano stated that if the plucking took place later in the fifth month, those remnants should be thrown away. Then, just before or during the rice harvest, he advised that the bushes be plucked once again. "Even if it is late, there will be no damage to the bush. Even though [the product] is just cheap steeped tea (*bancha*) and when picked late the color [of the leaf] is red and the taste bad . . . , there will be no damage to the bush. But if you pick the tea after the middle of the seventh month, there will be great injury to the tea bushes. If you repeat this for four or five years running the bush will die." In modern Akita prefecture, the northernmost area producing tea, the end of July is still the latest period for plucking tea.[13]

Kano's writing suggests that tea was rapidly becoming ingrained in northern Japanese culture. "On the day of the funeral of your grandfather or grandmother and you prepare tea for the gods and buddhas, or when you are turning your hand to a superior or lord for hospitality, you should truly take care in a marvelous way. Never show hurried behavior in your face or roll the tea without washing your feet and hands or fail to inspect the mat [for drying the tea leaves] for filth." Even for peasants from northeastern Japan in the early eighteenth century, tea retained its ceremonial aura. As a concluding remark, Kano advised planting tea seeds in the late tenth month in round holes, using manure, oils, or ash.[14]

Finally, Miyamoto Shōun, a resident of the northern province of Etchū, completed *Discussions of Household Agriculture* (*Shika nōgyō dan*) in 1789. While he referred to the standard works of Miyazaki Yasusada (see below), Miyamoto adapted the classic book to the conditions of Etchū Province and the far north. He was pointed in his concern for tea production in Etchū: "Near Toyama in this province there is . . . a region suitable for tea. The Lord of Toyama Domain . . . ordered that tea be planted there. Recently in the Zen temples of this land tea processing has been carried out and appreciated by people named 'Hitomaro.' It has become the brand of tea from this region."

Miyamoto took special care with the cultivation techniques for Etchū. Again, his attention to detail is remarkable:

> At the end of the tenth month, just before the first snowfall, sprinkle two or three inches (*sun*) of rice hulls around the roots [of the tea plant], or cover the roots with compost from dry fields. . . .
>
> The trunk of the tea bush should never stick out to any height. When the trunk stands high, the nutrients are taken only by the branches and not by the tea leaves, and in addition, it is easy for the cold winds of a bad year to do damage. . . . When you make it [the shrub] round until you see that the trunk is like that of bowl-shaped wild azalea, then you can pluck the center as it spreads out to the sides. The branches will be beyond

> counting and during the three months of winter even if much snow piles up the branches will not break. As they will be confined beneath the snow, the tea bush will pass the winter without damage or withering.[15]

Such care was necessary in northeastern Honshu where the winters were long and snowfall great. In fact, it is amazing that the farmers of the northlands were able to devise any method at all that would work under such inhospitable conditions.

When it came to tea plucking and processing, Miyamoto advocated that the first picking begin about the eighth day of the fourth month, later than most of Japan. The author described using chopsticks to stir-roast tea. Next, Miyamoto turned his attention to what he called "miscellaneous tea" (*zatcha*), consumed daily by the families of northeastern Honshu on their farms. First, he advised plucking at the height of summer. There followed four instructions: (1) wash tea leaves in a pot with water, a bamboo mat placed on top, and then have the whole concoction steamed; (2) dry after removal from the pot and, taking the hot water left in the pot and putting it in a flat-bottomed bucket, pour the water on the tea leaves and over and over again roll the leaves; (3); then loosen the leaves that have stuck together with your hand, spread them out on a mat, and let them dry in the shade; (4) when the leaves have generally dried, heat them in a stir-roaster pot.[16]

The aforementioned agricultural writings speak to the issue of the Tokugawa "industrious revolution" in complex ways. Certainly, the attention to detail and the emphasis on meticulous labor may suggest that tea-drinking commoners of the Tohoku were working harder and more efficiently than ever before. Tohoku tea production betrays what several scholars have recognized as the "handicraft" character of so many Tokugawa enterprises. At the same time, it is unclear how much of this new tea production ever passed through the market. Miyamoto's *zatcha* is a good example of this point. If the end of tea production in the Tohoku was home consumption and import substitution was the rule, then Franck's demand-pull "virtuous circle" would not have operated.[17] It is prudent to note that, even in the 1930s, home production and consumption of tea were widespread.

Not all tea in the Tohoku, however, was bound for domestic use, as Miyamoto makes clear in the following passage:

> No matter whether you are highborn or humble, rich or poor, you must drink tea after a meal morning and evening. Thus, beginning with Uji and Shigaraki, in Mino and Hida, or even from the villages of Echigo every year there is no limit to the expenses paid out to move tea. . . .

> Old farmers should all the more put their heart into making tea fields and leave them to their descendants. After your death, during the funeral rites (*tsuizen kuyō*) the tea can be used for the expenses of a chapel.[18]

At least some Tohoku tea production went to the market, thus encouraging the desired economic ripple effects.

The most that can be said of Miyamoto's essay is that it served to promote tea production and consumption in northeastern Japan. He offered words of advice about the wonderful effects of tea and the religious purpose attached to tea production. Although Miyamoto may have described cultivation and processing methods unique to northeastern Japan, his belief in the health effects of the beverage and its religious significance struck chords that went deep into the past.[19] By 1800, tea drinking had become a habit that northeastern Japanese peasants and city dwellers shared with the rest of the archipelago.

## CULTIVATION AND PROCESSING PRIOR TO THE RISE OF GENUINE STEEPED TEA (*SENCHA*) IN 1740: SHADES OF THE LATE MEDIEVAL PERIOD

During 1400–1600, many commoners came to drink tea for the first time in Japanese history. It is unclear how many consumers there were or exactly what kind of beverage they were imbibing. Sources such as comic skits (*kyōgen*) and scroll paintings indicate that the drink was "steeped" or boiled (*senjimono; senjicha*) and perhaps even crushed on a stone grinder. The concoction normally consisted of roasted tea leaves heated in water; peddlers often added orange peels, bits of gingerroot, and parts of persimmon to enhance the flavor of a liquid that may have been brownish-black in color. Some of the leaves may even have undergone partial oxidation as they dried in the sun.

The development of true steeped tea (*sencha*), familiar to modern tastes, was one of the critical innovations of the mid-eighteenth century. By tradition invented around 1740 in Uji, this steeped tea was green in color and tasted much sweeter, eventually acquiring a huge following in the archipelago. The beverage not only served to improve the general health of the populace by another notch and to multiply tea's effects in the "industrious revolution" but also helped open the way to Japan's first consumer society.

The invention of *sencha* is best understood in the context of the increasing diversity and sophistication of tea cultivation and processing that began during the expansionary times of the late 1600s. The story is a complex one with much detail; to aid the reader, I will deal with the story of tea before 1740 in two parts. First, I will examine those writings that betray signs of tea's medieval past; the main writing here is Hitomi Hitsudai's *Food Mirror for This Dynasty*, composed in 1697. Second, I will address the work of Miyazaki Yasusada, whose tea descriptions bring the reader up to the world just before true steeped leaf tea was invented.

Tea production during the early and middle 1600s was not much different from the prior two centuries according to available sources. Two early agricultural treatises, *A Collection of Monthly Agrarian Instructions for a New People* (*Shinmin kangetsu shū*, compiled around 1650 in Iyo) and *A Peasant's Life* (*Hyakushō denki*, written in 1680 in Totōmi), read more like medieval texts than later works. The first devotes little time to tea and is concerned almost exclusively with the labor requirements for planting seeds and making stir-roasted tea.[20] Even though tea farming had likely been known in Iyo for some time, the efforts to conserve labor apparent in this work may suggest that tea production was not a major enterprise in the region.

*A Peasant's Life* contains several familiar points concerning the cultivation of the herb:

> Tea is a useful thing for all people, low and high. It can be planted on the borders of dry fields, or as mountain dry fields (*yamabatake*), or in places where the soil is bad and cropping cannot be done, or within household yards, or in any open place (*akichi*).
>
> Tea seeds should be properly planted during the second month. One should plant tea seeds in the amount of about twenty or thirty seeds by digging a hole eight or nine inches (*sun*) in diameter and about three or four around, and deeply. . . . On the sixth or seventh day water them and they will grow well. After planting one should take care in covering the seeds. . . .
>
> If you fertilize them well, the plant will grow even better. Farmers, however, . . . often do not have enough for tea bushes. In winter, dig around the roots of the tea bush and put in pine needles; also place in compost and rubbish and replace the earth, and this will then become fertilizer. These are the secrets.[21]

Like the previous treatise, *A Peasant's Life* is reminiscent of earlier centuries. First, the opening description of the diverse locations for tea patches could have come right out of late medieval times. Second, the method of planting (twenty to thirty seeds) probably harkened back to the same epoch. Because about 70–80 percent of the seeds could be expected to germinate, the author knew the value of planting large amounts together. Third, the lack of fertilizer, another holdover from the medieval era, may also have been one reason that so many seeds were planted in one hole at a time. Finally, in a later passage that also recalls the medieval era, the author wrote that "stone is the best for a tea grinder because the tea will stick in the grooves of the grinder well. Such stone may be seen around the beach." In sum, the early and mid-seventeenth century looks like a continuation of medieval trends insofar as tea cultivation is concerned.[22]

By the late seventeenth century that began to change somewhat. In 1697, samurai-turned-doctor Hitomi Hitsudai brushed *A Food Mirror for This Dynasty* (*Honchō shokkan*), modeled on a Ming Chinese book of the sixteenth century. *Food Mirror* was a major work and is thought to have included details portraying tea production, exchange, and consumption accurately for the late 1600s; this account shows, even in my abbreviated translations, the great attention to detail practiced by tea workers around this time. Overall, however, Hitomi's work suggests some changes within a larger continuity linked to earlier practices. Accordingly, the author gave primacy to powdered green tea as the preferred beverage and depicted "steeped tea," which he confusingly named *sencha,* as a highly popular but inferior brand.

After briefly describing tea as a plant, Hitomi authored a relatively long section on the virtues of powdered tea. He summarized the history of the tea ceremony from Ashikaga Yoshimasa through the early Edo period. Then, he pointed out that Uji tea was the best in the realm, as managed by the Kanbayashi family. He gave the brand name as "falcon claws," a term also noted by European visitors to the archipelago. He stated that Uji tea was so good that it was paid as tribute to nobles and warriors, especially the Tokugawa house; it was also sold throughout the vicinity around both Kyoto and Edo. According to Hitomi, no other region besides Uji produced powdered tea any longer, but other regions grew and processed what he called steeped tea. (Hitomi's word is *sencha* but is not to be confused with the modern drink invented after 1740.) These other regions producing inferior tea included the Kanto, Mandokoro in Ōmi, Kumano in Kii, Abe in Suruga, the previously noted Iyo, and the western provinces including western Honshu to central Kyushu.

Hitomi described the cultivation and processing for all types of tea together, but in his narrative his preference for powdered tea and relative disdain for his kind of "steeped tea" is apparent, first in this detailed examination of tea cultivation:

> In tea, there is wild and the cultivated variety. If you move wild tea to good soil and fertilize it, you can pick the leaves, but the taste is not good.

> For cultivating tea, gather good tea seeds, till a nice garden, and plant the seeds. The best land is sandy. During the ninth or tenth month, break up the soil into fine particles, make the soil level with pathways, set up a string, and plant the seeds. Plant two measures (*gō*) of tea seeds in one place. . . . In planting the seeds, . . . cover them with at least three inches of sandy dirt. Or, alternatively, you can plant them in the second month. . . . [Hitomi goes on to describe the other method.] In either case whittle some bamboo and shape it like a trap and set this up on all four sides. This is to protect against the pecking of wild birds.
>
> When the seedlings are one foot high, for the first time fertilize the roots. For fertilizer, you may use summer grasses or horse dung. Open the soil around the roots and place the manure in there. After about one day replace the soil. When the stalks have become longer and three or four years have passed, one plucks the shoots, but when it is the year to pluck these stalks, use night soil as fertilizer. . . .
>
> [There follows a discussion of tea grades, from best to worst: several types of powdered tea and lastly "steeped" tea.]
>
> . . . In general, you should beware of spring frost or excessive cold in tea fields. For that purpose, you should weave together reeds or straw and make a blind. Weave them close together, and be careful not to allow the sun in. . . . [Instructions follow as to when to remove the roof.]
>
> When it comes time to pluck the . . . shoots, . . . [f]irst pluck the smaller [ones], process and try them. If the taste is good, then gradually pluck [the rest].[23]

This passage on tea cultivation is notable both for its overall portrayal of tea farming and for its distinctions among types of the beverage. Under general points, Hitomi showed care for the timing and placement for seed planting; the number of tea seeds was fewer than in *A Peasant's Life,* possibly indicating an improvement in the efficiency of these Tokugawa farmers over their medieval counterparts. The stress placed on the frequent use of fertilizer certainly marked an advance over medieval times. This passage also describes the roof-over method adopted for preventing damage to the tea bush and for producing a tastier beverage.

For Hitomi, however, all teas were not created equal. For example, the author distinguished between "wild" and "cultivated" tea, suggesting that the former was not even drinkable. Some country folk probably consumed "wild" tea, but that did not fit the author's agenda. Most important, Hitomi paid considerable attention to grades of tea, but note that the tea leaves for "steeped tea" (Hitomi's *sencha*) were listed last, probably meaning that they were plucked from lower down on the plant where the leaves were tougher and more leathery. In this vein, the author also wrote: "Currently, people plant tea in the back gardens of their houses, they pluck and process it; alternatively, temples and shrines make tea in their own plots, but neither is good."[24]

There follows a passage in which Hitomi discusses the processing of tea, again worthy of citation at some length:

> For storage of tea leaves, you can use an old porcelain. . . .
>
> To process the tea leaves, first you pluck the shoots, spread them out on a board, and separate them into high and low qualities. The better is called *goku* ("best" or powdered) and the lesser is called steeped tea (*sencha*). You steam both in the same way. . . . Consequently, in families where they process tea, they keep a deep secret of how long they boil the shoots and do not casually convey this.
>
> When you have finished steaming the tea shoots, spread out a wooden plate and gradually cool them with a fan. When the shoots are cool, prepare a roaster, place down paper, and without allowing the shoots to overlap roast them above the fire, turning them with your hands. . . . After doing this for a while, gather the shoots in one place in a basket, and carefully turn them with bamboo chopsticks. When the shoots have come out well, move them to the roaster above a simmering flame and gently turn them.
>
> When the tea shoots have been roasted in this way, spread out a winnowing fan . . . , and taking only the good shoots, remove any bad shoots mixed in with the good ones using bamboo chopsticks. When you have finished separating the [bad] shoots, gradually divide the [remaining] shoots onto nine types of winnowing fans. . . . When you have finished winnowing the shoots in this way, once again get rid of the powder using a horse's tail winnow, and choosing the shoots with a pheasant's feather, group them into seven grades. [The names of the grades are then listed.][25]

This passage encompasses the most complete and detailed description of the processing of tea leaves for both powdered and steeped tea to 1697, but reduced to its essentials, it repeats a familiar procedure: pluck, steam, and roast. To be sure, there are many details as to the proper methods for keeping the flame at the right temperature, turning the roasting leaves with the hands and chopsticks, separating the different grades onto nine winnowing fans, and obtaining the right firewood, but the basic process was the same as it had been since 1200. Apparently, this conclusion holds true even for inferior grades drunk by commoners, such as low-grade steeped tea (*bancha*) and "stalk tea" (*kukicha*).[26] Hitomi left no doubt, however, that powdered tea was the best and his "steeped tea" was a lesser brand. He then commented on tea marketing and consumption:

> The steeped tea [Hitomi's *sencha*] sold at markets in Edo comes from Suruga, Shinano, Kai, Shimōsa, and Mutsu. Recently, the custom in Edo is that people always drink several bowls of steeped tea (*sencha*) before the

> morning meal and they call this morning tea (*asacha*). Wives and women drink it the most. The custom in Kyoto and western Japan is not like this. The custom in Nara is to boil some rice, stir-roast some soybeans and black or red beans and mix them in. From all directions people praise this practice and call it Nara tea.[27]

According to Hitomi, steeped tea may have comprised a lesser brand, but commoners imbibed it as part of their daily routine. This passage constitutes anecdotal evidence that almost everyone was drinking tea by the late 1600s.

Being a doctor, Hitomi could not avoid promoting the health benefits of regular tea consumption. When a person had drunk too much rice wine, imbibing one or two bowls of thick powdered tea or two or three bowls of steeped tea would quickly cure any hangover and one's innards would start to feel pleasant. As long as one did not drink too much tea, no damage to the kidneys would occur. If the elderly drank several bowls of steeped tea with a pinch of salt every morning, they would live long, and there would be no damage to either their kidneys or their stomachs. As a doctor working before the scientific revolution, he could not have given better advice.[28]

Hitomi's meticulous description of the world of tea at the end of the seventeenth century was generally accurate for its time, despite the author's strong preference for powdered tea. Like the agrarian treatises written in the Tohoku, Hitomi's work relates in a complex way to the hypothesis about an "industrious revolution" in Tokugawa Japan. To be sure, the author portrayed a workforce that undoubtedly consumed tea and labored with precise attention to timing and the smallest details. The reader can infer that tea drinking was enabling and even stimulating a labor force that worked harder, more efficiently, and for longer hours.

The issue is whether or not the tea produced with this more intensive labor was entering the market and engaging Penelope Francks' demand-pull "virtuous circle." Hitomi referred both to tea production for domestic use and that which was sold on the market. If the "industrious revolution" was to have economic effects that multiplied throughout society, then something more than just harder work was required. Therefore, my view is that tea contributed to the industrious revolution in 1697, but not to the full extent it might have.

In sum, Hitomi discussed at length the farming and processing of both powdered and "steeped tea." His preference for the former is notable, even though most people consumed the latter. In other words, Hitomi was looking backward from the present. The appearance of what modern tea drinkers know as true steeped tea (*sencha*) was still a few steps away from realization. When true *sencha* was invented, tea's effects on consumption and the market reached a higher level.

## CULTIVATION AND PROCESSING PRIOR TO THE RISE OF GENUINE STEEPED TEA (*SENCHA*): LOOKING FORWARD WITH MIYAZAKI YASUSADA

As fate would have it, the year 1697 was an important one for Japanese agriculture generally and tea specifically. Besides Hitomi's *Food Mirror,* Miyazaki Yasusada published his *Complete Works on Agriculture,* the most well known of all agricultural treatises. He lived most of his life in Fukuoka in northern Kyushu, but traveled Japan from Kyushu to the Kanto plain, picking up tips as he went. *Complete Works* includes a chapter on tea as one of the four trees. Because the book repeats much of Hitomi's description, I will concentrate on those parts of Miyazaki's *Complete Works* that were new. Overall, Miyazaki portrayed an even more complex world of tea than Hitomi did, and the steeped tea that he depicted was a bit more advanced than his fellow author's. Miyazaki also advocated tea growing as a means to add value to farming and enter the market for increased income.

Miyazaki began with advice about planting and cultivation. After briefly noting the appropriate times to collect and plant tea seeds, Miyazaki stressed that "the northern shadow was good" and that the "tea bush did not do well in direct sunlight." He encouraged the use of fertilizer and opined that the "seed should be planted deeply." When the plant began to sprout, the "branches "should not grow up but out." He also wrote that "the three fields in Yamashiro [meaning Uji, Daigo, and Toganoo] all have red dirt mixed with stones and are shaded grounds where the wind and frost are extreme."[29]

He followed the views of his fellow agricultural specialists in stating that tea could be planted in a patch by itself, along the paths of fields of other grains, or in plots mixed in with other cultivars. He advocated a "three-foot (*shaku*) distance" between the holes for seeds. Miyazaki also believed that the holes should be dug the previous year and fertilized well with compost and human waste to the depth of "seven or eight inches" (*sun*) before putting in about twenty or thirty seeds. By the third year, the cultivator could pluck the longest shoots. "If there is drought that year, water well and put on wet manure or ash beneath the roots." Miyazaki also felt that sloping fields with good drainage were essential.[30]

Continuing with Miyazaki's general observations about planting, one notes that the agrarian expert urged that "in the mountains where the wind and cold were fierce" farmers should plant the bushes close to each other in double rows. In a passage reminiscent of Hitomi, the author seems to have shied away from wild mountain patches, instead stating that large "tea fields were the best" because they were easiest to harvest. In the cultivation of tea, Miyazaki also advocated that for every platter of seeds the cultivator planted in a circular way, after they had begun to sprout in a year, he should prune back the bush by keeping "seven or eight thick shoots and pulling the rest." This represents the first known reference to pruning the young tea bush, a practice still followed today. Finally on cultivation, Miyazaki also suggested that "about thirty days before plucking, the planter should lightly fertilize around the roots and in twenty days the shoots would increase." This idea has come down to tea farmers to this day.[31]

Miyazaki's great improvement on Hitomi's *Food Mirror for This Dynasty* was his division of processing into four distinct types.[32] In other words, he did not concentrate mostly on the methods for powdered tea. Miyazaki's four categories included: (1) a mode to make high-grade (powdered) tea (*jōcha*); (2) the processing of parboiled tea (*yubikucha*); (3) the steeped tea way (*senjicha*); and (4) a method for stir-roasted tea (*tōcha*). Of these four designations, the first was essentially the same as explained by Hitomi. The only real difference was that Hitomi advocated the turning of the leaves early in the process and then later with bamboo chopsticks. Miyazaki wrote instead that when the leaves are in the roaster (*hoiro*), "after a while, using an instrument called a *nen*—a piece of bamboo cut two fingers wide and three feet long, split in two on the tip about five or six inches, slightly bent and shaved and woven together with a string—take the broad end and, on the shaved portion, spread out the leaves so that they do not bend or break, and then turn them over."[33]

The second method was for processing parboiled tea (*yubiku cha*), using slightly tough or thick leaves:

> Pluck without leaving any shoots and boil water in a kettle. Place the leaves in two baskets with handles, half each. First place one in the boiling water. Mixing them above and below using chopsticks until the leaves are sticking to the chopsticks, raise the basket out of the boiling water and cool it by dunking it in a bucket of cool water.
>
> When the leaves have dried somewhat, put them in a roaster, where the fire is stronger than in Method One. When the leaves are being parboiled, if you place straw ash or volcanic ash—just a little—the color will turn blue-green. . . . If the steam was not hot enough the tea is not good and the color is bad. When you are changing the two baskets, always count one-two-three in rhythm.[34]

The instructions concluded with advice about parboiling leaves of different ages. This method was popular in Suruga in the mid-nineteenth century, when the leaves may well have been slightly rolled by hand.[35] Miyazaki had described the processing mode for yet another new, heretofore unmentioned kind of tea.

Third, Miyazaki addressed the method for producing what he called steeped tea (*senjicha*), probably the most widely consumed of all:

> Pluck new and old leaves without distinction, and steaming them quickly in ash, also cool these leaves with water. When they have dried out well, spread them out on a mat and dry them more. When the juice has dried a little more, roll (*momu*) the leaves on the mat, or make a straw mat and crumble them somewhat there. After three times, when the leaves are good and dry, one may also place them on a sieve. It is even better to place the leaves in a roaster for one time. Afterwards, put them in a bag. . . .
>
> In general, six *kan* [of this tea] is worth twenty *monme* of silver. One tea patch of one *tan* produces thirty bags, on average. Thus, thirty bags can yield 500–600 *monme*.[36]

Miyazaki had probably seen many villages where farmers processed tea in this way, even mountain villages where much of the leaf drying was done in the sun. Note that he advocated rolling (*momu*) the tea leaves on mats. As such, Miyazaki's description advanced one step closer to producing genuine *sencha* as it is known today. The economic calculations at the end suggest the value that this tea had in trade for Miyazaki. In this expert's opinion, hard work yielded a product to be sold on the market, and in turn raised farm incomes. It is hard to imagine a better definition of the "industrious revolution."

Method Four was, according to Miyazaki, stir-roasted tea. He wrote about the manner of processing in terms more explicit than any before employed:

> Use a Chinese pot (*tōgama*) for processing. First, make a boiler (*kamado*) molded high in the back and stick paper on the surface of the sides. Put one or two *shō* of leaves in the pot depending upon its size, and being careful to keep the flame low, stir them with your hands. Just as you stir the tea leaves as they stick to the sides, when the leaves are withered take them out.
>
> Then, using a mat from Kagoshima or Dejima or other mat, gently roll (*momu*) the tea leaves so that they do not break apart. When you have rolled them to a good point, put them back in the pot and, as before, stir the leaves without resting your hands so that they do not stick, and then after a while put them on a mat and roll again. Repeat this five or six times. Putting the leaves in the pot runs to seven or eight times.

> Most importantly, because when you stir-roast in the pot [frequently] . . . the leaves will dry out and shred, rolling the leaves normally should cease at four or five times. When you stir-roast, keep the flame low and the leaves repeatedly stir-roasted will have a good smell, and when placed in hot water the tea will come out well. Also, if the flame is low the quantity of tea leaves will not decrease.[37]

Being a resident of Kyushu, Miyazaki undoubtedly had learned much about stir-roasting from the producers at Ureshino and his description is mindful of their methods. He concluded his remarks on stir-roasted tea by writing that "in well-fertilized plots where growth is good, the grade of tea is high, and when young shoots are plucked and processed, the taste and fragrance is especially fine."[38]

Miyazaki rounded out his chapter by calling "Uji, Daigo, and Toganoo" of Yamashiro the three famous tea fields in Japan. Most notably, he served as an advocate for tea production, writing that "no matter whether city, country, or mountainside, if you have a small place that can be turned into a tea patch, you should without fail plant tea in any amount. . . . If you plant it once it will never die out no matter how many years pass. The wealthy will find comfort and the poor will find property."[39] Miyazaki's advocacy of the economic benefits of tea production not only shows the continued advancement of agriculture but also suggests that peasants could enter the growing consumer market to their advantage. His work describes a hard-working peasant labor force willing to sell the tea that they had produced to thirsty consumers, characteristic of "industrious" commoners.

To sum up, Miyazaki's main achievement was to discuss the plethora of teas available to residents of the islands in his day. What is more, he envisioned a peasant class that reaped economic benefits from the labor expended to produce the beverage. While he included "steeped" tea (*senjicha*) among his teas, however, the feat of producing true *sencha* was left for a somewhat later time and a different place. After Miyazaki, no one wrote so completely on tea for the next fifty years.[40]

## THE INVENTION OF TRUE *SENCHA* AND ITS AFTERMATH

Despite the efforts of Hitomi and Miyazaki, the creation of a more delicious, steeped leaf-green tea (*sencha*) needed literally "a final twist." By tradition, this accomplishment has been assigned to Nagatani Yoshihiro (or Sōen, 1681–1778), a native of Uji Tawara village in Tsutsuki district in Yamashiro. For his invention he has been called "the father of steeped tea (*sencha*)." Relatively little is known about this man who so profoundly influenced the development of tea in Japan.[41] Apparently, he was the descendant of a family that had moved to the area during the 1590s and famously opened new tea fields there and made a living processing tea for generations.

In 1738, at the age of forty, Nagatani conducted a long series of trials and experiments and developed an excellent brand of steamed, steeped leaf tea (*sencha*). It was different from the Chinese stir-roasted variety that was then being produced in Ureshino and had been described by Miyazaki, and that, with the addition of those processed leaves to hot water, became a brand of "steeped" or boiled tea. Nor was it like any of the teas (*senjicha; senjimono*) that I have discussed thus far.

Nagatani's innovation consisted of two parts. First, and unlike Hitomi, he refused to mix mostly the old and tough leaves but chose only the new, soft shoots used for powdered tea. These he steamed right away rather than following accepted procedure and soaking them before boiling. Second, he refined the former rough method of rolling the leaves with the feet and hands (implied in Miyazaki's treatise) and perfected a method for crumpling the steamed leaves by hand (*temomu*) to permit the constituent juices of the leaves to infuse the cup of tea later. Nagatani carried out his rolling on top of a roaster, an implement just like the one used for powdered tea. The roaster helped to dry the leaves as they were crumbled, yielding a sweeter beverage. Nagatani's method of rolling the leaves while they were roasting was a significant improvement over older methods that used the sun or wind for drying the leaves. In sum, Nagatani helped perfect a method of steaming leaves used for steeped tea that earned it equal status with the formerly ascendant powdered tea. The invention of genuine steeped tea (*sencha*) in the mid-1700s ranks as one of the greatest innovations in Japanese tea history and was destined to multiply the numbers of consumers many times.

By the time of Nagatani's work, steeped tea was growing rapidly in popularity in Japan among the elite, because it came along with the latest in Chinese Confucian culture.[42] As early as 1654, the Ming loyalist Yin Yuan (1592–1673) had fled to Japan, bringing with him the Ōbaku sect of Zen and the Ming custom of drinking steeped tea. His tea, however, appears to have been processed in the stir-roasted manner, even though he cultivated tea patches and made tea at his new home in Manpukuji in Kyoto. Ming literati undoubtedly provided cultural cachet for steeped tea, so long consumed in one form or another by commoners in Japan, but it was Nagatani who developed the new process. Eventually, Ōeda Ryūhō (died ca. 1756), author of *Tea Chats on an Azure Bay* (*Seiwan chawa*) could boldly write: "This book is solely for the purpose of boiled tea (meaning *sencha*). I will not discuss powdered tea."[43]

The following story also suggests the impact of Nagatani's work. In 1742, the Japanese Shibayama Kikusen, better known by his name of choice, Baisaō (1675–1763), and for his tireless advocacy of the "Way of Steeped Leaf Tea" (*sencha*), visited Nagatani and stayed the night. He is reported to have said to his host: "Old man Nagatani Sōen! You have put me up in a room and brought forth new tea from your own garden. How marvelous! How wonderful! Upon first trying it, it has a beautiful fresh fragrance and there can be nothing in the realm to compare to it!" Although there are claims that steamed, steeped leaf tea was invented earlier or in another place, at present Nagatani's place as its inventor appears to be secure.[44]

Nagatani's innovations opened the way for steeped tea to acquire a large following. For instance, just after his meeting with Nagatani, Baisaō (also known as Kōyūgai) wrote a book on steeped tea entitled *The Lineage of Toganoo Teas* (*Baizan shucha furyaku*). Born to a doctor's family in northern Kyushu, Baisaō took vows as a Zen monk at age eleven. At thirty-three, he watched the Chinese of Nagasaki boiling steeped tea and took to the custom. In 1731, at fifty-seven, he went to Kyoto and started selling steeped tea throughout the city. It is unclear whether the steeped tea was steamed or stir-roasted. He authored his book in 1748 and clearly preferred the former, writing: "In the fifth month of this year, I was blessed with hand-made new tea from some important personage (*inshu*). For the first time I tasted the best brand from Toganoo. Its fragrance and subtle taste was better than all the others. I do not doubt that it is called the best brand in all Japan." Apparently the Toganoo brand still retained some of its former reputation.[45]

With writings like these stressing the advantages of steeped tea, demand for that kind of tea expanded throughout Japan, especially in Kyoto. A certain Kamisaka Seiichi (b. 1824) received permission from a steeped tea master–producer named Ogawa Kashin (1786–1855) to produce a type of *sencha* for daily use. Kamisaka was from Uji but sold his tea in the northerly provinces of Kaga, Noto, and Echigo. In 1834, Kamisaka plucked the finest new leaves and shoots from fields employing the roof-over method of cultivation and then processed the product according to Nagatani's procedure. The fine fragrance led to widespread praise for the drink. The next year, in 1835, an Edo merchant named Yamamoto Kihei produced the same fine tea. According to tradition, the following year Sakamoto Tōkichi, from a village in Shizuoka, went to an Uji producer and learned Uji methods for steeped tea from a processor there. In 1840, he studied the methods for a special type of steeped tea called "jeweled dew" (*gyokuro*).[46]

It probably does not matter which of these stories is true, but "jeweled dew" tea became the beverage of choice during the 1830s in various places in Japan. The process had pickers pluck the finest young shoots grown in the roof-over method and then roll them on a roaster and make steeped tea. While no single person can be given credit for "inventing" *gyokuro,* it clearly developed from improvements made in the methods of processing by many people in Uji Tawara. "Jeweled dew" tea eventually became the highest and most revered brand of tea in Japan.[47]

David Howell provides an example of the effects of these new, improved teas on village life in late Tokugawa Japan. According to Ōtaka Zenbei, headman of Tomida village in Kazusa in 1860, "the number of tea merchants has increased steadily." The appearance of these merchants had altered village life considerably. About a hundred years before, "all the farmers" planted tea plants on the raised boundaries between their fields. They drank much of the tea and sold the surplus. Then tea merchants came, selling high-grade tea. "Now the villagers buy the high-grade tea and will not grow their own. Tea plants have virtually disappeared from the levies."[48] In other words, high-grade teas like those discussed above discouraged raising tea for domestic use and enticed those with the extra income to buy their tea on the market. This scene was probably repeated over and over again as the new, improved *sencha* and *gyokuro* made their impact felt in many parts of the archipelago.

Soon others followed Nagatani, mixing and matching processes and brands as they pleased. Ueda Akinari (1734–1809), a scholar from Osaka, in 1794 published another book dealing with the process for making *sencha* entitled *Miscellaneous Comments on the Way of Pure Elegance* (*Seifū sagen*). This excerpt is a neat summary of methods available for making "steeped" tea at that time:

> for tea, there is the method of steaming and roasting, stir-roasting, and drying in the sun. Roasting tea produces the best brand, stir-roasting the next, and tea dried in the sun is an inferior grade. Uji and Shigaraki do only steaming and roasting, while the tea of other regions is of various kinds. But I have heard that Kyushu and Shikoku do only stir-roasted tea. Roasted tea is good for boiling, while stir-roasting tea is good for steeping. These are the so-called types of steeped tea (*dashicha,* here meaning *sencha*). In both roasting and stir-roasting the leaves, these methods value the green color.[49]

Ueda's advocacy of steaming steeped tea as the most flavorful method is reminiscent of Nagatani. It stands in contrast to the Chinese preference for stir-roasting. Ueda also listed the brands of both powdered and steeped teas and mentioned that there were "leaf teas and stalk and leaf teas" and mixtures of both. If the tea consisted of merely the leaf point, the taste was poor. He even discussed pear-apple tea (*nashicha*), but said that, contrary to word of mouth, the taste was bad. By 1800, there were more brands of tea than anyone could count.

Ueda also wrote of the best tea-producing areas. He said that steamed steeped tea from Shigaraki was the best. Also good were teas from Kawakami in Ise, Hatori in Iga, Murō in Yamato, Kōya in Kii, Utsutsu in Owari, Yōrō in Mino, Rokubo in Suruga, and Ureshino in Hizen. He had also heard of teas from Higo and Chikuzen. This list is important because it repeats place-names that had been known for fine tea since the 1300s. Teas from Tanba, Harima, and Hyūga were good with meals but lacked elegance. Ueda concluded his evaluation of teas by noting that "in recent years commercial ships brought *tōcha* [a brand of Chinese stir-roasted steeped tea] but that it was not good."

Abe Masanobu wrote *The Suruga Journal* (*Suruga zasshi*) in 1843, adding his name to the chorus of writers waxing lyrical about the abundance of tea brands. He outlined three new methods that were really variations on earlier work by Miyazaki. In the first, called "green tea" (*seicha*), pickers plucked the tea leaves in the fourth month, parboiled it, squeezed it by wrapping it in a hemp cloth and using a stick, crumpled the product on a grass mat, roasted it dry, and then selected three grades of leaves and placed them on separate mats. In the second, named *ibiricha*, the processor washed the leaves and stir-roasted them while still damp. In the third method, simply dubbed coarse steeped tea (*bancha*), workers steamed the leaves and then dried them in the sun. They were then boiled in a pot. This process began in the middle of the fourth month and was commonly called "tea of the third picking" (*sanbancha*). In the first picking two leaves were taken, in the second three, while the third picking was simply *bancha*. A roaster could be used for the best leaves, but in other cases a pot was used. Methods two and three seem similar to stir-roasted tea, but as the leaves were washed, it was really a combination of stir-roasting and steaming methods.[50]

Evidently, by the mid-nineteenth century Japan was awash in numerous types of tea as well as advanced expertise for farming and processing the plant. It should come as no surprise that people began to think of the tea industry as a commercial asset for producers and the archipelago-wide economy. The task of making this apparent fell to the final great tea expert of the Edo period, Ōkura Nagatsune, who authored *A Consideration for Broadly Profiting the National Industry* (*Kōeki kokusan kō*, 1844). This work was written in a period when tea had become part of a booming commercial economy and mostly addressed methods of cultivation for special cultivars. Ōkura himself was born to a peasant home in northern Kyushu, pursued Dutch studies in the Osaka region, and traveled widely in the Kanto, western Honshu, and northern Japan to learn about farming there. In his view, "there were no families that did not use tea daily."[51] For those poor peasants who had "few dry fields or wet paddies, if they would just plant five to seven bushes within their household lots, it would be a great aid."[52] This passage surely denoted the raising of tea plants for domestic use.

Ōkura first addressed a simple manner of cultivation available to those who consumed coarse boiled tea (*bancha*), the beverage of the peasantry. He advocated tea processing for both home and market:

> In Hyūga, they make lots of tea called *bancha,* use it morning and evening, and send it to Osaka. Then, too, in Ise they make lots of tea like Hyūga's and ship it to Edo. The way of making this tea is unlike that of Uji. Just as with cultivating wheat and other dry field crops, stand on the border (*aze*) of a wet paddy and, as thickly as one scatters wheat seeds, plant tea seeds in the spring. In the autumn, thin out the places that have grown too thick and let them grow in places 1.4 or 1.5 inches (*sun*) and one foot (*shaku*) apart.[53]

There followed instructions on fertilizing with dried fish, vegetable oils, or night soil, and ways to keep the plants warm in the winter. Ōkura also advised the cultivator to weed constantly. The author also states that "[i]f you do not grow the cultivar as you have planted it, unlike others its growth will be poor. Even for one bush, rather than replanting the seedlings, it is better to leave them where you have sown them."[54]

After discussing the best kind of soil for the tea bush, Ōkura suggested that the plant did the best in "dry fields in the mountains where the sun shines brightly."[55] Then the author indicated the need for a completely new procedure: "During the third or fourth month of the fourth year, cut down all the bushes with a sickle without leaving anything. During the autumn, the remains that have been cut down will sprout from the beginning. Then the next year you may pluck and produce steeped tea" (*sencha*).[56] In other words, Ōkura was advocating cutting down the bush every fourth year for a fresh start. Advocacy of this procedure was Ōkura's most enduring legacy for tea.

Most of the processes for making tea advanced by this author have already been discussed: parboiling and the half-steamed, half-stir-roasted methods. Ōkura, however, described stir-roasting as especially fine, perhaps to set it off from the coarse steeped tea (*bancha*) described above:

> If you want to make *good* tea, pluck the shoots that have just barely started to appear during the third and early fourth month. Wash them quickly in water, place them in a flat-bottomed pot and stir-roast them. . . . When the leaves have become just like boiled vegetables, open up thin paper and cool them.
>
> Then put them back in the pot and this time make the flame a bit weak from the beginning. With your hands change the shoots around from top to bottom so that they do not stick together and then again put them in thin paper and cool the shoots. Place them in a pot. This third time stir-roast them with an even weaker flame. Then open paper again and cool the shoots. During this third time the leaves will dry out and curl. . . . On the fifth time [of repeating this], the leaves' shape will seem just like they came from Uji. But they will be a bit soft and appear as though they have been chewed with teeth. Taking this and stir-roasting the leaves a sixth time with a low flame, the leaves will be all crumpled up. Then it's done!
>
> This is the teaching of a previous Zen monk. This also appears to be "Chinese tea." (*tōcha*).[57]

Even though it was stir-roasted tea and had been prepared in Japan for centuries, Ōkura denominated it a "Chinese" beverage. When comparing Miyazaki's and Ōkura's varying descriptions of method, note that in Miyazaki's discussion of stir-roasted tea, the worker did not use paper and constantly rolled the tea leaves on a mat outside of the pot between roasts. For Ōkura, apparently, the crumpling took place during the actual routine of stir-roasting. Ōkura's stir-roasted method had originated with an old Zen monk as "good tea," he wrote, and he touted his brand of stir-roasted tea as the most economical and as good for sale on the market.

In the event, Ōkura's tea-making processes were somewhat different from both Abe Masanobu's and the Uji methods. Ōkura's upbringing in northern Kyushu or his position as an adviser to two domains in Shizuoka may have had something to do with this. As a final note, Ōkura's book contains pictures, one of which shows the workers transplanting seedlings. It was the first such reference to this method of farming tea in a Japanese work and may have stemmed from his work in Dutch studies.[58]

By the mid-nineteenth century, residents of the archipelago were consuming a plethora of tea varieties cultivated in the most efficient and productive ways possible. Beverages were processed in so many different and meticulous ways that it is impossible to do justice to them all. To be sure, powdered tea still existed for a portion of the elite, but most of the populace drank steeped tea noted for its deep-green color and marvelous fragrance and taste. Beginning in 1800, Japan possessed a nascent consumer society supplied by a hardworking, efficient workforce, and tea, especially *sencha,* was a big part of that development.

## ONE METHOD FOR ESTIMATING TEA CONSUMPTION: THE GEOGRAPHICAL SPREAD OF THE INDUSTRY

The wide number of tea brands and the multifarious, subtle methods for farming and processing the plant certainly leave an impression of nearly universal consumption of the caffeinated drink in Japan by as early as 1800. Even at that date, of course, Japan had no general statistical compilations to measure consumption; the historian must fall back on the available materials to draw an inference. In the following two sections, I am going to attempt to gauge tea consumption through the use of two types of materials: descriptive accounts of tea production and trade centers and the ubiquity of cultural references to tea in literature, art, and advertisements. This section will also provide additional examples of tea grown and processed for home use and for the market.

One way to track consumption is to describe briefly the geographical network of production and trade. Just as in the medieval age, certain places became famous for their special brands of tea. The litany of these regions shows the marked growth of tea production during the Tokugawa epoch. In fact, Japanese tea growers never produced, *in all of Japanese history,* so many brands of tea as they did during the Edo epoch. A summary of these regions and their various characteristics follows, beginning with the special place of what was considered by many to be Japan's best tea, that of Uji. Then I shall describe some of the most famous Tokugawa-era teas, moving from western Japan eastward.[59]

Uji tea was clearly the brand against which all others were measured during the Tokugawa era.[60] The process by which Uji tea eventually came to surpass that of Toganoo after the 1460s was discussed at the end of chapter 2. Beginning in the late sixteenth century, Uji became the place that maintained the "best practice" for tea production, as suggested by the work of Nagatani Yoshihiro. Perhaps as many as 170 roasters were in use during high season, and the managers at Uji might employ over one thousand workers in this processing. Another measure of the great value associated with Uji tea was its place in Tokugawa rituals of legitimacy.

To elaborate, the *bakufu* implemented laws regulating those who handled the elite's tea and establishing a rite known as *chatsubo dōchū* (the tea-jar journey). This political ritual accompanied the presentations of Uji tea to the imperial family, the shogun's house, and various daimyo every year around the middle of the fourth month. It first took place in 1613, but was not institutionalized until the reign of the third shogun Iemitsu in 1633.

Every year during the fourth month, thirty to forty people walked the entire distance along the Eastern Sea Route (Tōkaidō) from Edo, filled special stoneware jars with Uji tea, and then returned to the shogun's capital several days later. This display of political power took thirteen days one way. While this ritual had great political meaning for the various members of the elite, it was also *the* great ceremony that took place in Uji. There was a placard that stood alongside Uji bridge stating, "No sending out of new tea before dispatching of the ritual (*mimono*) tea."

Under the Tokugawa, the Kanbayashi household became the local representative (*daikan*) of Uji. Using skills that they had learned tending tea in Tanba, they took charge of production for the Tokugawa ceremony. At first Uji supplied powdered tea only, but as demand for steeped tea grew, they became major producers of it too. The lands under Kanbayashi control spread throughout the basins of the Uji and Kizu Rivers.

This ceremony was essentially a Tokugawa shogunal affair. That family was the first to visit Uji, and all the others followed after them. Consider the case of Owari domain. Owari was a territory granted to one of the Tokugawa relatives fit to provide an heir should the position of shogun fall vacant. There are accounts of the Owari domain representatives that survive today and show how important the tea rite was for the legitimacy of the Tokugawa family.

The Owari representative was accustomed to arriving the day after the shoguns, so important was the domain in the political system. The shipping of the jars from Owari took place each year during the late fourth or early fifth month, and usually about twenty-six persons made the trip from Owari. These included the leader, several retainers, five to seven handlers for the jars, and about ten corvee laborers from all over Owari.

Jars sent from Owari were then entrusted to various tea producers on an alternating basis. The Owari leader made a ceremonial inspection of each jar after its arrival in Uji. Once this task was finished, the handlers and laborers moved to Fushimi near Kyoto, where the party stayed for the duration. In the meantime, tea producers held a banquet for the party's leader and he stayed one night in Uji. The next day he too set off for Kyoto.

The sealing of the jars took place several days after the party had arrived. The process of sealing occupied three days that involved a meeting with Owari officials and the eventual sealing of the jars by the Kanbayashi. According to finely worked-out precedent, the Owari jars were never sealed before the *bakufu*'s; sometimes this meant that the Owari leader had to wait for several days at his inn. At last, several days after the official sealing of the jars was completed, the jars were shipped to Owari.

On the day before shipment, there was another banquet for the party's leader at the inn where he was staying. On the next day the party leader and the tea producers saw to the packaging of the jars in a palanquin-like parcel over which a curtain had been draped. The phrase "lasts a long time" (*nagamochi*) was also apparent. Following the packaging, the jars were sent back to Owari after a process that had taken about a month. This means that the Owari leader had waited about one month in inns in Uji and Kyoto. The ritual importance of Uji powdered tea only increased during the Edo period.

Uji was the leader, but as is evident from the following narrative, different brands of tea originated from almost every nook and cranny of the islands. In Kyushu, Fukuoka had a long tradition of tea cultivation stretching back to the eleventh century and the immigrant Chinese who brought their tea and methods with them. During the Tokugawa era, Fukuoka continued to be a major center of production. In the late sixteenth century, the Ōtomo family, rulers of northern Kyushu, received tea from their domain. Between 1750 and 1770, large amounts of tea were shipped to Kyoto and Osaka, while in the mid-nineteenth century Fukuoka supplied tea to Okinawa. After the American Commodore Perry arrived with his fleet in Japan in 1853, Nagasaki became a major port. Almost all of the tea produced in Fukuoka was of the stir-roasted variety.

Miyazaki, located in southeastern Kyushu, started producing tea during the 1600s. The ruling Shimazu household ordered tea from this part of their giant domain. By 1687, tea was being taxed. In 1757, Uji-style tea fields appeared in the area, and some of the beverage processed there was presented to the emperor. The Shimazu eventually took over these fields. Miyazaki had many mountain patches (*yamacha*) and they were taxed, but farmers there processed stir-roasted tea for local use, unlike the Uji-style production that took place on level lands.[61]

Kagoshima in southern Kyushu was blessed with a climate and soil that made for some of the best tea in Japan. There were many mountain patches. The origin of tea from Kagoshima (Satsuma) harkens back to the mid-sixteenth century, and by 1617 the tea there was an object of the tax collector, the rate rising noticeably by 1644. Between 1644 and 1648, the ruling daimyo family ordered seeds from Uji and established tea fields, and added more in 1718. During the 1770s, there are many sources indicating the introduction of Uji methods. Around 1800, there are records of tea parties, and it is clear that the Shimazu family enjoyed the tea ceremony and possessed many fine tea bowls. For this purpose, naturally they used powdered tea processed in the Uji style. In 1866, a Satsuma native went to Uji and learned about *gyokuro,* the popular type of steeped tea using the roof-over method. Yet the local tea was stir-roasted cheap steeped tea (*bancha*), dried in the sun.

Like Kyushu, Shikoku possessed numerous mountain patches and had its own traditions for growing and processing the beverage in all four provinces on the island. As early as 1587, the local daimyo family, the Chōsokabe, carried out cadastral surveys including tea patches. Tea was traded from Tosa during the medieval period and was also the object of taxation. Tosa had numerous local varieties of tea, all valued for their high quality. One author wrote in the early nineteenth century that "along the roads in western Honshu and all the small islands all the way to Kyushu, there is not a place that does not consume Tosa tea. Truly it is a famous brand produced in large quantity."[62] When the Yamauchi took over from the Chōsokabe in the early 1600s, they issued orders concerning tea gathering. Peasants were directed to collect tea from all the mountain patches in the province. Most of the processed tea was sent to the Kyoto-Osaka area. Like the Shimazu, the Yamauchi preferred Uji-style tea, bought by domain procurement. In 1843, 3,210 *kin* of steeped tea (*sencha*) cost from .45 to .86 *monme* per *kin,* but since the purchase was done by government procurement, the price was lower than would have prevailed on the open market.

Tosa supplied three types of tea: high-quality steeped tea (*sencha*); low-quality coarse, steeped tea (*bancha*); and an oxidized tea known as *tarecha.* By 1873, production figures are available (see table 3).

In the same newspaper that reported these figures, the author wrote: "Among the many products of Tosa . . . they are all of the greatest beauty. Tea especially is a product that grows naturally in the mountains, and there are places where the patches occupy over forty miles (*ri*). . . . Now we have employed seventy teachers of processing from Tanba and are learning to process tea in the Yamashiro (Uji) style, measuring heat and cold and the season. We have established processing plants north and

**Table 3** Tea produced in Tosa at the end of the Tokugawa period

| | *Amount** | *Price†* |
|---|---|---|
| Total tea production | 12,739,348 | 4,124,463.76 |
| *Bancha* | 1,507,360 | 92,123.00 |
| Powdered tea | 487,551 | 9,520.43 |

*Source:* Ōishi, *Chagyō hattatsu shi,* p. 297.
**Kin*
†Yen

south in two grades." Another oxidized tea (*Awa cha*) was also traded continuously throughout the Edo period.

Uji was indeed the most famous production center of tea in the Kyoto-Osaka region of Japan, in part for its early technological and economic advantages and in part because of its meaning in ritual politics. As is apparent from this narrative, however, many other places in central Japan produced teas of great variety. Tanba Province was also near Kyoto, a province first charged with supplying tea to Emperor Saga in the early ninth century. Tanba was also the home of the Kanbayashi, chief innovators at Uji. In 1614, a cadastral survey noted that there were more than 41.5 *chō* of tea fields yielding almost thirteen *koku* in tea taxes, mostly steamed and other types (*yudecha*). Tea farmers tended to be among the upper class of peasants, but by the 1700s mid-level cultivators also grew tea and traded it to Hyōgo and Osaka. In 1714, 35 percent of the productive value of Ōsawa village in Sasayama domain was counted in tea. By the early 1800s, the domain produced 100,000 *kan* of processed tea and tea acreage occupied 6.7 percent of all cultivated land. Mountain patches were also common both for local consumption and as a source of a commodity to be traded.

Nara encompassed a region that had perhaps the longest tradition of tea production and consumption in all Japan. Going by the cadastral survey of 1594, at least sixteen villages in the Nara area were suppliers of tea. In similar surveys of 1615 and 1639, villages that either paid taxes in tea or furnished labor for tea occupied every district (*gun*) in Nara. Two hundred and two villages furnished almost 12 *koku* in revenue. Again, according to cadastral surveys of the 1590s and 1670s, the acreage devoted to tea in Nishino village in southern Nara increased by more than twenty times to 10.5 *chō*, and Niizumi village (also in southern Nara) doubled to almost seven *chō*. Then there were places like Shinohara for which the survey simply stated: "This place has tea everywhere."[63]

Peasants had long experience with tea:

> Tea does best in poor soil (*yasechi*). There's no reason to tend the bushes; just leave them alone and they grow large. Villagers who live almost the whole year by slash-and-burn dry fields are well off. A long time ago the office of the local samurai (*daikansho*) carried out a cadastral survey using a six-foot pole. Places that yielded good tea were called "top dry fields" (*jōbatake*), and the fields were divided into three classes (also *chūbatake* and *gebatake*). We also bought some seeds from Uji.[64]

Apparently, even farmers in the mountains of Nara respected the reputation of Uji tea.

By the 1730s, the Nara region had become famous for its steeped tea throughout Japan. By the late 1700s, food and roadside tea shops increased greatly along with the populations of such large cities as Edo and Osaka. Eateries in Edo served buckwheat noodles and hot rice bathed in tea called *chazuke.* One name for the tea-rice dish was Nara *chazuke,* as mentioned by Hitomi Hitsudai. It filled hungry customers' stomachs. By 1824, in Edo there were sixty restaurants, twenty shops serving *chazuke,* eighty tea shops, forty bars, and forty tobacco stores. Shops serving tea and *chazuke* ranked together as the most popular centers.

As the narrative addresses places east of the capital region, Ise was another notable tea-producing area. Ise tea from at least four different places was sent to the northern provinces through Tsuruga in the 1600s. In 1736, Ise tea was shipped to Osaka, and then to Edo by 1818. Central Ise is quite mountainous, and there were many mountain tea patches (*yamacha*) there. Peasants competed to enter these mountains and pluck tea, in one day picking as much as ten to eighteen kilograms.

One place in southern Ise known as Kabata Valley was heavily forested and known for its tea. During the Edo period, it belonged to Kii domain and was near several production sites in Nara, and so tea spread there naturally. Every year farmers would cut the vegetation and burn the grasses so that the next year tea shoots would appear. In 1751, the daimyo of Kii domain placed a tax on tea bushes. Many farmers became angry and buried their tea bushes.

As for northern Ise, in 1598 the samurai official also placed a tax of three coins per bush on tea production. Producers suffered from this burdensome tax, so they gradually quit working and the fields fell into disuse. Inside the village, however, a person named Ōtani Genuemon feared the tea bushes would be abandoned and asked for, and received, a revenue reduction. He then suggested drying the tea in the sun naturally (rather than using a roaster), and thus the tea fields escaped destruction. In other words, the farmers made a go of it by reducing their costs.

Just over the mountains from Kyoto, Ōmi was a major center of tea production for the Tokugawa period. Through the Muromachi era, farmers probably managed the tea lands there through slash-and-burn agriculture. From a small village named Ogura, Mandokoro tea started in six wild patches. Gradually farmers learned to cultivate it, and later they even produced refined steeped tea (*gyokuro*). Tea from Mandokoro in Ōmi was sold far and wide by lumbermen. The renowned philosopher Motoori Norinaga noted a song from Mandokoro: "The tea plucked here—will it be whisked to a froth by Akita girls when it arrives there?"[65] One possible source for the tea in Ōmi is in Sakamoto in front of Hiyoshi Shrine. About

Ōmi tea, Ueda Akinari wrote that "there are many types of tea in Shigaraki. Mountain villagers opened fields and processed the tea. Steeped tea [from Mandokoro] is without doubt the best in the realm."[66]

East of the capital region and Ise and Ōmi lay the famous "Tōkaidō" running from Mino to Shizuoka along the Pacific Ocean. In general, well-known centers of production included Kiyomi and Ashikubo in Suruga, Wachigai and Yōrō in Mino, and Utsutsu in Owari. In Mino, the valleys along the Ibi River were tea centers in olden days, holding many mountain patches (*yamacha*). The earliest notation of a tea field in the area refers to the temple Ryūtokuji in 1511 in Ikeda town. In 1601, a samurai placed a placard stating that "there should be no disturbance of trees or tea fields" at Tōkōji along the Ibi River.[67] In 1793, a farmer from Ikeda town had two *chō,* and in 1818 he invited processors (*chashi*) from Uji to introduce their methods. A record from 1857 suggests that sales were brisk. Mikawa also possessed mountain patches throughout the province and was a famous center of production. In 1653 Mikawa farmers sent their tea to Shinano, and documents show that the Ina route was quite a bustling region for trade in tea and other items. In Kären Wigen's insightful study of the Shimoina region in Shinano, in 1763 tea comprised almost 45 percent of the region's imports measured by the number of packhorses (10,756).[68]

Shizuoka was a major place producing tea and had been so since at least the fourteenth century. The region was renowned for its fine leaves of deep green. Moreover, along the Tenryū, Ōi, and Abe Rivers mountain patches were distributed widely, farmed in slash-and-burn style by the late 1500s. When Ieyasu became shogun in 1603, he often stayed in his ancestral castle at Sunpu, and large amounts of tea from Ashikubo and Ōi were sent to Edo especially for the shogun (*goyōcha;* see below). At Nakagawane village along the Ōi River records from 1602 and 1603 state that taxes were collected on tea at the rates of 1,366 coins for 25 *kin* and 46 *kin,* respectively. If one *kin* was equivalent to 160 *monme,* then it would have come to about 4 *kan,* or more than 1 *ryō.* In a record from 1738 from Abe district, tea production was worth 8 *ryō;* in one from Sukumodahara in 1784, Yoshioka village produced 24 *ryō* in tea (over 1,000 *kan*).

According to records from the district where Mount Fuji towered, that area had produced coarse steeped tea (*bancha*) for three hundred years by the 1600s and first sold both to nearby villages and as far away as Kai and Shinano Provinces. Beginning in 1716, the region had sent its tea to Edo, with trade at its most frequent in the mid-1700s. One village named Kageyama sent sixty packhorses carrying *bancha* to Edo during that time. As one packhorse carried four loads and one load contained eight *kan,* the shipments to Edo and elsewhere must have been truly gigantic.

Along the Tenryū River, a certain Tarōzaemon farmed over nine units of inferior-grade tea fields in 1677. Mountain patches were common along this river. Along the Ōta River in 1673, a survey shows tea fields of various grades under cultivation. They were said to date back to the late fifteenth century. Suruga tea, it will be recalled, appeared in *A Food Mirror for This Dynasty* (1697). In his piece of fiction entitled *Irozato mitokoro zetai* (Households from Three Places in the Red-Light District) dated to 1688, Ihara Saikaku portrayed a scene in which "four or five men in a household made rice in rotation and saw a peddler carrying Abe tea. He was one of several who had traveled from Suruga. Twenty-five or -six of them had red-flushed faces and wore loincloths."[69]

By the Tokugawa period, shipments from Shizuoka to Edo were so common that the region had its own commercial organizations (*kabu nakama*) in the shogun's capital, as well as several more (*cha ton'ya*) in the regional capital, Sunpu. Local tea movers were also organized. The chief official (*bugyō*) in Sunpu gave government approval to the trade arrangements. Sunpu became such a center of the tea trade to Edo that a "tea town" (*chamachi*) developed there and in other localities. Tea shops were plentiful, too. As early as 1695 boat service "supplying lots of tea," mostly to Edo, was in operation. In 1824, the Bunsei Tea Incident erupted when tea producers from 3,800 households in Shizuoka protested against unfair treatment by the merchant organizations (*ton'ya*) and other merchants in Sunpu. This incident is examined below.

As our narrative moves along to the Kanto region, there were two areas of great importance: Sayama and Ibaragi. Chapter 2 showed that tea production in the Kanto region dated back at least to 1300. The construction of the shogun's capital at Edo gave the early development of tea production in the Kanto a giant boost. In 1696 tea was plucked from the temple Tafukuji and named Mitomi tea. Mountain patches were prevalent in Chichibu and Tama and farmed in swidden style. Sayama tea is well known today, but evidence regarding its origin is sparse. It may have started as early as 1802, but by 1813 there were fifty-four tea households possessing more than two hundred tea roasters (*hoiro*). In 1819, when Sayama established its own merchant organization (*cha ton'ya*) in Edo, the region was known for cultivating tea in the Uji style and was listed as a major producer of fine steeped tea too.

Ibaraki had at least two local varieties of tea, cultivation of which dated back to the 1660s. Producers shipped Ibaraki tea to Shinano, Kōzuke, and all over northeastern Honshu. During the early 1800s, the price of tea dropped and production in Ibaraki ground to a halt, but during the Tenpō famine of the 1830s, farmers were encouraged to plant and sell tea to help their families survive. Local officials brought in Uji cultivation techniques, and in 1851, Sekiyado domain located in Shimōsa Province opened its own wholesale shop within the domain estate in Edo. In another case, farmers from Kuji in Hitachi Province imported seeds from Uji and spread them widely throughout the area. More recent inspection of the flowers and seeds from Kuji suggests that the tea dated back at least three hundred years and was botanically unlike the Uji plant. Ibaraki tea must be the oldest in the Kanto.[70]

The northernmost limit for tea cultivation is located on the northern tip of Honshu, but as noted previously, peasants of northeastern Japan experimented with, and were somewhat successful at, cultivation there. As of this writing, the northernmost tea tree stands at the temple Zenryūji in Hokkaido at a northern latitude of 43 degrees, 10 minutes, although it probably does not date from the Edo epoch. It was over sixty years old in the 1980s. There were a few bushes in Aomori that actually produced tea (40 degrees north, 35 minutes). In Akita in the eighteenth century the daimyo (Tagaya) brought in seeds from Uji and tried to sell tea as an aid to increasingly indebted samurai. There were apparently five *chō* there. The low temperature during the winter is -19 degrees C, but 60–80 centimeters of snowfall blankets the tea trunks and allows the tea to mature. In processing, the farmers of Akita followed the Uji method of steaming, roasting, and rolling the leaves, but unlike in Shizuoka, for example, the Uji method was not the most recent available at the time. The Satake daimyo family also used its connections with Kyoto to import Uji seeds and had many of their retainers plant tea. Even northerly Tsugaru domain cultivated small amounts of tea by 1700 and optimistically established a tea official (*chabatake bugyō*).

Along the Pacific Ocean, there is little snowfall and so there was practically no production north of the limit. One exceptional area is Yonezaki town near modern Takada, where there are some bushes attached to temple grounds. It is said that production there harks back before 1772. In the early years after the fall of the *bakufu* in 1868, Miyagi prefecture in northeastern Japan was the fourth-leading producer of tea, behind only Mie, Kyoto, and Shizuoka. There were also a couple of tea bushes in Iwate prefecture. According to one story, tea stopped coming to northeastern Japan during the Warring States period, and so locals tried to import seeds from Uji, and even planted them, but the bushes died. Later there was some success at Nanbu domain, and local legend attributes some tea fields to Ryūsenji near Miyako city in Iwate.

To summarize, during the Edo period, tea producers thrived from Kyushu to the Kanto and the southern part of northeastern Japan. Farmers even tried to produce tea north of this line, but with limited success. Practically speaking, a line drawn through Ibaraki and Niigata prefectures marks off the northern limit of Tokugawa tea cultivation, with the tea fields around Kuji in Ibaraki covering about two hundred hectares and those around Murakami town in Niigata about forty hectares. As already noted, there was some production at Takada city in southern Iwate and also in Miyagi prefecture, but these places were exceptional. The growth in tea production witnessed during the Tokugawa period may truly be said to be the final stage in the expansion of tea production that had begun during the 1300s.

The nearly archipelago-wide production of large amounts of this beverage suggests that numerous residents—perhaps almost all—were also consumers as early as 1800. Many farmers both of rice and other grains in valleys and on plains, and mountain peoples utilizing slash-and-burn agriculture had their own small tea plots and supplied their own versions of the beverage to their households and villages. As the population grew rapidly and urbanization took place during the 1600s, tea consumption and commerce increased at a rapid rate. The reader has already seen the role played by the towns of Obama and Tsuruga in supplying tea to thirsty residents in northeastern Japan, where not much tea could be cultivated.

By the 1700s, the large cities of Kyoto-Osaka in the western part of Japan and Edo in the Kanto came to dominate trade. Generally speaking, tea from Kyushu, Shikoku, and western Honshu flowed through Osaka, while Edo merchants dealt in tea from Shizuoka, Shinano, Kai, the Kanto, and the southern reaches of northeastern Honshu. Tea towns sprang up in local cities such as Tsuruga and Sunpu. These various centers of the tea trade came to handle truly immense amounts of tea. For example, in 1714 Osaka managed 1,478,000 *kin* of tea worth more than 1,460 strings of cash, while Sunpu in 1856 transshipped about 196 tons of processed tea, netting 16,000 *ryō* in gold.[71]

For most of the Edo period, the three main trade routes were through Tsuruga and Obama to the northeast, from western Japan through Osaka and Kyoto, and from central and eastern Japan through Edo. The first route was operational mostly during the seventeenth and early eighteenth centuries, until a safer and speedier way from central Japan through Osaka by boat to northeastern Japan was discovered around 1700. The second and third routes through Osaka and Edo, respectively, used mercantile organizations (*kabu nakama* and *cha ton'ya*) to control the tea trade most completely during the seventeenth and eighteenth centuries. Eventually, however, producers from Kyushu to the Kanto became dissatisfied with the monopolistic merchant groups and tried marketing tea directly to consumers where they lived.[72] In the event, whether viewed from the perspective of production or of commercial value, tea seems to have been a crucial item consumed by almost all residents of the islands by 1800.

## A SECOND METHOD FOR MEASURING TEA CONSUMPTION: THROUGH A CULTURAL LENS

The beginning of a consumer-oriented, leisure economy is one of the most well-documented developments of the Edo period. In large cities such as Kyoto, Osaka, and Edo, entertainment districts flourished, offering people chances to visit tea shops of numerous varieties, theaters, restaurants, and many other venues for personal enjoyment.[73] Even in rural areas and smaller towns, the elite of the countryside engaged in all sorts of pursuits that indicated they had time on their hands and money to spend. This world has come down to modern readers through references in literature, drama, poetry, art, and even advertisements.

Tea of diverse brands played a central role in the incipient consumer society. Tea shops (*chaya*) specializing in everything from the beverage to prostitution could be found all over the islands, but most especially in the "floating world," the colorful name given to red-light districts in the big cities. Haiku poets brushed an almost unending number of paeans to tea, and tea designs found their way onto family crests. There was even a female hairdo named "the tea whisk." Artists producing wood-block prints left the modern world with representations of the world of tea at each stage from production to consumption. Advertisements ranked tea among the growing list of items for popular consumption. Gauged by these measures, tea was an integral part of everyday life and probably imbibed by almost all residents of the archipelago by the 1800s.

Tea shops comprised an almost unending variety.[74] Of course, many evolved into restaurants (*ryōri chaya*) offering a wide variety (*banji*) of foods, including boiled fare, fresh fish, liquor, and so on. The best of these restaurants was concentrated in the three great cities, and their praises were endlessly sung by the mid-1800s. Tea rest stops (*kake chaya; cha mise*) were small and flimsily constructed; they could be found near the famous shrines of Kyoto, Osaka, and especially Edo. Related to the "hospitality stations" of the late medieval epoch, these tea shops numbered thirty or forty in Kyoto and twenty to thirty in Osaka. Young girls dressed in beautiful clothes sold tea cakes and other light foods to go along with tea. These tea shops also printed their names and locations on the sides of rectangular boxes.

Tea seemed to find its way into all corners of food consumption. Of course, there were many tea peddlers walking the streets of the big cities, selling tea poured over rice or other grains. Tea shops and peddlers specializing in a bowl of rice, soybean curd, and tea (*narazuke*) were also common. People ate tea gruel (*chagayu*) and preferred tea cakes (*chagashi*), with sugar being an important ingredient. The society participated in many festivals and holidays where tea was featured; on 7/10 festivalgoers were treated to steeped tea (*sencha*) at Sensōji in the Asakusa part of Edo.[75] On New Year's Day, many residents of Osaka and Kyoto consumed *fukucha,* tea that included a pickled plum and kelp.

Famously, tea and the tea shops acquired associations that had little to do with the beverage. In the early nineteenth century, an employee of the Dutch East India Company stationed in Nagasaki, Philip Franz von Siebold, wrote:

> Sometimes the Dutchman and his whole party resort to a tea-house: a licensed place of entertainment, where there are drinking and music. These places are also made the scenes of the most abominable licentiousness.
>
> The number of these tea-houses appears to be beyond all conception. The Dutch writers state that at Nagasaki, a town with a population of from sixty to seventy thousand souls, there are no less than 750; and that upon the road to [E]do the inns are almost invariably houses of this description, or have such attached to them. It is from these houses that the members of the Dutch factory obtain their female servants or companions.[76]

In the red-light districts, sex shops (*kago chaya* and *tenjin chaya*) offered their services to the willing; according to one source from the mid-1800s, in Nakano-chō in Yoshiwara in Edo, there were at least 88 such enterprises.[77] For those interested in a little privacy, there were "meeting tea shops" (*deai chaya*) catering especially to gay men. Tea shops even found their way on board river cruisers. In Osaka alone, there were over 47 theater tea shops by 1700, while Edo boasted 58 in 1714 and 142 by 1842.[78]

In regard to theater, there was at least one famous kabuki play that focused on tea. Entitled *Yari no Gonza kasane katabira* (Pikeman Gonza), the plot revolved around the tea ceremony and competition to land a lucrative job in service.[79] To summarize the plot, the main character, Gonza, became betrothed to Oyuki, who gave him her sash as a sign of the promise. Her brother, Bannojō, was a student of the tea master Asaka Ichinoshin, as was Gonza. At the time, Asaka was looking for someone to carry out the secretive ritual, and both men wanted the job.

Asaka's wife, Osai, was alone in Edo with her daughters. When she met Gonza, she immediately wanted him as a husband for one of her daughters. She agreed to teach Gonza the rituals if only he would assent to her proposal. Osai and Gonza had their meeting, but in the meantime Osai had found out about Gonza's previous engagement and the gift sash from Oyuki. While Bannojō watched furtively, Osai flung first the gift sash and then her own at Gonza, suggestive of sexual impropriety on her part. As might be imagined, Gonza and Osai fled and ultimately met their deaths at the hands of her husband. Chikamatsu's play suggests that the audience must have been familiar with what was by then a tea pastime engaged in by numerous adherents, including wealthy peasants and middling merchants and artisans.[80]

Poetry is another literary art form that frequently featured tea. Haiku, the seventeen-syllable verse popular during the Edo period, contained all sorts of references to both the plant and the beverage. To elaborate, over five hundred haiku masters brushed poems using tea. Matsuo Bashō, the most famous haiku poet, wrote fifty-seven. Poets took the tea flower as a subject 180 times, tea plucking 110, the tea roaster also 110, new tea 50, tea processing 30, and tea hospitality 24.[81]

For example, during his travels in Shizuoka, Bashō wrote:

> Snoozing on a horse, remnants of a dream,
> The moon is distant—
> The smoke of roasting tea.[82]

Another master wrote:

> Going on a trip for a whole year!
> If only I have tea along the way;[83]

and yet another:

> Plucking and plucking, a person appears.
> Is this a tea patch?[84]

Notably, the first two haiku were composed during leisurely travels, suggesting that tourism was an integral part of the incipient consumer society.

Although they had the most associations with tea, haiku were not the only poetical form to contain such allusions however. Consider these brief lyrics (*senryū*):

> Too much tea-soaked rice (*chahan*)
> Three helpings will be more than a bellyful![85]

Or:

The tea bowl on the edge of the well
Might fall!
The serving girl is drunk.[86]

Again:

Until the dried plum (*umeboshi*) appears,
The New Year's tea (*fukucha*) will be imbibed with beans.[87]

In particular, the author who compiled the last set of poems noted that the custom of "New Year's tea" had mostly died out in the cities. The poem serves as a reminder that, even though they lived in rural Japan, country folk consumed tea too.

One-man comedic skits (*rakugo*) also featured tea, especially bawdy stories concerning tea shops. Some selected titles include "Parent and Child Tea Shop," "Wasabi Tea Shop," "Chinese Tea Shop," "Teeth-pulling Tea Shop," and "Drawing Tea." In one story, the plot revolves around some yokels from Osaka who went sightseeing in Edo. Seeing that the price of tea was more than the two or three coins that they were prepared to pay, the leader of the band offered six or eight coins, using numbers in his comrades' names as signals to the owner to indicate how much they could give. In the outcome, the tea-shop owner asks for "Mr. One Hundred" (one hundred coins), but of course the visitors have only "Mr. Thirty-two" (thirty-two coins). By the way, the comedian always had a bowl of tea to drink while he told his tale.[88]

Visual artists were just as taken with the beverage and the plant. The use of the tea flower and seeds for family crests may seem like an unusual purpose for tea, but one source has listed at least forty-five different emblems for individuals or families that utilized part of the tea plant.[89] Unfortunately, it is unclear exactly which families or individuals wore such emblems of distinction, but they were popular in the status-conscious society that was Tokugawa Japan. One might speculate that these crests could have designated tea shops, tea merchant houses, or even prostitutes.

As the acting in kabuki plays became a profession that attracted attention, printers composed advertisements and handbills that were distributed around the big cities. By the end of the Edo period, these advertisements (*mitate banzuke*) ranked not only famous members of acting troupes but also almost everything imaginable. Several included tea or dishes that included tea. In "Visual Evaluations All about Fish: First Installment," dated to the 1860s, the bottom row features "famous

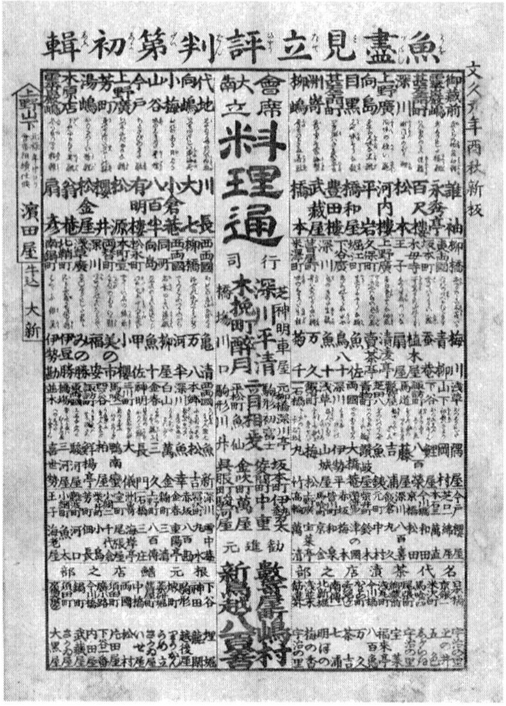


Figure 7. This "ad" from the Edo period is modeled after posters of sumo wrestler rankings. The references to tea dishes appear at the lower bottom right half. *Source*: Tokyo toritsu chūō toshokan.

shops for *chazuke*"—fourteen from all over Japan (figure 7).[90] In another entitled "A View of Numerous Products from the Provinces," modeled after a sumo-wrestling ranking chart and dated to 1840, the top line under *maegashira* (senior champion) shows Uji tea, right after sugar and whale.[91] If advertising is one measure of the vitality of a consumer society, Edo Japan was home to one of the world's first and most competitive markets.

Wood-block prints (*ukiyo-e*) reveal just how deeply entrenched tea was among the archipelago's residents. Hundreds of these images portray tea in all kinds of settings, showing tea peddlers, serving girls, tea workers, tea shops, tea imbibed on a journey, an actor drinking his tea after a performance, a bather imbibing the beverage, enthusiasts engaged in the tea ceremony, and more implements than one can name. Unfortunately, only a few can be described here. In the first print, a serving girl from a tea shop (*chaya*) offers up tea on a tray (figure 8). Pictured next is a scene representing tea plucking underneath far-off Fuji. In the final print, an actor rests with his bowl of tea after removing his make-up. As recorded in the medium of wood-block prints, tea seems to have been a common feature of everyday life in Tokugawa Japan.[92]

Figure 8. Tea-serving woman. From Kitagawa Utamaro, *A Collection of Six Famous Beauties (Okita of Nanbaya).* TNM Image Archives.

To be honest, no one can compute what proportion of Japanese consumed tea routinely by the early 1800s. Statistics are simply not available. Then, too, real per capita consumption of *commercial* tea increased more than sixfold between 1890 and 1920, indicating that consumption had a way to go yet to attract everyone shopping in a market on a daily basis.[93] Residents of the Japanese islands were still a fair distance from the heights of tea consumption reached during the first half of the twentieth century. Evidence about tea production and cultural norms suggests, however, that tea consumption for the last decades of the Edo epoch had attained a new high, extending to a large majority of Japan's inhabitants.

As a final measure of tea consumption, the testimony of some members of the Dutch East India Company is instructive:

> It is, nevertheless, the most useful among the plants inasmuch as the daily beverage consumed in homes and inns is boiled from its baked, rough leaves.[94]

> Because a traveler rarely drinks anything else, tea is served in all inns, taverns, roadside food stalls, and in many huts set up in the fields and mountains.[95]

> Tea is drunk throughout the whole country for the purpose of quenching thirst, for which reason they keep, in every house and more especially in every inn, a kettle upon the fire all day long, with boiling water and ground tea.[96]

> But the grand object of cultivation, next to rice, is the tea plant. . . . Its consumption now is almost unlimited. To supply this demand, in addition to the large plantations where it is grown and prepared for sale, every hedge on every farm is formed of the tea plant, and furnishes the drink of the farmer's family and labourers.[97]

> Tea made in the ordinary way, that is, boiled in the teakettle, is drunk at all their meals, and, indeed, at all times in the day, by every class.[98]

To be sure, these observers did not often escape their factory on Dejima, and their comments are subject to the usual doubts attached to cross-cultural misinterpretations. Made over two centuries, however, they undoubtedly contain no small portion of truth. By the early 1800s, Japan possessed a nascent consumer society in which a wide variety of tea brands produced by an efficient workforce was readily available.

## THE BUNSEI TEA INCIDENT OF 1824

In 1824, 115 villages producing tea in a wide swath of mountainous districts in Shizuoka filed a lawsuit with the Edo *bakufu* (or shogunate) against merchant organizations (*cha ton'ya*) in Sunpu and other local traders (*zaikata shōnin*) charging unfair business tactics.[99] Coming as it did toward the end of the Tokugawa period, the protest was one of many similar conflicts taking place throughout Japan at that time. This grievance was a long-drawn-out affair, not completely resolved until 1857 after Commodore Matthew Perry had pressured the shogunate to open Japanese ports to foreign commerce and in some sense forced the hand of the official (*kanjō bugyō*) dealing with the issue.

As the commodity involved was tea, however, the incident reveals many interesting aspects of its cultivation and trade during the late Edo period. An analysis of the so-called Bunsei Tea Incident lays bare not simply the inner workings of the *bakufu* but also the way in which conflicts between lowly producers and predatory merchants gave rise to frictions in the early and mid-nineteenth century. The shogunate collapsed, to some degree, because it was unable to negotiate a settlement that resolved the core problem.

As already noted, tea was a major product of Shizuoka. In fact, in the seventeenth century the village of Ashikubo was granted the high privilege of providing the Tokugawa household with the commodity (*goyōcha*). Shizuoka was *bakufu* domain (*tenryō*), and many villages paid their taxes to the shogunate in tea. Furthermore, as production increased during the Edo period, merchants specializing in tea rose to prominence and formed organizations (*chaton'ya*) in Sunpu and Edo. Eventually, peasants used proceeds from their tea sales to pay their taxes, and close relationships developed among local producers and the merchant organizations in Sunpu and Edo. Some wealthy peasants and landlords (*zaikata shōnin*) participated directly in trade to Edo and Kai Province too. Thus, there were various groups with economic stakes in the Shizuoka tea trade.

The lawsuit (*ōryō deiri*) of 1824 named fifteen commercial organizations in Sunpu and fifty-seven local peasant merchants for taking unfair advantages in trade.[100] Plaintiffs included sixty-four villages near Ashikubo, thirty near Ieyama, fifteen near Uzuna, and six near Mizukami, all of which were under the jurisdiction of local samurai officials (*daikan*). Two landlords represented all these peasants in the suit.

The grievance began by describing the area where the tea producers lived in both Tōtōmi and Suruga Provinces. Tōtōmi was a mountainous thirty square miles (*ri*) including Akiba and Senzu mountains, while in Suruga petitioners hailed from the river valleys of the Ōi and Abe Rivers, altogether forty square miles marked by the great mountain Azaikawa. Villages were strewn amid valleys of this mountainous region, often separated by two miles or more. The grievance points out that there were few rice paddies in such terrain and that almost all plots were unirrigated dry fields. Even for these patches the harvest was often poor, as boars, deer, and monkeys did great damage to the crops.

Therefore, from olden times peasants considered tea cultivation their primary occupation. They paid not simply their taxes but also for their living necessities with the proceeds of the tea harvest. Traditionally, there were two ways of doing business. First, many local growers of appropriately wealthy means and resources sent shipments straight to tea markets in Edo. These more fortunate tea producers had the resources to bypass the Sunpu associations and deal directly in a major consumption center (Edo). Even these peasants, however, objected to the high-handed mercantile tactics described below.

Most tea producers in Shizuoka, however, lacked the wealth to take advantage of the first method. They handled their situation in one of two ways. Ideally, as the tea harvest was ready each year, producers would hand over the tea to one group of defendants named in the suit—the

Sunpu commercial organizations—and from there the products would be variously consumed or shipped to Edo. Producers would take what was due them according to the settled-upon price.

In reality, though, many tea producers were too poor to wait for the harvest in the spring and took an agreed-upon prepayment at the first of the year so that they could continue to meet their living expenses, and eventually, their taxes. The prevalence of such an arrangement—bound to benefit Sunpu mercantile associations—suggests the straitened conditions in which many farmers found themselves. In any case, the petition stressed that most farmers could not make ends meet without fair treatment by commercial interests.

Since 1813, however, circumstances had become particularly difficult for tea producers, as merchants cheated farmers in one of three ways. First, they often simply refused to ship the tea delivered to them. To elaborate, in 1813 Edo commercial organizations (*chaton'ya*) formed a new league of twenty shops, and they reported that they had to pay an added tax (*myōgakin*). This tax was widely collected on commercial organizations and meted out to the shogunate as "thank money" for being allowed to handle certain trade items exclusively. After 1813, when the tea producers of Shizuoka sent their shipments of the commodity directly to Edo, they were treated as "outside shipments" (*sotoni*) and simply left on the ground to rot. For example, shipments bound for Edo every year during the fifth or sixth months languished until the seventh or eighth month of the next year—or for even two or three *years* at a time. When Sunpu local merchants acting as middlemen paid out the final price for the tea, they tallied it at a special low rate and refused under any circumstances to bargain face-to-face. Because of this, in recent years there were no shipments from tea producers directly to Edo.

Instead, peasants had no choice but to send their tea indirectly through the merchant organizations in Sunpu. Sunpu traders took advantage of their monopolistic position to pay for the tea at prices below production costs, the second method of cheating the farmers. The price dropped continuously, so that compared to previous years the scandalously low price was not half of what it had been. Farmers had difficulty paying not only their taxes but even for food and provisions. Peasants surmised that the defendants (viz., the Sunpu merchant organizations) and the Edo *cha ton'ya* had conspired to establish their own arbitrary rules for the monopolistic buying and selling of tea.

One method of calculating unfair prices was as follows. The farmers reasoned that they were preparing and handing over tea shipments of eight *kan*, 400 *me* at Sunpu, but that the defendants were lying, protesting falsely that the Edo merchant associations were taking more than two *kanme* as handling fees, computing the shipment to Sunpu at only six *kan* 300, 400 *me*. This "recalculation" of the shipment to Sunpu amounted to a reduction of over 25 percent in the amount the Sunpu merchants paid local tea producers.

The grievance outlined a third dishonest commercial practice. Since 1813, when the Edo merchant associations had been formed, no matter what the grade of tea, or whether it was dubbed an "outside shipment" or not, Sunpu and Edo merchants conspired to take large amounts of silver for each package of tea (*hon*) and divide it among themselves. As was clear from commercial books of the various Sunpu merchant organizations, these middlemen were simply appropriating these large sums for their own profits. According to the Sunpu books, Sunpu middlemen dubbed these sums "handling fees" (*kusen* and *kurashiki*) and collected them at the rate of six *monme* per unit (*hon*). From these "handling fees" the Sunpu *chaton'ya* subtracted the fee due to the *bakufu*, the "thank money" (*myōgakin*), at the rate of one *monme* for each unit of tea (*hon*). The farmers went on to calculate that every year they sent more than 20,000 *hon* of tea to Sunpu and then Edo. Even if the thank money was one hundred *ryō* of silver, the total really collected was 330 *ryō*, or 230 *ryō* taken without reason as "handling fees" by the middlemen of Sunpu.

It was naturally difficult for farmers to do nothing when they heard about the avarice and misappropriation of their shipments. At first, cultivators raced over to the establishments of merchants living in the "tea town" (*chamachi*) of Sunpu. The Sunpu organizations would not even greet the peasants. The peasants then felt that they had no choice but to go to the shops of two merchants in Edo. Edo traders stated that, even though they had subtracted one *kanme* for each tea unit as handling charges, they knew nothing at all about the other fees.

On 11/25/1824, the *bakufu* official conducted a hearing among the quarreling parties. The decision satisfied no one and settled nothing. The responsible official (*kanjō bugyō*) decided that the suit "lacked proof" and fined both parties to the suit for their excesses. The shogunate had essentially evaded the suit brought before them; the root of the problem remained.

Various historians have looked at this first suit and, using the names of the defendants and plaintiffs, have reached different conclusions. The first analysis, completed in 1959, viewed the suit as the result of a conflict between average and poor peasants (the plaintiffs) and wealthy peasants (the defendants *zaikata shōnin* who had the resources to ship their tea directly to Edo; also known as *gōnō*).[101] The Sunpu and Edo commercial organizations that were taking such exorbitant fees for doing so little came in for less criticism. Then, in 1988, a scholar discovered that the wealthy peasants had communicated secretly with the plaintiffs, providing information from Sunpu and Edo that the plaintiffs could not possibly have known, such as the amount of *myōgakin* taken by the merchants.[102]

At present, historians have noted that, as the petition neared completion, many of the landlords and wealthier farmers were dropped from the suit as defendants. They have also shown that almost 95 percent of the population of the villages in Tōtōmi and almost 60 percent of the villagers in Suruga participated in the suit as plaintiffs. Current descriptions of this conflict view it almost exclusively as a protest initiated by the tea producers against the high-handed actions of the commercial organizations (*chaton'ya*) of Sunpu and, to a lesser extent, Edo. In other words, it was a geographical conflict between rural village dwellers and urban merchants in Sunpu and Edo who were colluding in illegal trade activities.[103] The sequence of events following the 1824 nondecision supports this conclusion, too.

In 1841, reformers came to power in the Edo *bakufu* and, led by Mizuno Tadakuni (1794–1851), abolished all commercial organizations such as the *chaton'ya* that had lain at the root of the problem in Shizuoka. Traders of all sorts, including the tea producers of Shizuoka, anticipated being able to ship their goods to Edo and engage in "free trade." To be sure, there was much resistance among the former organization members as they tried to protect themselves. In Sunpu, however, tea producers enjoyed open and free mercantile relations with the former members of the associations. Shipments of tea expanded as a result of the abolition of these *chaton'ya*.[104]

In 1845, however, Mizuno was driven from power and the economic policies of the Edo shogunate changed again. In 1851, the mercantile associations of Edo were reformulated, and in the next year those of Sunpu were re-created. Almost immediately trouble between the tea producers of Shizuoka and the Sunpu and Edo *chaton'ya* erupted again. The central issue was that, whereas the Edo associations and the producers had agreed to allow the Edo groups to collect handling fees that would be subtracted from the price of the tea delivered to Edo, the Sunpu associations now once again stepped in to take their percentage as "handling fees"—a double whammy! Unlike the previous suit, this time the defendants were all members of the objectionable Sunpu mercantile associations.

In the second month of 1853, about four months before the American Commodore Perry arrived in Edo seeking commercial and diplomatic relations with Japan, sixty-three villages in the Abe and Warashina regions of Shizuoka filed a second protest against nineteen newly created merchant organizations operating in Sunpu.[105] The tea producers repeated much of their argument of 1824, adding two new points.

First, the plaintiffs outlined their traditional route for shipping tea. From of old many had transported the leaves to Sunpu and then had it sent on to the two ports of Shimizu and Yaizu for shipping to the Edo market. They argued that the distance from their homes in the mountains to Sunpu was eight to ten "miles" (*ri*) along treacherous paths. Farmers carried one or two bundles (*hon*) at a time to Sunpu, and shipped their tea cargo by oxen or horse to a port at Shimizu. Since the reorganization of the Sunpu mercantile organizations, however, the merchants had effectively cut off the road to Edo at Sunpu and demanded the two types of handling fees.

Second, the tea farmers then did what they had not done in 1824: they explained the history of their enterprise to the Edo *bakufu* court with supporting documents going back to the early seventeenth century. The plaintiffs showed that all throughout the past they had paid the tea tax without excessive "handling fees." The plaintiffs then appended numerous types of supporting records. This time the tea farmers of Shizuoka were determined to win.

The protest was presented to both the main Sunpu official (*bugyō*) and the Edo government during the second month of 1853. Soon it would be time to pick tea, and the plaintiffs stated that they had no idea what sort of treatment they would face in Sunpu. They feared that there would be delays and once again their tea would sit in Sunpu and rot. For this reason, the peasants filed their grievance in both places.

The *bakufu* office that heard the case (*kanjō bugyō*), however, rebuffed the plaintiffs. A diary has survived that details the office's dealings with the tea producers of Shizuoka.[106] The first meeting between protesters and the shogunate's official took place on 2/16, noting the reception of the grievance. Then the court stalled. Eventually, the true aim of the Edo office became apparent as Ōhara village began using the Sunpu associations and refused to pay for the lawsuit. All the delaying, requests for more documentation, and communication with the Sunpu office had resulted in a split in the ranks of the peasant plaintiffs. Then, on 6/3, the very day that Commodore Perry's ships arrived in Tokyo Bay, the Shizuoka tea producers reported that all tea shipments bound for Shimizu and Yaizu, and eventually Edo, had been stopped and were being delayed by the Sunpu organizations. Peasant representations to Edo continued until 7/11, but it made no difference—they had lost again. The newly formed Sunpu mercantile associations, with the help of shogunate inefficiency, had succeeded in blocking free access to the markets in Sunpu and Edo for the Shizuoka tea producers. Undoubtedly, in the great excitement caused by Perry's arrival the case was doomed.

Angered by this defeat, on 3/1854 the peasants of the sixty-three villages party to the suit sent a document to the Sunpu official (*bugyō*), who tried to put a pretty face on an ugly situation.[107] The peasants would have none of it, but said that they would no longer accept advances on the tea harvest from the Sunpu merchants. Instead, farmers established "gathering places" (*cha kaisho*) where they would assemble shipments to Shimizu or Yaizu and take care of delivery on their own. Tea producers were now going around the Sunpu *chaton'ya* and thus avoiding the handling fees and the monopoly on shipment through Sunpu that so threatened the farmers' livelihood.

In the long run, however, Perry's arrival had positive effects for the plaintiffs, because it delivered a harsh blow to the *bakufu* itself and all the mercantile associations that relied upon it and other governments to maintain their iron grip on trade. Undaunted, on 7/1854, the tea producers of Shizuoka filed a third suit. Plaintiffs included the tea producers and wealthier merchant-farmers of 122 villages, virtually the entire area from Mt. Fuji westward to Shida district in Suruga Province. The defendants were eighteen members of the Sunpu mercantile associations.

This time the petition essentially repeated themes stressed in 1824 and 1853. It even noted that tea farmers attempted to sell eighty *kan* of tea to cover their legal expenses, but could not get the tea through to port because the Sunpu merchants had held back shipment. The merchants had "locked hands," not allowing free sales to merchants from other parts of Japan. As a consequence, sales had plummeted, and several tens of villages and thousands of farmers had slid into poverty. Most important, the peasants could neither pay their taxes nor pass along their enterprises to their descendants. Among peasants with smallholdings, their forests and dry fields had to be pawned one after another. Former farmers fled to other places and scattered everywhere in great numbers. They had lost their homes in the villages, and both poor and wealthy producers suffered great confusion in the hostile economic environment. Edo must act![108] For the next five years, the war of lawsuits continued.[109]

At last, in 1857, the *bakufu* came to a decision on the tea producers' long-standing grievance. The decision allowed the producers to ship their tea directly to Edo and freely at Sunpu, but the closing statement, written in 2/1859, was a vague document. The shogunate official (*kanjō bugyō*), the reform-minded Kawaji Toshiakira, stated that "the villages of Abe and Warashina districts could sell their tea freely in Edo as in the past," and that the result would be that "sales items within the city would become plentiful."[110] At the same time, however, Kawaji allowed the mercantile associations of Sunpu to remain in existence. Tea producers of Shizuoka called the decision "the ultimate victory," but mercantile associations tried to cause more trouble thereafter.

The main reason the farmers eventually won out was their strong unity in the face of hostility from both commercial adversaries and governmental bureaucrats. For example, in 4/1857, peasants agreed to divide the costs of the lawsuit, including the lodging and food for their representatives in Edo, equally among themselves. This agreement recognized the fact that some farmers were too poor to keep paying their taxes as well as the added costs and made allowances for this problem. Instead of assessing the payments for the lawsuit costs by individual, the assessment was done according to village productivity, essentially making the wealthier producers pay on a sliding scale. The method of payment, along with such devices as the "gathering places" where tea shipments were assembled for transport to Edo, showed the strong group solidarity of the tea producers and their determination to win.[111]

Despite their seeming victory in 1857, tea producers did not have an easy time of it. In 5/1862, peasants submitted the following sad request for assistance to the samurai official (*daikan*) responsible for overseeing these many villages. It is revealing of the hardships suffered by the plaintiffs to all these suits. Peasant representatives sent to Edo for the suit incurred large expenses and were forced to sell and pawn family possessions. All during the years of the suit there was never any rotation of the representatives. In 1857, even though the shogunate had recognized the validity of the peasants' assertions and allowed them to send their shipments directly to Edo, tea sent to Kōfu and Mishima was still held up by the mercantile associations of Sunpu.

During these long-drawn-out suits, three or four of the representatives in Edo had died and there were no observances of New Year's or the Rite for the Return of the Souls of the Dead (*obon*). Two or three years after the decision, the price of tea rose and the standard of living for the village tea producers began to improve. Therefore, the villages planned to take care of the souls (*tsuizen kuyō*) of those who had lost their lives in Edo, give thanks to the various villages that had prayed for victory in the lawsuit, buy back the lands pawned to pay for the suit and other costs, and arrange a ceremony for the return of the status quo. There were numerous consultations about carrying out these activities, but they were postponed and had not been completed even as late as 1862.

As for the price of tea, while previously it had been one or two *ryō* for a parcel, now producers received five or six *ryō* and an observer would expect that the economic conditions of the villages would be good. Indeed, the farmers who had relied on their legal representatives when this conflict flared were now blessed with a good economic life, but they had forgotten their duties and obligations. Plans to recompense the representatives' families for their sacrifices remained unfinished. The wives and children, along with the parents of the former legal representatives who had died doing their duty, moaned sadly for assistance, but nothing was done.[112]

The tea producers had paid a heavy price for their victory in the lawsuit. As Engelbert Kaempfer, a representative of the Dutch East India Company, had written over a century earlier: "Tea-preparers complain mightily of the unhappiness of their profession, for nothing, they say, can be got cheaper in the Country than Tea, and yet no work is more tiresome and fatiguing."[113] Ever since tea had become an economic commodity in the 1300s, the status of tea laborers seems to have been low. They were often abused by their employers and tea merchants and ignored by government officials. It is important to realize that the creation of markets for a consumer society can have its disadvantages for producers too.

The Bunsei Tea Incident of 1824 and the ensuing events in the conflict between the tea producers of Shizuoka and the mercantile associations of Sunpu may admit of many different conclusions. Certainly, they tell us much about the everyday life of tea farmers in the late Edo period, as farmers often sold rights to their tea in advance to pay their taxes and obtain their living necessities. This way of doing business suggests the penetration of mercantile capital from Edo and Sunpu into the nearly inaccessible villages of Shizuoka. The Bunsei Tea Incident also shows the solidarity of the tea farmers of a wide region ranging from the foot of Mount Fuji to Abe and Shida districts in Suruga Province. In the face of hostility from merchants and the paralysis of the shogunate officials, peasants had to work together for thirty-three years to beat the odds against them. They shared costs, both monetary and otherwise, overcame the deaths of their legal representatives, and won "the ultimate victory." Struggles like these were not in vain, because when the Tokugawa *bakufu* fell in 1868, the new regime headed by Emperor Meiji would have great use for these and other tea producers.

The Edo period constituted the high point of tea production, trade, and consumption before the arrival of modern techniques and markets to the islands after 1868. Tea had "seeped down" to all classes in Japan even more than it had during the late medieval era. As such, the Edo period, perhaps more than any other epoch, witnessed the development and maturation of the three social and economic trends stressed in the introduction and mentioned throughout this book. Farming intensification and improvements, the "industrious revolution," and the creation of an incipient consumer society comprised mutually reinforcing occurrences.

First, not even the late medieval epoch (1400–1600) comprised an era of more widespread and more meticulous agricultural development than the Tokugawa period. By 1700, agrarian experts were writing on many aspects of tea cultivation and processing; Hitomi Hitsudai epitomized this work as he raised tea farming to a high art of measurements and timing. At the same time, Miyazaki Yasusada had begun to recognize the bounty of tea types by narrating the details for his four processing methods. Nagatani Yoshihiro invented *sencha,* and more brands were to follow in the next century. It is generally known that Japanese farming was productive and well organized by 1850; tea cultivation provides a good example of the how and why of this favorable outcome.

Second, the growing consumption of tea overlapped with the "industrious revolution," which was undoubtedly already under way by 1600. While intensified agrarian development was proceeding, it is well to remember that a large sector of the populace was drinking the beverage. Boiling water to imbibe a caffeinated concoction, peasants and townspeople alike achieved an unexpected health benefit that redounded to their economic advantage. Hitomi wrote that the women of Edo could not start their day without their morning bowls of tea; a century later Ōkura Nagatsune opined that "everybody consumed tea daily." The herb played a subtle but meaningful role in Japan's industrious revolution by stimulating workers—both agricultural and protoindustrial—to labor harder, more efficiently, and for more prolonged periods.

A caveat about tea's role in the Edo-period industrious revolution is in order, however. Most of the writers on tea describe the beverage's production for both domestic drinking and selling on the market. Though most of the populace undoubtedly consumed tea at some point, even in the 1800s a large percentage of tea was cultivated and processed for household use. Because perhaps as much as half of all tea was domestically consumed, it did not engage the market or Francks' demand-pull "virtuous circle." The full economic impact of tea would have to wait until after World War II. Yet consumption of tea was one of the factors that endowed the archipelago with a disciplined, efficient workforce for employment in the European-style industrial revolution occurring later.

Third, tea was a central commodity in Japan's incipient consumer society. Bountiful agriculture and an "industrious" populace required some outlet for their products. This outlet became increasingly available by 1800 in the form of a consumer society in which tea had a prominent position. No one will ever know how many tea drinkers inhabited Edo Japan at that date, but production indicates that the herb was available, either through the market, taxes, or domestically, from southern Kyushu to the northern tip of the Tohoku. Tea shops ranged throughout the archipelago, and poets, playwrights, and artists gave tea its rightful high profile in their cultural representations. Even Dutch observers commented on the widespread consumption of the herb, especially through shops.

As with the industrious revolution, however, one must not press this argument too far. Consumer societies require sellers and buyers. If as much as half the tea was grown and imbibed for household use and so never entered the market, then Japan's consumer society was not as large as it might have been. As adumbrated above, this trend toward consumerism took a long time to work itself out for Japan, probably not coming to fruition until after World War II. It is notable, though, that by 1800 another building block was in place for Japan's social and economic modernity.

Then, too, Japan's development of a modern tea industry was also beginning to redound, however slowly, to the world's benefit. Now that the country was producing so much delicious tea and was connected even tangentially to a worldwide market through the Dutch, it was only a matter of time before the commodity would make its way to Europe. In 1610, the Dutch shipped the very first boxes of Japanese tea to that continent.[114] The first mention of Japanese tea being sent to England was in a letter of the English East India Company dated to 1615. In 1664 the same corporation sent tea to Charles II as a gift. Soon, though, the English gave up on Japan as a market, and references to Japanese tea in England disappear. Nonetheless, the modern era would bring Japanese tea to the whole world.

CHAPTER FOUR

# Modern Tea: From Triumph to Uncertainty

The sudden arrival of Commodore Perry's "black ships" in Tokyo Bay in 1853 signaled the beginning of the end for the Edo shogunate, in part by kicking off a price revolution that the *bakufu* could not contain. By 1868, the new Meiji government, under the yoke of unequal treaties with the Europeans and Americans, moved to reform Japan. The samurai class was abolished, the government centralized, and a new land tax established to provide the regime with revenues. A draft of commoners supplied a modern military machine. By 1890, the Meiji Constitution provided a political structure modeled on that of Prussia and the way lay open for rapid economic development to catch up with the Great Powers. For several decades before and after 1890, Japanese intellectuals debated the benefits of liberal democracy and the legacy of their own traditions.

The Meiji reforms, often enacted on a trial-and-error basis, proved to be generally successful. During 1894–1895 in the Sino-Japanese War and again during 1904–1905 in the Russo-Japanese War, the Japanese fought and won two imperialist wars of aggression, acquiring for themselves an empire in Asia. Around 1895, the economy achieved takeoff, or self-sustaining economic growth, and expanded quickly and greatly until 1920. Modern inventions such as the railroad, telegraph, radio, phonograph, and so on were introduced to the archipelago. Socially, everything from hairstyles to shoe brands changed, as the old society gave way to the fashionable figures of "modern boys" and "modern girls."

Under political parties during the 1920s, the economy performed less well. In 1930, the Great Depression hit, and the military, fearful of a reviving China and Soviet Russia abroad and "un-Japanese" thoughts at home, forced its way into power and led Japan down the primrose path of war and destruction. Between 1931 and 1945 in World War II, Japan was thoroughly defeated and the military repudiated. The country lay in ruins and the empire was gone. Americans occupied Japan as conquerors during 1945–1952 and implemented a series of reforms to demilitarize and democratize the country.

Under adroit leadership, Japan rose from the ashes of defeat. Between 1950 and 1990, the economic "miracle" occurred in which growth averaged about 10 percent per year. Social changes followed in the wake of economic expansion such as the world had never seen, and most Japanese became middle-class, able to afford to travel, live in nice homes with air-conditioning, and send their sons and daughters to university. An American scholar classified Japan in 1980 as "number one" in the industrialized world.

All of this came to an abrupt end in the 1990s. The economy stalled and stasis replaced growth. The population, already the oldest in the world, began to shrink. Under the US occupation, the constitution of 1947 had granted the people new rights and sovereignty, and rule by conservatives had been the rule. When the economy slowed to a standstill, people tried other political parties, but the conservatives remained powerful. At present, the conservatives rule a Japan still mired in no growth and more divided between the haves and have-nots. As if to symbolize the malaise of the current era, on March 11, 2011, a powerful earthquake shook Japan, killing twenty thousand in a giant tsunami and wrecking a nuclear power plant in Fukushima, causing multiple meltdowns. Today the Japanese remain affluent, and there is much to admire about their society. Increasingly, however, they are concerned about environmental matters and wondering what their fate in Asia and the world really will be.

The jewel that was the traditional tea industry has turned out to be a great asset to modern Japan. Early on, tea became one of three major exports from the islands along with silk and coal, helping to finance the growth of the prewar Japanese economy. As tea became an industry essential to national welfare, inventors began to mechanize cultivation and processing and scientists attempted to rationalize production in other ways. During the prewar years, domestic consumption of the beverage was slow to become commercialized, as many farms made their own tea. Even so, tea drinking inside Japan was ubiquitous by the 1960s, taking place daily at home and in the office. By 1980, the country was producing 100,000 tons of tea, the peak of postwar totals. Japanese green tea became a quotidian item hardly worth notice in a newly enriched Japan.

As consumers became wealthier, tea increasingly faced a powerful competitor in imported coffee, which comprised a large share of Japan's nonalcoholic beverage market by the 1970s. Producers of Japanese tea tried many tactics to regain popularity, the most successful of which was the adoption of PET bottles dispensed from vending machines and convenience stores by 1990. Due to the success of this strategy, contemporary tea drinkers hardly know how to use a teakettle. The process by which Japanese tea went from the dominant beverage to just another drink has been skillfully recorded in Japanese literature, art, and radio and TV advertisements.[1]

## EXPORTS DRIVE A MODERN TRANSFORMATION OF THE TEA INDUSTRY

As noted at the end of chapter 3, Japanese tea was being traded to the Netherlands and England as early as the 1600s, although in small amounts. The year 1858, when the United States and Japan joined in a treaty of amity and trade, serves as the beginning of the modern era for Japanese tea. In that year, as soon as commercial relations with Europe opened, six tons were shipped to England from Nagasaki. One year later, in 1859, Japan commenced exporting tea to its American partner. The United States became an especially valuable customer. Next to raw silk, tea was the number two export from Japan, ranging from 20 to 70 percent of total exports. Low wages were partially responsible for a Japanese cost advantage, but by 1900 that benefit was disappearing. At first profits were as high as 40 percent for Euro-American firms, but they nosedived during the period 1875–1885.

As Shinya Sugiyama has noted, many factors in the international system favored Japan's export drive in the period 1850–1900.[2] First, there was a general decline in ocean freight rates, especially after the Suez Canal was opened in 1869. Second, a depreciation of gold in terms of silver helped Japan, because European and American powers adhered to the gold standard whereas Japan used silver; therefore, Euro-Americans were encouraged by costs to buy East Asian imports and discouraged from exporting to the region. Third, although the imperialist threat greatly motivated Japanese leaders and business people, because of the scarcity of coaling stations, not even Great Britain could project much military power into East Asia or Japan. Fourth, the construction of telegraphic lines to East Asia in 1871 provided added incentive for business firms to open there.

The commercial agreements established "treaty ports" in Japan, of which the most important for tea were Yokohama, Kobe, and Nagasaki.

These three ports housed 50, 30, and 10 percent of Euro-American merchants, respectively. The ports included a twenty-five-mile radius in which foreigners—mostly British—could live and carry out business. As Sugiyama has pointed out, although the ports were intended to facilitate trade for the Euro-Americans, they actually protected Japan and gave life to internal Japanese trade networks because they prevented foreigners from accessing Japan's interior regions. The treaty ports amounted to a nontariff barrier to the Euro-Americans.[3] Japan's well-developed transport system, plentiful water supplies, and excellent irrigation systems took over from there.

A brief outline of the tea trade during the latter half of the nineteenth century is in order. Japan shipped its tea primarily from factories located in the treaty ports. Euro-American agents bought export tea in Yokohama (from eastern Japan) or in Kobe (from western Japan) and refired the tea at stations in those ports. At Yokohama, well-paid workers daily used 880 large pots to re-dry the tea for the long journey to Europe or the United States. Foreign powers such as England and the United States built commercial halls to facilitate the tea trade.[4] Shippers attached colorful labels to their shipping containers (figure 9).

Figure 9. Tea shipping box with label. Sunpu Museum.

Japan's chief customers were the United States, Great Britain, Russia, Canada, and Australia. The United States was a particularly important buyer of Japanese green tea during the 1860s, taking 87 percent of exports during 1865–1866. From 1871–1875 through 1891–1895, Americans increased their consumption of Japanese tea from sixty million pounds to ninety-one million, as the superior quality and lower cost of Japanese tea ousted China from the US market. Residents of New York, Chicago, and San Francisco were consumers of plentiful amounts of Japanese green tea. The demand not simply from the United States but from other countries all over the world was strong and soon led to great changes in industrial structure, technology, and the location of tea fields. Taken together, these and other changes constitute the modern transformation of the tea industry in Japan.

To understand this transformation, it is helpful to survey the industry on the eve of the Meiji Restoration around 1858. At that time, Japan was producing tea throughout the archipelago, from southern Kyushu to a line running through Honshu reaching just north of the Kanto and Niigata prefecture. Of these regions, the Kyoto-Osaka region and provinces along the Pacific Ocean ranging from Ise to Suruga maintained their positions as the leading tea-producing regions, but there were some surprises as well. Cold Miyagi prefecture in northern Honshu ranked fourth, while Niigata was twelfth, and Ishikawa was twenty-fourth. In other words, production in the frigid northern part of Japan was surprisingly high. This trend was a tribute to the growth of the industry in the Tohoku during the Edo period, as shown in chapter 3.

Another characteristic of tea production during the early years of the Meiji period was the processing of all sorts of tea, also noted in chapter 3. Each local region produced its own unique brand of tea, and people acquired a taste for each. The various methods of processing were related to the price of tea in each region. Generally speaking, tea was more expensive in the cold regions of northeastern Honshu, at 34 *sen* per 600 grams, even though production was high in some areas. The reverse trend was especially true of western Japan—Kyushu and Shikoku—where stir-roasted teas were prepared and the cost was merely 10 *sen* per 600 grams. On a nationwide basis, tea cost 16.7 *sen* per 600 grams. At that time, money spent for one kilogram of tea (27.8 *sen*) could have bought 4.6 *shō* of rice, a considerable volume. Growers of tea must have found their businesses to have been fairly lucrative.[5]

In the first years of the Meiji period, Japan produced 9,522 tons of tea. The Kyoto-Osaka region led the way with 28.5 percent of production, while Shizuoka, Owari, and Mino yielded 22.3 percent. Yamanashi prefecture had a mere .1 percent of the total, while the Kanto region produced 9.9 percent. Surprisingly, northern Japan produced 11.2 percent, while western Honshu grew about 7 percent of the total. Shikoku grew 6.5 percent. Northern Kyushu had a 9.9 percent share, while southern Kyushu produced about 5 percent. In other words, mapped upon modern tea production, cultivation was spread all over the islands. Regional specialization based on comparative advantage had not yet taken place.

The advent of a large export trade resulted in many changes for Japan's tea industry over the long run. First, the acreage of tea production in Japan underwent a complete transformation. Reliable statistics are available from 1892, and, at first, it seems as though the land area producing tea changed very little between 1892 and the late twentieth century (1980). The 1892 total probably included an increase of 1,000 hectares per year from 1858, and so it seems that at the outset the export trade led to more land being used for tea cultivation.[6] It must be remembered, however, that before 1858 there were many "mountain patches," border fields, and mixed plots containing tea and other cultivars. Thus, the two figures are not really comparable. Today statisticians list both fields exclusively given over to tea and those that have multiple uses. Around 1892, 63 percent of tea fields produced nothing but that plant; in 1970, the comparable figure was 74 percent.

This relatively small increase masks important long-term changes, however. Farmers began to cultivate tea in new areas and to abandon older, less productive regions. Many of these new fields were constructed on flat highlands and rolling hills, such as those at Shizuoka. Farmers began to experiment with different strains of tea and increased the numbers of varieties. In terms of production, Japan apparently harvested about 10,000 tons in the early years of Meiji. As exports to the United States increased, that figure became 30,000 tons, where production remained until the end of the Meiji period in 1912. Soon thereafter, exports of Japanese green tea exploded, the industry became more mechanized, and the amount of tea produced in Japan reached 38,000 to 40,000 tons in the 1910s. When Japan became involved in World War II, however, the amount of tea fell back to about 30,000 tons and did not assume prewar levels again until 1955 or 1960. Then domestic consumption took off, and by 1975–1980 production was over 100,000 tons.

To produce so much more tea on about the same acreage, productivity had to increase dramatically. Since the Meiji period, productivity has risen every year except for the war years and their immediate aftermath. In 1892, ten ares yielded 50.6 kilograms of raw tea (*aracha*); in 1975, the same figure was 173.3 kilograms, an increase of 3.4 times. As tea leaves contain 75 percent water, this means that the amount of raw tea leaves produced would be four times that 1975 figure. It is important to note, however, that productivity per region of Japan varied widely, depending on how many harvests the climate allowed the farmers to retrieve. The most productive areas have traditionally been the Kyoto-Osaka region and Shizuoka, followed by northern Kyushu, southern Kyushu, and the Japan Sea littoral. Productivity in the Kanto and northeastern Japan has lagged. Shikoku and the rest of western Honshu rate low productivity because of the lack of rain and the effects of erosion.

The transfer of production from mountainsides to flatland was another important trend. Makinohara in Shizuoka, developed by soon-to-be unemployed samurai families between 1870 and 1884, is the best example of this phenomenon.[7] In 1959, there were 47,814 hectares of tea fields in Japan, and 53 percent were located on sloped land, 32 percent on highland, and 24 percent fell into both categories. These figures suggest that about 50 to 70 percent of tea cultivation took place on relatively flat land. The days of "mountain patches" situated far from roads and other transportation nodes are now long gone.

Of the types of tea that Japan has produced during the modern era, the overwhelming majority has been steeped leaf tea, whether steamed, parboiled, or stir-roasted (see table 4). Coarse steeped tea (*bancha*) was always next, ranging from 4,000 to about 13,000 tons throughout the modern era. "Jeweled dew," or *gyokuro,* developed in Uji during the late Edo period, was a distant third, ranging from 187 to 340 tons during the Meiji era and gradually expanding to over 500 tons in 1980. Although not noted in table 4, Japan produced black tea over the entire modern period, with amounts varying from 7 tons in 1925 and again in 1980, to 3,725 tons in 1955. Surprisingly, powdered tea was not even made in large amounts during much of the Meiji period, and was processed in decreasing amounts from 48 to 24 tons before 1900. It becomes clear that collapsing the analysis of tea in Japan to include only powdered tea significantly distorts the place of teas in modern Japanese society.[8]

In terms of the geographical distribution of production centers for these various teas, powdered tea has been processed most abundantly in Aichi prefecture and Kyoto is no longer the leader in this area. Shiga, Fukuoka, and Mie also make powdered tea. *Gyokuro* has been a good export for Fukuoka and Shizuoka, ahead of the Tokugawa center in Kyoto. Regions that use straw or netting to guard against frost may be found throughout the archipelago, and that tea is known as *kabusecha,* a sort of middle ground between regular steeped tea and "jeweled mist."

**Table 4** Tea production by type, 1884–1980

| *Year* | *Total* | *Steeped* | *Coarse steeped* | *Powdered* | *Gyokuro* |
|---|---|---|---|---|---|
| 1884 | 21,552 | 11,293 | 7,827 | 48 | 187 |
| 1890 | 25,080 | 13,616 | 8,144 | 34 | 208 |
| 1895 | 29,356 | 17,956 | 7,108 | 26 | 340 |
| 1900 | 30,393 | 20,684 | 4,041 | – | 284 |
| 1905 | 25,596 | 17,510 | 7,682 | – | 265 |
| 1910 | 28,533 | 19,386 | 8,776 | – | 274 |
| 1915 | 33,107 | 23,531 | 9,166 | – | 309 |
| 1920 | 38,434 | 28,022 | 9,379 | – | 281 |
| 1925 | 28,735 | 26,690 | 7,916 | 60 | 265 |
| 1930 | 38,064 | 30,080 | 7,478 | – | 262 |
| 1935 | 42,408 | 33,615 | 7,824 | – | 289 |
| 1940 | 54,455 | 39,290 | 10,658 | – | 291 |
| 1945 | 50,026 | 37,619 | 8,471 | 222 | 352 |
| 1950 | 28,778 | 19,682 | 6,659 | 145 | 449 |
| 1955 | 59,662 | 38,617 | 8,772 | 187 | 183 |
| 1960 | 74,953 | 55,463 | 8,733 | 269 | 268 |
| 1965 | 80,132 | 62,972 | 9,075 | 327 | 338 |
| 1970 | 86,814 | 68,363 | 12,298 | 361 | 407 |
| 1975 | 97,956 | 77,726 | 13,794 | 338 | 499 |
| 1980 | 101,487 | 79,996 | 13,582 | 389 | 527 |

*Source:* Ōishi, *Chagyō hattatsu shi,* p. 326.
*Note:* All figures are averages given in tons.

Surveying the entire modern period, scholars have noted that the production of *gyokuro* has grown by 2.8 times and powdered tea has grown by a factor of eight; but taken together in 1980 these teas did not even equal 1 percent of total tea production. *Sencha* has grown by seven times and stir-roasted tea by three. Coarse steeped tea (*bancha*) has about doubled. A major reason that steamed, steeped leaf tea has grown so quickly and occupies such a large proportion of Japan's total tea output is that almost all tea given over to export has been *sencha* (table 5). Usually about 30 to 40 percent of all steeped tea was shipped abroad as an export, with the rest consumed domestically. Eventually, Japan added homemade black teas, oolong tea sent to the United States, green teas shipped to Russia and North Africa, and powdered tea dispatched to Mongolia.[9]

**Table 5** Tea exports, 1884–1980

| *Year* | *Total produced* | *Total exported* | *Percent exported* |
|---|---|---|---|
| 1884 | 18,803 | 17,037 | 90.6 |
| 1890 | 25,080 | 20,326 | 81.6 |
| 1895 | 29,355 | 22,831 | 78.1 |
| 1900 | 30,394 | 19,641 | 64.3 |
| 1905 | 25,596 | 20,035 | 77.2 |
| 1910 | 28,533 | 18,128 | 63.7 |
| 1915 | 33,107 | 18,143 | 54.8 |
| 1920 | 38,434 | 20,414 | 52.9 |
| 1925 | 35,756 | 11,200 | 31.2 |
| 1930 | 37,944 | 10,420 | 27.6 |
| 1935 | 42,407 | 13,917 | 32.7 |
| 1940 | 54,455 | 19,508 | 35.9 |
| 1945 | 50,026 | 6,223 | 11.6 |
| 1950 | 28,778 | 3,792 | 17.9 |
| 1955 | 59,662 | 12,734 | 21.3 |
| 1960 | 74,953 | 9,398 | 12.6 |
| 1965 | 80,132 | 5,686 | 7.2 |
| 1970 | 86,814 | 1,803 | 2.1 |
| 1975 | 98,156 | 2,214 | 1.5 |
| 1980 | 101,487 | 3,043 | 3.1 |

*Source:* Ōishi, *Chagyō hattatsu shi,* p. 329.
*Note:* Amounts are averages given in tons. Figures for total production differ slightly from those listed in table 4. Because amounts are averages, percentages sometimes vary.

The proportion of raw tea (*aracha*) exported ranged from 60 to 90 percent during the Meiji period, but declined steadily thereafter. The main reason for the decline was the establishment of tea plantations in India, Sri Lanka, and Indonesia and the increasing popularity of other beverages, especially coffee. Tea exports also peaked around World War I, as England imported Japanese green teas in place of the more customary black teas that were then less available. The effects of the Great Depression and World War II are also apparent. Japan tried to replace previous markets by sending green tea to the Soviet Union and North Africa, but with few results. At different times, businessmen and government officials tried various experiments with techniques from China as well as domestic methods, but the outcomes were not long-lasting.[10] Production dropped precipitously right after World War II, partially because Americans in great numbers took up the habit of drinking coffee. During the period 1950–1980, production grew to new heights, but it was almost completely for domestic consumption.

The modern era naturally falls into three subperiods with the following general characteristics. Between 1868 and 1925, most commercial tea went to the export market; techniques of cultivation and processing saw many improvements and partial mechanization; a large (mostly female) workforce tended to the harvest and processing; and domestic consumption included lots of the beverage made at home. Between 1925 and 1980, rationalization and mechanization of cultivation and processing reached a peak and eliminated the need for most of the female laborers; drinkers imbibed tea primarily through purchase as the country urbanized and incomes multiplied; and more affluent consumers turned increasingly to imported coffee instead of tea beginning in the late 1960s. After 1980, tea production and consumption faced decline in Japan, and exports revived somewhat as green tea found a niche market around the world. The recent creation of new foreign markets partially explains how Japanese green tea ended up in destinations as disparate as Cape Town, South Africa, and St. Louis, Missouri.

## TEA CULTIVATION AND PROCESSING, 1868–1925

The period from 1868 through 1925 evinced several new trends in the production of tea. The first of these has already been mentioned: the opening of new tea fields on flatter lands. In 1869, about 250 samurai—nearly a thousand people including their families—began laboring at Makinohara in Shizuoka. With the help of local farmers, the work advanced quickly. In 1871 there were 200 *chō;* in 1877, 500; by 1890 the figure had grown to 600 *chō;* by 1916 it was 1,600 *chō;* and in 1930, 2,987 *chō.* Sayama in Saitama prefecture, located on a low plateau, is another example. It has been developed since the late Edo period. By 1877, Sayama ranked eighth in Japan, producing 418 tons; and by 1883 that figure was 1,112 tons, placing Sayama fourth. In northern Ise, too, an area with low hills produced 759 tons of tea by 1877; and by 1883 that figure was 1,770 tons, ranking northern Ise third in Japan. Even Miyazaki and Kagoshima, regions where mountain patches had predominated, witnessed similar trends.

Improvements in the technology of tea-field management represented a second characteristic of the industry during 1868–1925. One advance was in the area of fertilizers. During the early Meiji era, farmers did not use fertilizers very much. In 1865, however, producers at Makinohara applied night soil, with good results. Without any fertilizer, scientists have determined that ten ares of land will produce no more than 400 kilograms, and for most of the Meiji period, yields were about half that. By 1925, the most advanced regions of tea production—Shizuoka and the Kyoto-Osaka region—reached 400 kilograms, mostly because of the application of fertilizers. By 1925, these fertilizers were often chemically produced, rather than guano or night soil. In 1903, the Experimental Laboratory for Tea Processing of the Agricultural Office (*Nōmukyoku seicha shikensho*) produced the results of a five-year study advocating fertilizing during the winter and in the spring when new shoots were just starting to appear.

Farmers also were advised to manage their lands better in other ways. In 1902, the same experimental laboratory advocated deep plowing during the tenth to eleventh months, turning the soil over to cover the roots of the tea bushes at the same time as the winter fertilization, and weeding during late April through late May. Veteran farmers also chimed in on this topic, referring to the need to cover the roots with straw.

Tea producers also created new ways to deal with insect infestations. Most farm households in the early Meiji period reserved notations for losses due to insects, and the general way to deal with them was to burn torches or fires, producing smoke to drive insects away. The Experimental Laboratory listed ten species that afflicted tea farmers. Beginning around 1900, chemical insecticides came into use, the early popular ones being coal derivatives and pine tar. Around 1920, sulfuric nicotine was imported from Singapore and the United States. Pamphlets detailing which insecticide (including simply trapping) worked best on each variety of insect appeared to aid farmers with this serious problem.

Another advance was the adoption of pruning to encourage the proper growth of the tea bush. Ōkura Nagatsune, whose work was discussed in chapter 3, had been the first advocate of pruning in the early nineteenth century. Yet throughout the period before 1868, pruning had rarely been practiced, and as a result tea bushes grew quite tall, especially in the mountains. At first the pruning took the form of merely chopping down the bush with a sickle. It was much easier to pluck the bushes at harvest time, as bushes grew in a more uniform way, quality improved, and the number of new tea leaves picked increased. Bushes might be taken at the roots, somewhere in the middle, or higher up. In 1883, Ōtsuka Giichirō (1844–?) became an early advocate of cutting the bush to the root about once every five years. In 1902, the Experimental Laboratory wrote that pruning should take place after the first plucking to encourage a better second harvest. It soon became standard practice at fields where steeped tea, "jeweled dew," and fine powdered teas were produced.[11]

Advancements in tea-leaf plucking encompass a third important development. Throughout history, this task had always been performed by hand, a highly labor-intensive procedure. To understand the variation in picking methods, a more detailed discussion of how the tea plant grows and matures is necessary. New soft shoots contain the highest concentration of the vital ingredients of tea—caffeine, tannin, and amino acids—while the more mature leaves have less. Traditionally, there had been five methods of handpicking the leaves, including placing the shoot between the thumb and forefinger and snapping it off, a method by which an individual could usually count on harvesting about ten kilograms per day. This was the standard and best method, but there were also methods that called for using the fingernail, reaching down farther in the bush to grasp stalks, and using both hands. The advantage of these other methods was that the picker could pluck more tea in a day, anywhere from fifteen to fifty kilograms. Usually for new shoots used in the finest teas, such as "jeweled dew" and powdered tea, the picker used the standard method. As the harvest progressed and new shoots disappeared, however, the other methods were employed to great benefit.

Beginning around 1883, though, Shizuoka farmers invited the expert Sakai Jinshirō (1842–1918) to instruct them about their tea cultivation, and he recommended using both scissors and a sickle to harvest the thicker, older stalks. By 1890, these instruments were also employed for pruning and cutting the bushes back after the harvest. The use of scissors to pluck tea stalks in later pickings helped to raise the efficiency of harvesting tea leaves somewhat.

Yet the use of scissors did not really change tea picking that much. Just as in the medieval and Edo eras, pickers took tea leaves at different times, first plucking the new soft shoots and then gradually progressing to the older, tougher stalks. Because tea shoots and stalks became harder (and thus less filled with their constituent compounds) at roughly the same time, even using scissors for the later harvests did not really change the job that much. Owners of large tea fields were required to employ lots of female pickers (*chazumi fu*) at one time. Typically, tea processors hired between two and twenty young women per household to pick tea. It was seasonal labor and embraced wide swaths of Japan where tea was a major business.

The use of scissors should not be entirely dismissed, however. Eventually, this tool came complete with a net to catch the tea leaves. Still, fears about quality continued, and the use of scissors did not really spread around Japan until 1918. Even then, tea scissors could only be used on relatively flat lands, where one picker might harvest up to 150 kilograms a day. The added efficiency (a factor of ten) made it worthwhile to sort out new shoots from older, harder, less tasty stalks and twigs.

The establishment of better methods for rolling leaves for steeped leaf tea (*sencha*) was a fourth development. In 1871, officials in Hikone domain located near Kyoto published *An Illustrated Explanation of Tea Processing* (*Seicha zukai*).[12] While the book contained advice on everything from planting seeds through storage of the finished product, its description of processing had the most import. According to this manual, picking should take place about eighty-eight to one hundred days after the start of spring according to the lunar calendar, and for every five or six new shoots pickers should leave one or two unplucked. These pickings comprised the best tea (*jōcha*). Steaming should be done according to the fragrance of the tea leaves and stopped when the leaves were no longer bright green. Then the steamed leaves should be spread out on a mat and cooled with a fan.

Next, the processor put the leaves into a device called a *jotan*. This was essentially a charcoal brazier with paper on top, where the leaves were rolled with a slow circular movement of the hands. In the next step, the worker separated leaves by size on the paper top using a winnow. After winnowing, processing was completed when old leaves were removed with chopsticks. The resulting product was then dried over a low flame and put in storage jars. The same process was then repeated for the remaining young shoots. In particular, there were two innovative pieces in the brazier above which the tea leaves were crumbled. To hold the paper at the top of the brazier in place, processors employed an iron grate and iron netting. These were likely developed in Uji.[13]

As a center where tea-processing technology was the most advanced, officials in Uji, along with others in Ōmi and Ise, named certain persons masters (*chashi*) and sent them to many places, including Shizuoka. These experts helped to spread the best practice to all regions where steeped tea was produced for export, and at fairs in Japan Uji and Shizuoka teas took top honors. It also assured that all steeped tea going for export met a high standard. It had at least one negative consequence, however, as the wide variety of different brands of tea celebrated in the Edo and early Meiji periods gradually dwindled. Moreover, during the late nineteenth and early twentieth centuries, teas of inferior grades, such as coarse steeped tea (*bancha*), gradually could no longer compete with regular or fine steeped tea, and many businesses producing exclusively these teas went bankrupt.[14]

Still, there was a problem with the Uji method of crumbling the steamed tea leaves, called *momikiri* or *yorikiri*. It required lots of labor, was inefficient, and the shape of the leaves in the final product was unappetizing. Then, too, different methods of processing the leaves left them in various colors and degrees of fine fragrance and eye appeal, depending on how much oxidation they underwent.

Soon tea experts (*chashi*) of the best regions went to work, visiting as many farmers' villages as they could. They taught the mostly female labor force to crumple their tea properly. In Ibaraki, Saitama, Shizuoka, Kyoto, and Mie, and any place possessing ten to twenty tea roasters, these masters sent their pupils, where they were hired in a huge operation to roll tea leaves the right way. Three times every day, tea rollers crumbled three to six kilograms per roaster, while female tea pickers could do the work of about two persons. In other words, a professionalized labor force came into existence, with its own rhythmic songs to ease the hard labor of tea plucking and crumbling. In 1877, a new and better method of rolling the steamed tea leaves was developed. The most popular was rotational crumbling (*kaitenmomi*), developed in Shizuoka; this method is the direct ancestor of the rolling procedure used today.[15] It did not hurt that rotating crumpling was two or three times as efficient as the Uji method. Tea processed by rotating (also called *tenguri*) had the added advantage of producing a more beautiful product (figure 10).

Figure 10. Rolling tea by hand. From *Sayama cha no seisan yōgu: Hōkokusho* (Iruma: Iruma Museum, 2009), p. 24.

The workforce that came into existence for plucking and rolling tea leaves was composed of true professionals, requiring as long as ten years of training. Even then, competition for jobs was keen, as several thousand *chazumi fu* and *chamomi fu,* wearing their characteristic red headbands and organized in units of about five persons, descended upon Shizuoka or Ise during harvest time. In Ise, each tea producer might employ thirty to forty female tea pickers during the season. These women sang songs in rhythm that told of their labors:

> When the tea is gone, tea pluckers go home;
> All that's left is their baskets and hats.[16]
>
> When the weather is good,
> Tea pluckers with their red straps
> Are in a great uproar![17]
>
> If you are going to pick tea shoots,
> Pluck properly from the root.
> Unskilled pluckers all run away![18]

While these workers from all sorts of places were in a village, it was an exciting time, with lots of news from outside the area. For this hard labor tea pickers were paid about eight *sen,* and the leaders (*chashi*) about 20–30 *sen* per day. Moreover, workers stayed in the owner's home, allotted a bag of rice per day. They usually signed contracts at the start of the year, and even though their labor was difficult, there were often more workers than employers.

In 1905, the Ministry of Agriculture and Commerce standardized the procedure for rolling tea. It was quite an achievement, encompassing nine steps and taking 2.5 hours for one *kanme* of tea leaves. As a result, by 1922 the price of tea had risen by 3.3 times. Tea rollers also sang while they worked:

> Aaae! Roll! Roll! Roll!
> Eeee! Must roll to arrange the leaves.
> Aaaa! If you crumple them even old leaves will make tea![19]

Unfortunately, the cost of fuel, wages, food, and other essentials had increased by a whopping factor of seven to nine. Since many farm households supplied their own items such as food, most were just barely running in the black. Romantic as it might have seemed, this system could not remain economically viable.

These harsh economic realities begot the fifth trend during 1868–1925, the initial drive toward mechanization of the industry. Inventor Takabayashi

Kenzō (1832–1901) tried his hand at tea processing during the early years of Meiji and developed a tea-leaf steamer and what he called a "tea processing friction machine" (*seicha massatsuki*) in 1885. He took out patents on the machinery and gathered about a thousand people for a demonstration; but because the cost was high and the end product not attractive enough for consumers, his inventions failed to arouse interest. In 1898, he received a patent for a prototype for a device (*sojūki*) for roughly rolling the steamed tea leaves. It would eventually turn out to be a revolutionary idea, but this first machine was too small and merely did the initial crumpling. This still left the processor to use his or her hands to roll steamed leaves on top of a roaster. Even then it reduced the workload for laborers, and several farm households adopted the machine. Takabayashi died penniless without realizing the true value of his contribution.

Still, the drive toward mechanization was on. In 1896, Mochizuki Hatsutarō (1864–1915) invented a device for rough rolling, and then in 1900 a machine for crumpling more finely in a rotating style. About the same time Usui Kiichirō (1872–1950) developed his own type for fine rolling. Then, in 1915, Akiba Yasukichi (dates unknown) made a great improvement by perfecting an automatic steamer.

Soon enterprising tea producers realized that they could work these machines together as a system. The Mochizuki machines used a steamer of three to four horsepower, employing water, electric, or gasoline power. Taken together, these machines performed the initial and fine crumpling in five steps, and in one twenty-four-hour period could produce 66 *kan* (1 *kan* = 3.75 kgs) of processed tea and reduced costs by 20 percent. The cost for these machines, however, was prohibitive for most farmers, and they continued to use Takabayashi's device for rough crumpling only. Thus, by the 1920s, methods for processing varied widely by enterprise, with small tea producers still relying on rolling by hand, while mid-sized businesses used just the device for rough crumbling, and larger producers such as those at Makinohara were more completely mechanized. Mechanization was primarily applied to fields on the flatter lands where the acreage was larger, while old methods using the hands prevailed in the mountains as before.

The advice and mentoring of experienced farmers who imparted their knowledge to other peasants was a sixth characteristic of these decades. These "old farmers" (*rōnō*) had likely been active throughout Japanese agrarian history; Miyazaki Yasusada, whose work on tea I discussed in chapter 3, was one such figure. In this epoch, the Japanese government sought to spread best practice around Japan. The standardization of the rolling process was just one such technique, most of which methods came from the Kyoto-Osaka region. Tea fairs and organizations helped accomplish this purpose. In 1877, the first domestic tea fair took place, and two years later the Organization for Progress in Tea Processing (Seicha kyōshin kai) was formed. The Japanese also sent their products to the St. Louis World's Fair in 1904 and to Portland and Seattle in 1905 and 1910, respectively.

This effort to spread best practice included the publication of various periodicals. The first such effort has already been described—*An Illustrated Explanation of Tea Processing*. In addition to the topics previously mentioned, this work showed farmers how to retrieve tea seeds and plant them, how to begin harvests (not before the fourth year), how to manage the soil by covering the base of the bushes with soil, how to transplant the denser plants in the autumn and spring, and how to fertilize in the spring, summer, and in some cases during the winter.[20] *An Illustrated Explanation of Tea Processing* showed and represented in the simplest way, with pictures illustrating how all these tasks were to be completed, the best practices as they had been developed in Uji. Other manuals soon appeared, including *New Explanations for Tea Processing* (*Seicha shinsetsu*) in 1873 and *Complete Tea Processing* (*Seicha ichiran*) in 1876. Their advice on planting seeds, tea picking, fighting frost and insects, and processing was invaluable.

In 1879, the first meeting of the Tea Industry Symposium (Chagyō shūdan kai) was held in Yokohama. Meetings were held regularly thereafter. During the earliest of these meetings, entrepreneurs learned about the low cost of drying in the sun, a traditional method that still seemed to have a place. At the third meeting in 1883, some thirty-one famous "old farmers" were in attendance. At that time, the Tea Industry Cooperative (Chagyō kumiai) was formed, adding its own rules and pressing issues to do with both domestic and international trade. Officials from national and local governments also attended to hear lectures about planting, processing, enterprise management, sales, and exports. Meetings of these various organizations also took place in 1915 when mechanization was the topic, and in 1921 when planting, mechanization, and storage were on the agenda. Altogether, these publications and organizations helped the tea industry prepare for the lean times that were manifest after the export boom of World War I.[21]

The seventh and final characteristic was a modest effort by the Japanese to enter the world market for black teas. Remember that Europe's initial experience with tea came in 1610 when the Tokugawa shogunate sent some green tea to the Netherlands. Since then, giant plantations producing black teas in India, Sri Lanka, and Indonesia had flooded the world market and greatly influenced European tastes. In 1874, Meiji oligarch

Ōkubo Toshimichi (1830–1878) ordered farmers to begin producing black tea on the Chinese model. The Japanese came up with plans for producing black tea, but when the United States population turned out to prefer Japanese green teas, the plan was dropped. The Japanese learned from their overview of world tea consumption, however, as Tada Motokichi (1829–1896) continued to experiment with black teas, and eventually they imported seeds from Assam in India, better suited to black teas because they had more tannin and emitted a fuller fragrance. Using the seeds from Assam and guidance from abroad, Japanese tea producers sent between fifty and two hundred tons of black tea abroad during the Meiji years.

During the first stage of Japan's modern tea production, cultivation and processing comprised a unified system. Primarily driven by the world export demand for Japanese tea, cultivators learned to use more and better fertilizers, tend their fields more productively, chase away those nagging insects, and prune to improve growth of the plant. Entrepreneurs and workers made numerous advances in tea plucking and crumpling, requiring the employment of thousands of mostly female field hands. Tea fairs, organizations, and publications spread the best practices as soon as they were available. Advances had truly made Japanese green tea competitive on the world market, but future changes, especially as anticipated by the first wave of mechanization, were to have an even more profound effect.

## MARKETING, CONSUMPTION, AND THE CULTURE OF TEA DURING THE MEIJI (1868–1912) AND TAISHŌ (1912–1926) ERAS

Until 1925, at least half the Japanese tea produced for market went for export to the United States or elsewhere. Therefore, domestic *commercial* demand for tea began as a small but ever-expanding portion of the overall market for tea. There were, however, innumerable producers of tea leaves or the actual beverage; as of 1930, 75 percent of the Japanese population was rural, and many simply grew and processed their own tea for home consumption (*jikayō cha*).[22] Viewed as a whole, therefore, Japan's tea industry was composed of innumerable small organizations producing for many purposes—everything from small amounts for home consumption to large quantities for export abroad. This market structure was in large part an inheritance from the Edo period and stood in strong contrast to that of India or Sri Lanka, where a few large plantations produced all the tea.

To elaborate, the market at Shizuoka, a major tea-producing area, shows just how complex a local structure could become.[23] Until about 1900, Japanese shippers (*hamaokuri*) in Shizuoka collected, sold, and transported most raw tea directly to Yokohama. From there foreign agents often reprocessed the product for the journey to foreign lands. In the less likely event that the raw tea was to be sold domestically, rural tea producers in Shizuoka went through a middleman (*cha nakagai shō*), who then collected and shipped the tea to market in the prefecture.

Around the turn of the century, however, Japanese producers and traders decided to take the export tea trade away from foreigners and developed tea-reprocessing plants in Shizuoka. From 1900 until 1925, market structure became even more intricate. Producers of raw tea typically went through one Japanese broker for reprocessing and then a second for the finished tea, who worked with yet a third wholesaler (*ton'ya*) for sale abroad or within Japan. All of this activity took place in Shizuoka. This complex industrial marketing structure would remain through 1931.

As the export market declined steadily, producers and wholesalers looked for methods to increase domestic sales. Beginning in the 1890s, tea firms in Uji turned to a new marketing strategy: sales by mail order.[24] It proved to be a good idea, as the number of Uji tea firms trading in this way grew from ten in 1914 to thirty-nine by 1925. Mail-order sales of green tea in Kyoto prefecture (which includes Uji) amounted to 1.6 million yen in 1919, or about 36 percent of all finished tea sales from the prefecture. When in 1924 it was asserted that green tea contained vitamin C, industry firms proclaimed that "this discovery amazed the middle class!"[25] A leading company in Uji wrote: "From 1916, the domestic consumption of Uji green tea grew at a dramatic rate because the practice of enjoying the drinking of tea had spread among ordinary people, and the population had also increased."[26] Uji tea was no longer just for the elite.

Because most Japanese tea was either exported or grown by consumers, newspaper advertisements for the domestic market were rare and not very exciting.[27] They were all black-and-white and frequently merely mentioned the name of the company where the tea could be bought. The first newspaper ad appeared in 1888 for *gyokuro* and *sencha* from Uji and was written in non-colloquial Japanese. Beginning in 1907, ads were published with somewhat greater frequency; Uji teas predominated. In 1919, a newspaper advertisement broke new ground by mentioning the advantages of drinking tea—that it was good for heart disease and regular excretion.

The most arresting advertisement appeared in 1922 and showed a serious man holding a bottle of "tea essence" (*chasei*). It stated: "Wake up!

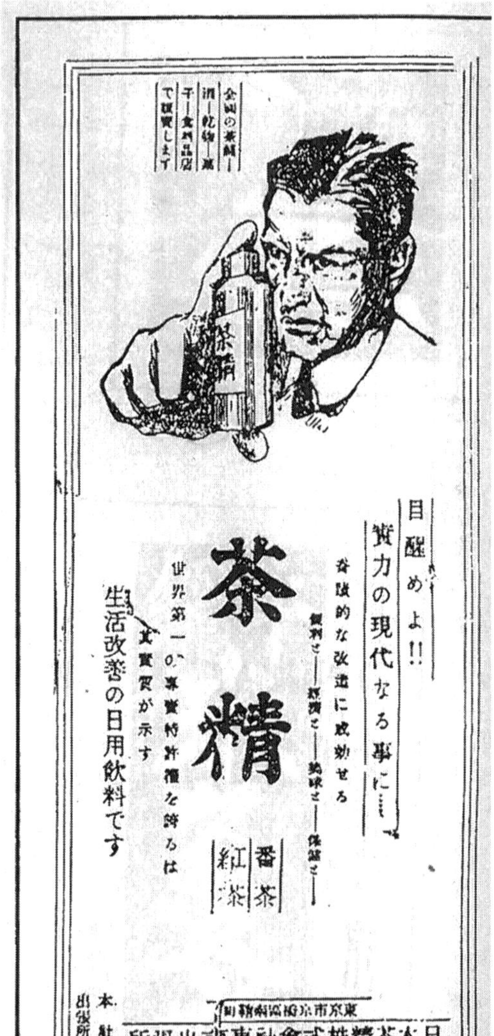


Figure 11. Newspaper ad for tea from the 1920s. From Hashima Tomoyuki, ed., *Shinbun kōkoku bijutsu taikei 7 Taishō hen: Inshoku shikōhin* (Tokyo: Ōzora sha, 2003), p. 250.

To the modern power! . . . A daily drink for the improvement of modern life!" In small characters, the ad pressed the advantages of this tea marketed through Tokyo; it was touted as "convenient, economical, delicious, and healthful" (figure 11). In 1927, after the discovery that Japanese green tea contained vitamin C, an advertisement notified readers of that point too. All in all, however, tea advertisements were rare compared to those for beer and tobacco—why advertise if the tea product was already being widely consumed?

Despite the relatively small commercial tea market at home, there can be little doubt that by 1925 tea of some variety was consumed in virtually every household in Japan. In late 1941, researchers from Seijō University in Tokyo conducted surveys for sample households all over the islands from Hokkaido to Okinawa. They asked about one hundred questions concerning diet in Japan; question 91 asked about the consumption of tea on a regular basis. Of the fifty-eight households in cities, villages, and towns, fifty-four (over 93 percent) answered that they consumed tea on many occasions, usually regularly. The only exceptions were households in one village each in Fukushima, Shimane, Okayama, and Nagasaki prefectures. (The village for Nagasaki was located on the isolated island of Tsushima.) In early 1942, however, when the same university conducted more surveys in about thirty-three villages stretching from Iwate in northern Japan to Kagoshima in the south, only eighteen (54.5 percent) answered with a similar positive answer. It should be noted, though, that not every household responded to the query.[28]

Comments about the survey question were often laconic, but some households gave details about their tea consumption. Most who specified a brand of tea indicated that they drank coarse steeped tea (*bancha*), although half a dozen noted that they preferred *sencha*. A few even imbibed black tea. One household consumed tea-rice gruel (*chagayu*), while those in Okinawa drank "Chinese tea." Most of the households that revealed where they obtained their tea stated that it was home-grown (*jikayō*), although, again, half a dozen responded that they bought their tea. Both Uji and Ureshino teas were singled out by name. Respondents generally said that they drank tea "all the time" or "three times a day," but at least one household said that they could afford tea only for special occasions or when guests visited. One householder said that "all the women of the village gather at one house to drink tea," while another stated that it was the drink of preference before going to work in the morning. In one village, all the "old people" drank tea. Only one household sold tea, but several noted that "tea is a necessity." Tea was plainly deeply intertwined with the customs of Japanese (especially rural) society.

Competition awaited, however. Japanese with ties to the Dutch East India Company first tried coffee during the Edo period, but found it bitter and did not like adding milk to it. After the Meiji Restoration in the late nineteenth century, however, coffee was seriously imported into Japan, and by 1888 an enterprising fellow had founded Japan's first "coffee house."[29] By 1901, about 145 "Western-style" cafés and eating places dotted Tokyo; by 1923 Japanese tea shops had been replaced by coffeehouses in the fashionable Ginza section of the capital. Japanese workers labored in Brazil, another source for Japan's coffee culture. In one Tokyo shop, there were 70 thousand coffee customers per month, while Osaka could manage only 52 thousand. To be sure, in 1925 coffee was not yet anything like a competitor for tea, but coffee's association with freedom from social hierarchy was a big attraction in the anomie of the big city. Instead of social gatherings, coffee became associated with the solitary individual, and Euro-American culture like jazz, eroticism, and avant-garde art. Two drinks could not have been any different or appealed in more unique ways to their various clienteles.[30]

Literature of the period from 1868 to 1925 reinforced the strong association between Japanese tea and sociability and hospitality. In the works of three famous authors, Natsume Soseki, Tanizaki Jūnichirō, and Nagai Kafū, tea almost always accompanied the initiation of social interaction. For example, in Natsume Soseki's *And Then,* there was an introductory scene with two men (Daisuke and Hiraoka) and an old woman. As the two men converged for conversation: "The old woman finally appeared with the tea, putting a tray on the table and apologizing all the while that it had taken so long because she had put cold water in the kettle."[31] Tea also appeared occasionally when Daisuke tried to court Michiyo, a major story line. Tea was also a drink tied to contemplation. In Soseki's *The Wayfarer,* the protagonist "sips tea" while sitting with his mother, but it was "black tea."[32]

Conversely, when something went wrong in a story, the breach was almost always reflected in the breakdown of tea etiquette. For example, Natsume Soseki also wrote the humorous *Botchan,* about a young man who journeyed to a rural school to become a schoolteacher. The locals mistreat him at every turn. When the main character arrives at his lodging, his landlord offers to make him "a nice cup of tea." The trouble is that the landlord is going to use, not his own tea, but some of his tenant's![33] Japanese writers of this time skillfully used the serving of tea to set the mood for each scene.

Tea served another function in the tales of Tanizaki and Nagai: it nostalgically reminded the reader of traditional Japanese culture. In Tanizaki's

*Some Prefer Nettles,* the story is set in Tokyo during the 1920s. The main character Kaname is a typical Japanese "anti-hero" going through a divorce as he struggles to define himself as modern and Euro-American or traditional Japanese. He is attracted to a Japanese geisha named O-hisa, and when she appears, she is often associated with tea: "She brought in tea and towels, almost noiselessly, and disappeared."[34] Of course, O-hisa works from a "teahouse." In Nagai Kafū's *Geisha in Rivalry,* the geisha Komayo and Kikuchiyo both toil and live at teahouses. In this case, the authors evoke a time gone by simply through the mechanism of tea or the old-fashioned "teahouse." In sum, even as tea production modernized, the appeal of the drink was tethered in a subtle way to the past.

## THE ROAD TO A SCIENTIFIC, MECHANIZED TEA INDUSTRY, 1925–1980

During the late nineteenth and early twentieth centuries, Japan's tea industry had made great strides toward modern production, including the standardization of rolling methods and first steps toward mechanization. The booming export trade had stimulated most of these changes. After 1925, however, tea gradually decreased as a major export item for the producers of Japan and instead became a beverage for home consumption. This transition encouraged those concerned with tea and Japan's economy to think big. The advent of the Great Depression and the disaster of World War II added to the stimulus for a thorough transformation. While Japanese cultivators and entrepreneurs continued to make improvements in farming methods, the real story of these decades is the application of botanical principles to and full-on mechanization of tea production.

Changes in the management of tea fields continued to characterize the era from 1925 through 1980.[35] One major change was the movement from planting with seeds to using seedlings. Even early on, tea farmers knew that producing seedlings by splicing (*tsugiki*), rooting (*nezashi*), layering (*toriki*), and cutting (*sashiki*) was possible. Taking a somewhat mature young branch, attaching one to three layers of leaves to a buried branch of a live bush in a well-drained plot with a temperature of about 20–25 degrees centigrade, and allowing the sun to shine on this project for a while, led to a rate of almost 100 percent attachment of the leaves. This process (layering) was utilized during the late 1920s, but proved less than perfect because the new shoots and roots did not do so well and often died.

From 1930 through 1955, farmers preferred to use layering rather than cutting to increase the numbers of their tea bushes. As already described, in this method a stem from the parent plant was cut and attached to a live branch, which was then buried with the cut branch above ground. Cultivators found that after two or three years the young seedlings could be layered once again. After about six months to one year, the new seedlings had grown plenty of roots, were quite large, and could then be used to plant new fields. In using this method, however, even taking twenty seedlings from one tea bush, for a field of ten ares that had 1,500 bushes the cultivator reaped only 30,000 seedlings, and one with 2,000 bushes only 40,000 seedlings. Moreover, there could be no harvest from the field where the seedlings had been taken and were growing like babies attached to the mother plant.

Soon farmers found that cutting was the answer. In other words, a branch was cut from the bush, planted in the earth, and the new seedling soon had roots. From the same sized field of ten ares, tea producers found that they could harvest 300,000 to 400,000 seedlings—ten times the amount acquired by layering. Under this method, once the cut seedlings had formed roots, fertilizer was applied. Seedlings cut in June had grown to twenty to thirty centimeters by the autumn and practically none died even three years into the process. Once they were planted in March, by the next November their roots reached a depth of sixty to seventy centimeters. Then, in 1960, farmers began placing black plastic and cloths over the growing saplings to produce even better results. The use of these seedlings gathered by cutting from the mother bush was a major advance over layering, and especially planting with seeds.

Another trend was the application of more and more fertilizer. Per *tan,* the new average was 26 kilograms of nitrogen fertilizers, 11 of phosphates, and 11–15 of potash in 1933. Organic fertilizers were applied as well. Fertilizer was hard to come by during World War II, but soon after the war the amount of fertilizer increased to double the prewar amount. Essentially farmers received an increase in their harvests of 200 kilograms for this investment. The timing of fertilizing also changed from early fall and late winter during the Meiji era to mid-September and early March during later eras. Because farmers used so much fertilizer, it became the chief cost of production for them.

Prevention of infestations by insects and blight also improved through the use of chemicals, traditional, and viral agents to get rid of pests. During the late 1930s, chemical agents became much more prevalent, especially soap liquids and pine resins. Lists were made of the major types of blights and insects infesting the tea plant. In 1958, a major paper on how different types of pests attacked different strains of tea was published. DDT came into use after World War II, despite the eventual realization of its threat to humans and the environment. Once these threats were investigated and known, however, farmers increasingly turned away from it and other chemicals. At the same time, blights and insects developed resistance to chemical agents. Another problem was that the cost of pesticides increased until it represented 8.7 percent of the total outlays of farmers. In other words, despite their problems, chemical agents still were used with great frequency during the early and middle decades after World War II.

The incremental changes in farm management represented continuity with the time before 1925. As noted earlier, however, the period from 1925 to 1980 encompassed a much larger transformation. One of the biggest developments was botanical—namely, the selection and collection of strains of the tea plant, initially from around Japan and eventually from around the world. Sugiyama Hikosaburō (1857–1941) was a major figure in the movement, as he collected teas from around Japan as faraway as Tanegashima. During the late 1880s and 1890s, he collected seeds from about two hundred to three hundred tea bushes, and then, beginning in 1914, attempted to propagate them in a small garden near his house by controlled pollination and selection. In 1920, he moved his research facilities to Shizuoka and the Ministry of Agriculture and Forestry (Nōrinshō chagyō shiken jō) took over his labors. Sugiyama was praised for his efforts at trying to improve the Japanese tea plant by breeding teas for early, middle, and late ripening seasons. Sugiyama also broke new ground by trying his hand at rooting, layering, splicing, and using cuttings, but his early experiments were failures.

Another important figure was Ōbayashi Yūya (1866–1937), who graduated from the School of Agriculture at Tokyo University after studying botany. Ōbayashi came at his botanical practices from the perspective of commerce and industry. He eventually traveled to India, China, and North America to observe the conditions under which tea was produced and consumed in various areas of the world. Ōbayashi became the first head of the government's Experimental Laboratory in 1896, but he was roundly critical of Sugiyama for trying to improve upon the native strains by separating out early-, middle-, and late-ripening teas. For his part, Ōbayashi incurred Sugiyama's wrath by advocating the interbreeding of all the various types of tea in Japan to harmonize their distinctive flavors. Ōbayashi clearly had an eye to reviving the Japanese export market, where he hoped that a single Japanese green tea would become the leader throughout the world.

It was only a matter of time before more Japanese botanists turned their attention to plant genetics. In 1932, Takezaki Yoshinori (1882–1975) put his knowledge about plant breeding to good use, differing in his opinions from both Sugiyama and Ōbayashi. Takezaki advocated the development of multiple tea strains that were adapted to different regions of Japan. He argued that breeding should first be conducted to separate native Japanese teas into different strains, so that the number of varieties could be increased. Then they could be blended in processing to produce a single beverage for mass consumption. For Takezaki, tea could be both a specialized beverage for niche markets in Japan and an object of mass consumption abroad. During the next decades, a greater number of strains was produced, and layering became the preferred method of carrying this out.

In the end, however, the tea industry did not really follow the fundamental vision of any one of these men, Sugiyama, Ōbayashi, or Takezaki. They all had in mind the giant tea plantations of India, Sri Lanka, and Indonesia and hoped that Japanese tea producers would produce a strain or strains of green tea to replicate that mass production method in Japan. For his part, Sugiyama advocated breeding early-, middle-, and late-ripening tea plants with soft saplings that could be harvested over a longer period of time and taste better for a mass market. Ōbayashi wanted to interbreed regional teas, utilizing their special characteristics to create a single tea variety to increase consumption. Takezaki argued for a little production from many strains and huge production for daily consumption, corresponding to consumers' tastes. For all three, the model was the large plantation such as those in India and Sri Lanka. Instead, the Japanese tea industry ultimately adopted the perspective that each Japanese raw tea leaf had a special flavor and fragrance attractive to Japanese consumers, so that producers united the production and the processing of each strain of raw tea into a single system, and therefore tended toward small factories, with even more refinements during sales. India had huge enterprises, while Japan's remained small.

The Japanese continued with native plants and tended toward the creation of numerous strains from them. At the Tea Processing Experimental Station under the Ministry of Agriculture and Commerce (Nōshōmushō seicha shiken sho), various strains were teased out. Three different brands were chosen from Uji alone, used primarily for export. Another came from Nara, given its own name in 1925. Still another came from Miyazaki and was used for stir-roasted teas. Around 1930, a mixture of teas from Kagoshima and Mie prefectures was successfully blended. There were also teas from Saitama, from Kyoto (used exclusively for powdered and "jeweled dew" teas), and so on. In any case, the Japanese tea industry chose the road of small centers of production and a wide variety of individual tea brands. Eventually, by the way, Sugiyama succeeded in having four strains registered with the government as early- or late-ripening teas.

Another reason for all this botanical work was concern for the health of tea bushes in Japan. Between 1936 and 1942, the government collected 150,000 strains of green tea and another 3,700 of black tea from around the world. The object of collecting all these strains during these years was to produce the healthiest tea plants possible. World War II put a stop to this effort at collection, but the efforts of men like Sugiyama were far ahead of their times, as they took cuttings from one tea bush and spliced them with another. In 1952, Japanese scientists used cuttings from Taiwanese plants to promote a healthier plant; plants from India and Sri Lanka were also made available. During the 1950s, about 30 percent of new plantings were done to improve the health of the tea bush; by the 1970s, all new planting had achieved this purpose. For these practices, cutting and splicing came into widespread use—gone were the days of mixing seeds.

By 1980, 55,311 hectares were planted in tea bushes, and 26,800 hectares, or 48 percent, were cropped in one newly teased-out strain or another. In snowy areas or those regions formed into slopes near mountains, the older native mixed strain of Japanese tea still held sway. In Shizuoka, however, the new individual strains made up about 40 percent, in Kagoshima 70 percent, in Mie 46 percent, and in Saitama 22 percent. One particular strain, called *yabukita* and developed by Sugiyama for its convenient harvest time, comprised 82 percent of tea fields under a newly developed strain. In this way, botanical work consumed the industry and comprised one of the essential characteristics of the Japanese green-tea industry between 1925 and 1980.[36]

The botanical work had a spin-off: it led to the renewed effort to develop a black-tea industry. Japan exported relatively small amounts of black tea during the Meiji period, ranging from 44 to 32 tons, with the most being 156 tons during the early 1890s. After decreasing during the 1920s, these amounts reached 3,075 tons between 1936 and 1940. After World War II, in 1955 Japan produced as much as 8,225 tons. All during these decades, however, Japan also imported black tea from Great Britain. It was becoming clear that Japan's native strains were unsuited for black tea.

In 1929, the Experimental Station under the Ministry of Agriculture and Forestry introduced Assam tea (*Assam indigenous*) from India. These seeds were entrusted to various experimental stations around Japan, and the Assam tea was interbred with native Japanese strains. Though the brands were registered, most of them did not taste very good. Eventually, there were thirteen brand names noted in government records before World War II.

Beginning in 1964, breeding, planting, and processing of black tea proceeded under the watchful eyes of scientists. The technology and standard methodology became established. A plan was hatched in 1959 to devote 10,000 hectares to the production of black teas. Most of the effort focused on southern Kyushu. Still, Shizuoka, with 7,089 tons and older methods, was the leader in production at this time. Then, in 1960, imports barriers were removed and gradually imported black teas increased and domestic production fell off. In 1969, the Ministry of Agriculture and Forestry succeeded in crossbreeding Chinese and native strains, and the tea seems to have had much promise as a black tea, but it was really too little too late. By 1972, Japan produced no more black tea, and within eight years the Japanese were importing 15,000 tons of black tea annually.[37]

Along with botanical work, engineers and entrepreneurs succeeded in completely mechanizing harvesting and processing. Concerning plucking, previously it was noted that tea scissors had been in use, but they had many problems, such as unevenness in the harvest. Then, during the 1950s, exports to the United States and Africa dropped off; the price of tea reached ten yen per kilogram. The tea industry was even called a "sunset industry." Moreover, labor costs continued to rise—some way had to be found to eliminate the costs of all those tea pickers (*chazumi fu*).

In 1950 in Nara, an electric picker was developed. By 1956, Katsumi Shinsaku (dates unknown) of Shizuoka invented a motorized rotating hand-held tea picker. It weighed about six to twelve kilograms and cost 45,000 to 65,000 yen. Yet it could pluck fifty to seventy kilograms per hour, about twice the amount that a worker with scissors could pick. It took some time for these machines to come into wide usage during 1965–1970. In 1965, a further improvement was made as Matsumoto Machines developed a mower operated by two persons. It soon spread to larger tea fields on relatively flat or somewhat sloping land. A smaller version was eventually developed for more mountainous regions, and later there was a riding version as well. In one eight-hour day, these later machines could harvest .6 to .8 hectare, six to eight times as much as the hand-held types. At the same time, however, it is well to remember that these machines could not be adapted to every topography, business structure, or enterprise size. In mountainous Kagoshima and Miyazaki prefectures a total of only 1,120 hectares used this machinery. Moreover, the machinery did not always produce the best leaves for niche markets such as powdered or "jeweled dew" teas. These machines did help to save Japan's tea industry from the problem of high costs during the immediate postwar period, though.

Farmers did not simply mechanize the harvesting of tea—soon processing evinced a similar devotion to machines.[38] The modern steamer with netting and adjustable temperature was developed during the late 1920s and early 1930s and essentially served most farmers during this era.

Figure 12. Tea-rolling machine. From *Sayama cha no seisan yōgu: Hōkokusho* (Iruma: Iruma Museum, 2009), p. 24.

After steaming, the leaves were placed in a rough rolling machine (*sojūki*), which, as we have seen, was invented around 1910 (figure 12). From this machine, the raw leaves went to a crumpling machine where the action was rotating, and this machine (*jūnenki*) was perfected around 1915 or so. The difficult process of rolling these raw leaves was still not finished even at this point, and so the product was moved along to a rolling machine that also dried the raw leaves (*chūjūki; saikanki*). This machine was also invented in its modern form around 1910. At last, the leaves, now crumpled into a mass, went on to a fine-rolling machine (*seijūki*), also completed in its current form around the same time.

By 1922, tea producers in Shizuoka possessed 14,667 rough-crumpling machines, 3,867 rotating crumpling machines, and 3,709 fine crumbling contraptions. Rough rolling was about 50 percent mechanized, showing that the process was partially mechanized in that proportion of households. In other words, about half the tea producers still relied on rolling the steamed leaves by hand. One factory could produce 450 kilograms of tea and could handle about 52 ares. Even in advanced Shizuoka, there were many households still doing much of the processing for steeped tea by hand. In 1927, the number of tea producers using power was 5,223 households.

Mechanization did not really take off until after World War II in the 1950s, however. Stir-roasted tea was a perfect candidate for machine use, as the process was likened to steeped tea. By the late 1940s after the war, inventors developed a mechanization process for stir-roasted tea in which the leaves were first mechanically stir-roasted, then underwent rotating crumbling, then drying, and finally stir-roasting in two steps. In one day, this mechanized process could handle 3,750 kilograms of tea. Still, in Kyushu in 1968, the average was more like 300 to 700 kilograms per day. In that same year in Kyushu, a better machine that could produce 4,800 kilograms per day was developed. Moreover, conveyor belts moved the raw leaves along from one machine to another.

Even the production of powdered tea became mechanized in 1948. Because powdered tea belonged to a niche market and high quality was a major concern, the leaves were steamed in a special steamer and then went through three stages of drying before being put in jars. To produce powdered tea, the leaves were then cut, separated out, and ground—all by machine. Yet, as with all types of green tea, small producers still preferred to do the work by hand, grinding powdered tea on a stone grinder, as in the 1300s.

In 1927 in Shizuoka, 10 percent of the tea producers did the rolling of their tea leaves by hand, 21 percent were half-mechanized, and 69 percent were more fully mechanized. This state of affairs produced households that simply grew the tea and harvested it and then sold it to some other larger producer who could process it with machines. At the same time, many producers wanted to process more than they cultivated and were buyers. Specialized sellers of tea also appeared. In any case, during the prewar period, tea processing by machine was not very efficient. One bottleneck was the rough-rolling machine, which could take only about fifteen kilograms or so of raw leaves.

After World War II, however, individual tea fields expanded and the amount of tea increased greatly. These changes led to demand for greater and more efficient mechanization during the 1950s. Between 1955 and 1960, machines were invented that supplied raw leaves to steamers and automatically dried them. Fuel switched from coal to oil. Between 1960 and 1963, more new machines were developed, including one to cool the steamed leaves, an automatic fine-crumpling machine, and a rough-crumpling machine run by propane gas. Air currents, conveyor belts, and vibrating machines connected one processor to the next. These new methods replaced the older method of moving the processed product along by hand using a winnowing fan. All these developments made the production of steeped leaf tea (*sencha*) much more efficient.

The crucial breakthrough, however, came in 1964 when an improved rough-rolling machine (*sojūki*) was invented that could process 35 to 50 kilograms. It moved raw, steamed leaves from a rear board using warm air currents and was a great improvement over machines that could handle only 5 to 10 kilograms at a time. This invention opened the way for larger machines all the way down the processing system, from rough crumpling to rotating crumbling to fine rolling of the raw tea. At one time, tea producers could put in 35 kilograms, and sometimes 50, in each of two rough rollers and form lines of machines on the factory floor.

By 1967, entrepreneurs had a system for large-scale machines in relatively big fields, such as the sloping lands of Shizuoka and the Kyoto-Osaka region. In 1968, small, motorized tea-picking machines could pluck 1.5 hectare per machine, and then a family of three could handle the work. Processing was carried out with several families using one factory with the outsized machines, and could easily handle twenty hectares in plenty of time. In 1968, inventors also perfected a rough crumbler that did up to 120 kilograms. Soon other processing machines for crumbling the raw leaves came into existence, and factories adopted the new machinery, utilizing three or four lines of the giants. This new technology spread throughout the 1960s and early 1970s.

In fact, rough rollers became so proficient that it was necessary to have trucks haul the picked leaves over some distances, just so long as the tea did not go bad. Here the rule was "pluck and process" in the same day. The adoption of large machines also still left plenty of room for crumbling by hand. Furthermore, sometimes drying was too fast and the flavor and fragrance became bitter. Gradually, though, entrepreneurs learned to adjust the temperature of the blowers on the rough-crumpling machines and the quality of tea improved.

Finally, during 1955–1965, inventors perfected a system by which all these processing machines, from the steamer to the fine-crumbling contraption, could be connected. In the late 1960s, tea processed using this system went on sale. In an hour, tea producers could process 200 to 300 kilograms of raw tea. Yet problems also arose with quality, and so this revolution was not widespread by 1980. Some pointed to the potential of computers for controlling advanced mechanization.[39]

The nub of the issue was the question of what was most economical. High machine efficiency did not necessarily mean greater economical value. To elaborate, the processing of tea was unlike other manufacturing systems because leaves varied in color, shape, fragrance, and water content. These variations required human processors to continue to be involved in the crumpling of the leaves as a check. Perhaps computers could be developed with programs to account for this, but as of 1980 this was not yet clear.

The era from 1925 through 1980 had witnessed the development of a second unified system of production for Japanese tea. Incremental changes in bush reproduction, fertilizer application, and insecticide usage still characterized farming, but concentration on plant genetics had led to the teasing out of multiple strains and the creation of an industry with innumerable small enterprises. An attempt was even made once again to produce black tea, but failed in the face of stronger competition. Most of all, tea production underwent much more mechanization than ever before, from the use of motorized tea mowers to the introduction of machines to handle every facet of tea processing. Changes in consumption patterns soon meant that quality became uppermost in producers' minds.

## TEA CONSUMPTION AND MARKETING, 1925–1980: THE DIETARY TRANSFORMATION

The half-century under consideration in this section encompasses what is known as the beginning of Japan's dietary transformation.[40] To explain further, this dietary or nutritional transition refers to a fundamental shift in what people around the world were eating and drinking; during the twentieth and early twenty-first centuries, as most of the world's population moved from being overwhelmingly rural with little disposable income to mostly urban and more affluent, the diet of men and women switched from starchy carbohydrate staples to high amounts of animal protein. Depending on how one chooses to define it, one could assert that the dietary transformation comprised a more advanced stage in the evolution of consumer society, which, as I argued in chapter 3, began in Japan in the early nineteenth century.

The era 1925–1980 in Japan sits almost perfectly astride this nutritional transformation. Before 1960, more than half Japan's population was rural and adhered to the traditional diet; by 1980 the nutritional transformation had begun, more than half the population was urban, and Japan's economy was the wonder of the world, with growth rates in excess of 10 percent per annum. By the early 1980s, many affluent consumers had become more discriminating, demanding a richer and more sophisticated diet.

For Japanese tea, the decade of the 1960s was the critical time, when exports dropped drastically and tea had to compete with coffee and other drinks for the newly enriched consumer in Japan and around the world. Most of the production changes described in the preceding section—genetic experimentation, more intensive field management, and the devotion to mechanization—took place in that context. In other words, Japanese tea producers faced a growing crisis by the 1960s, as exports continued to fall and attempts to process black teas failed. As noted in the preceding section, the Japanese government even went so far as to think of tea as a "sunset industry" shortly after World War II.

Consider first the marketing and consumption of tea before 1960, in many ways an extension of trends described previously. Until the imposition of wartime economic controls after 1931, the market was much as I characterized it earlier for Shizuoka, with layers of producers, brokers, middlemen, wholesalers, and retailers. Gradually, though, tea producers came to embrace (1) either those who produced or bought and processed tea for themselves and (2) those who sold tea leaves on a large scale on the market. Increasingly, these producers, in Shizuoka and elsewhere, took their tea directly to sell without going through brokers and the like. When wartime controls were imposed, tea farmers' organizations were linked directly to nearby tea merchants, and local markets all over Japan flourished. This situation obtained during the American occupation (1945–1952), and its aftermath too.[41]

In the years leading up to World War II, newspaper advertisements for tea were also similar to those of the 1920s—black-and-white, simple, and relatively rare. In one ad for 1942, Meiji Tea boasted of its "elegant fragrance and appealing color," but that was exceptional.[42] In that same year, however, Aozora Tea glorified itself as "the tea that makes the Japanese spirit" (*Yamato kokoro*), creating a nationalistic rationale for its beverage.[43] Recall that, as of 1941, most Japanese consumers were rural folk who cultivated tea (usually the coarse steeped brand) for home use.

During World War II and its aftermath, tea appears to have been one product that was not subject to rationing, although it seems to have been hard to come by. In *Leaves from an Autumn of Emergencies,* an anthology of diary entries from eight ordinary Japanese during the war, tea was mentioned as many as eight times by the same number of authors. Even as late as 1944, one diarist in Kyoto wrote that he had "poured a cup of *bancha* and ate half my rice ball."[44] One package of steeped tea (*sencha*) in Kyoto in late 1944 cost five *sen,* a quarter the price of bean paste (*miso*) and one-sixty-fifth that of a bag of rice. During the last year of the war, one recipe recommended serving used tea leaves with a little sugar, soy sauce, and dried bonito flakes both as a side dish and a drink.[45] Tea remained available right up until Japan's surrender in August 1945.[46]

As noted, the 1960s was the pivotal decade for tea in Japan's dietary transformation. For one thing, tea faced its first truly serious competition from coffee. Ironically, a Japanese scientist living in Chicago invented instant coffee, and by the 1950s the beverage was being mass-produced in the United States. By the 1960s, the drink was popular in Japan, where it was imbibed at home and in offices for the first time. By 1970, freeze-dried coffee was available. By 1975, the residents of Japan were drinking more coffee than tea by weight and Japan became the world's third largest importer of coffee behind the United States and Germany.[47] Around 1980, there were 154,680 cafés with 575,768 employees. Coffee culture assumed a major role in Japan's dietary and social matrix.[48]

To combat fears of decline and entice consumers to drink more tea, in 1961 thirty-three tea retailers announced the formation of the All-Japan Tea Merchants' Club (ZenNihon chashō kurabu) in *Japan Economic Newspaper* (*Nihon keizai shinbun*).[49] In the announcement, the group stated that at present their best seller was small amounts of tea (100 grams) for fifty yen; the club argued that at that rate most would barely survive. They aimed to sell the same amount for double the price within five years.

To carry out this dramatic change, the club wrote that merchants needed to communicate to consumers "how up-market and high quality" their teas were. These teas were from the first plucking, and second and third teas were to be priced on a sliding scale. In the words of the club's chair, Ikeda Shūji, consumers were asking for teas that had a "fine fragrance" and "good taste." High-end consumers wanted something better than coarse steeped tea for which they paid a little; they wanted a more luxurious beverage (*shikōhin*) appealing to young and old alike, a drink that would be consumed in Japanese households day and night.

In Japan's rapidly growing economy of the 1960s and 1970s, the strategy seemed to have had a positive effect. The Tea Merchants' Club grew to forty-six members, ranging from Aomori to Kumamoto, by the early 1980s. A sample of the membership shows how tea retailers tried to meet the tastes of the urban consumer with money to spend and delicious alternatives such as coffee to consider. Takamori meicha dō, located in Aomori prefecture in the north, was founded in 1901 as a tea shop (*cha mise*) and incorporated in 1955. Between 1956 and 1971, it opened four branches and adopted three principles: (1) strive to please the customer; (2) strive to do business with the best information and according to contemporary trends; and (3) develop a spirit for pleasing local customers.

Machidaen honten in Sayama in Saitama prefecture was started in 1898 and at first sold its tea in northern Honshu. Eventually, sales centered on Tokyo, Kanagawa, Nagano, and Gunma prefectures. Incorporated in 1954, it opened two retail shops and a wholesale division. It built a processing factory, a reprocessing factory, cold-storage facilities, and another store. The company owned three hectares of tea fields from which it gathered tea leaves. Later, Machidaen diversified by sponsoring a driving school and store for field athletics. The company's motto was Drinking Tea Is Based on Trust.

Ippodō Tea Shop started in Kyoto in 1721. Originally from Shiga, its owners called it the Ōmi ya and sold Uji tea. By 1964, it was a stock company with three million yen in capital, increasing to ten million yen by 1970. The company president was a fifth-generation descendant of the founder. Sales policy included these rules: (1) adhere to set prices; (2) place importance on the product and sell according to the customer's preference; (3) because workers who come and go are important customers, treat them right and make them happy.

Haraguchien in Fukuoka was founded in 1936, beginning from a store in front of Fukuoka Station. It became a joint stock company in 1950 and opened a new store in 1966, along with a reprocessing factory. In 1976, it opened another store in Yaotome and established a large storage facility on one thousand *tsubo* of land. In 1977 it became a joint-stock company and increased the size of its main headquarters too. Selling mainly *sencha* and *gyokuro,* Haraguchien had laid stress on becoming the chief collection point for raw tea in all of Kyushu, as well as being a major retailer. Its motto was "Contributing to local society through tea."

The reader may well ask: How could coffee make such inroads with Japanese customers while retailers of green tea of all types continued to see their market grow? Remember that, until 1980, production of Japanese tea had grown to 100,000 tons with a drastically shrinking export market. The answers must be found in the continuing growth of Japan's population, especially in the cities, and the rapid per capita rise of incomes. In other words, for both coffee and tea there was a "win-win" set of circumstances in which both could grow. This confluence of factors, however, would not continue long after 1980.

In addition, beginning in the 1960s, tea companies began to advertise more effectively, especially on radio and television. For instance, in 1968 Myōkōen, one of the forty-six companies in the Tea Merchants' Club, won a silver medal for its TV ad broadcasting in central western Japan.[50] "A man said, 'I went to see Europe and America and the thing that moved me most. . . .' A woman replied, 'I can drink Japanese tea here.' Myōkōen Tea!" In 1980, Haraguchien's TV ad showing rolling tea fields, a female tea plucker, and then a cup of tea won an excellence prize (*yūsaku shō*). The voice-over said, "The fragrance of Yame, won't you try it?" And then, "Just, won't you try drinking some tea? Haraguchien." In the final scene, over a cup of steaming tea appeared the words "O! To be Japanese!"[51]

Consumption of Japanese tea expanded markedly from 1960 to 1980, as tea producers and merchants met the challenge they faced from the decline of the export market and the beginning of stiff competition from coffee and other nonalcoholic beverages. A second survey of Japanese diet conducted during the 1980s confirms the unshakable hold that tea had on the populace. Carried out for all forty-seven Japanese prefectures from

Hokkaido to Okinawa, the survey revealed that tea and food dishes prepared with tea were intimate parts of the food culture in thirty-eight of the forty-seven prefectures; as might be surmised, the only areas left out of this picture were in northern Japan, where it was too cold to grow tea and the tradition of tea drinking was not nearly as old. Moreover, a total of 109 locales, both urban and rural, within the thirty-eight prefectures had traditional dishes that included green tea.

The polymorphous state of tea dishes was truly astounding. Of course, drinking tea was central, but depending upon the region the tea might be powdered, steeped, stir-roasted, or mixed with beans (*mamecha*), potatoes (*imocha*), or something else. In the Kyoto-Osaka region and westward, people ate tea gruel (*chagayu; chagai*). Consumers in other regions liked tea poured over their rice (*chahan*) or tea with pickles (*chazuke*). There were lots of ceremonial uses for tea too, beginning with New Year's Day's *fukucha*. The long list of tea dishes and the many varieties of tea stand in contrast to the survey of 1941, when most tea was homegrown, coarse steeped tea.[52]

As seen in the survey and the appeal to "Japaneseness" made in the TV ads, in 1980 tea occupied much the same cultural niche that it had fifty or a hundred years earlier. In Japanese literature and film of the era, the chief role of tea was to represent daily sociability and hospitality, as it had earlier. In Tanizaki's *The Makioka Sisters,* the story of an Osaka family including four daughters, for example, tea frequently introduces a scene where there is interaction among the characters. Speaking of a "young wife" living near to her, the character Sachiko remarks that "[n]ot a minute later she was back with tea for me. . . . And how would you like a cup of tea? she said."[53] In Kawabata's *The Sound of the Mountain,* the main character is an old man tending to family responsibilities in postwar Japan. He is close to his daughter-in-law Kikuko, who is always supplying him with tea: "When they got home from viewing the sunflowers she hurried for his tea."[54] In Kurosawa's *Ikiru,* a film about an aging bureaucrat struggling with the meaning of life, the stage direction for an early scene in the municipal office states: "Dissolve to the office. Two of the staff are eating their lunch and drinking tea as they talk."[55] Up to 1980, there was room for tea to grow in this traditional role along with Japan's population and economy, but soon enough all that would be tested.

## JAPANESE TEA PRODUCTION AND CONSUMPTION, 1980–PRESENT

During the last decades, the amount of tea produced in Japan has diminished and then stabilized at just over 80,000 tons per year (see table 6).

**Table 6** Tea production in Japan, 1980–2009

| *Year* | *Total* | *Steeped* | *Coarse steeped* | *Powdered* | *Gyokuro* |
|---|---|---|---|---|---|
| 1980 | 102,300 | 81,400 | 12,100 | 415 | 553 |
| 1985 | 95,500 | 74,700 | 11,500 | 552 | 420 |
| 1990 | 89,900 | 72,700 | 8,020 | 896 | 357 |
| 1995 | 80,400 | 63,900 | 8,020 | 820 | 305 |
| 2000 | 84,700 | 63,500 | 11,400 | 1,010 | 207 |
| 2005 | 100,000 | 70,200 | 18,200 | 1,630 | 227 |
| 2009 | 86,000 | 58,600 | 17,600 | * | * |
| 2013† | 82,849 | * | * | * | * |

*Source: Cha kankei shiryō* (Nihon chagyō chūō kai, 2010), p. 10.
*Note:* All figures are given in tons.
*Asterisks indicate that no figures were available.
†Figure for 2013 is from the Ministry for Agriculture, Forestry, and Fisheries.

This amount is about 9.5 percent of world production of green tea, with China growing 80.6 percent, Vietnam 6.8, and Indonesia 2.1.

By far the largest proportion is still steeped leaf tea (*sencha*), and coarse tea (*bancha*) has shown some increase during the last decade. So has powdered tea, although the amount (in tons) is still very small. Surprisingly, "jeweled dew" tea has fallen in popularity, but that may be because the amount of a less expensive knockoff (*kabusecha*) has doubled, from about two thousand to four thousand tons, at the same time. An elderly scholar summed up the situation for Japanese tea over the last fifty years: "Once we drank green tea morning, noon, and night, but now people have coffee with breakfast, black tea with lunch, and green tea in the evening."[56]

Another important trend has been the dramatic decline in households producing tea. According to the Ministry for Agriculture, Forestry, and Fisheries, the number of households growing tea in 1970 was over 1.1 million. By 2001, the number had shrunk by 90 percent to 102,400. Of course, these figures denote a huge growth in productivity, since one-tenth the number of farmers are now cultivating about the same amount of tea as thirty years ago. They also suggest that few farmers now grow tea for home consumption, but instead they go through the market. The same ministry today designates tea as a "crafted agricultural product" (*kōgei nōsakubutsu*).

Despite this decline in growers, as shown in table 7, almost all production is for domestic consumption. To be sure, there has been a modest increase over the last decade, but the amounts are still very small. Earnings

**Table 7** Japanese tea exports, 1980–2013

| *Year* | *Total* | *Exports* |
|---|---|---|
| 1980 | 102,300 | 2,080 |
| 1985 | 95,500 | 1,762 |
| 1990 | 89,900 | 283 |
| 1995 | 84,800 | 461 |
| 2000 | 89,300 | 684 |
| 2005 | 100,000 | 1,096 |
| 2009 | 86,000 | 1,958 |
| 2011† | 82,100 | 2,387 |
| 2013† | 82,849 | * |

*Source: Cha kankei shiryō* (Nihon chagyō chūō kai, 2010), p. 47.
*Note:* All figures are given in tons.
*Asterisk indicates that no figures were available.
†Figures for 2011 and 2013 come from the Ministry for Agriculture, Forestry, and Fisheries.

range from six to eight billion yen in good years. For these exports, the United States is the best customer, far ahead of other places such as Canada, Singapore, Hong Kong, or Taiwan. The green tea on the menu at the St. Louis restaurant mentioned in the introduction could well have come from Japan. As for Cape Town, I can be less certain, although Japanese exports to South Africa increased by 50 percent between 1999 and 2009.[57]

Faced with a static or diminishing home market due to a stable and then shrinking population, a lifeless economy (after 1990), and the growing popularity of other beverages, the tea industry tried to capture new consumers and hold on to old ones. The most effective marketing tool was developed by tea giant Itoen, that is, the utilization of PET bottles beginning in 1990. To elaborate, by that year convenience stores like 7-Eleven and Lawson, as well as vending machines, were located at almost every street corner of towns and cities. The coffee industry had been ahead of the curve because it first sold canned coffee from vending machines as early as 1973. Now tea joined the fray. The result has been that bottled *sencha* and *gyokuro* of high quality have become immediately available and remain relatively popular.[58]

The strategy has been so successful that the older generation in Japan worries that those aged thirty and younger will only know PET bottles and be unable to recognize tea leaves or how to use a kettle for steeped tea. The adoption of this strategy, however, ranks as one of the most important changes in the history of Japanese tea, along with the introduction of the tea grinder around 1250 and the invention of steamed, steeped tea around 1740. It has probably been a major reason that tea has at least held its own in the domestic market since 1990.

More effective advertising has also held the market for Japanese teas steady. During 1997–2013, tea advertisements for television won prizes in fourteen of seventeen years. In 2007, Japan's giant beverage company Suntory won a gold medal for an ad for its tea called Iemon.[59] In the TV spot, a Japanese man and woman are pictured wearing traditional garb in breathtaking natural surroundings. The appeal, however, is more than just a pitch to traditional Japanese values. The beautiful wife says: "How wonderful!" a sentiment with which the husband Iemon agrees. Then the wife comments: "It's nice to do this every once in a while and forget all about work", as Iemon grunts his approval and replies, "Let's come again." In the frantic modern world where coffee and "power drinks" have become associated with a long workweek and exhausting schedules, Suntory has succeeded in casting its excellent tea as a way to relax. Of course, drinking green tea from a PET bottle as one hurries to catch a subway train hardly qualifies as relaxation. Other ads associate traditional Japanese scenes nostalgically with a slower, saner pace of life.

When I was doing research in Kyoto in 2014, I saw what I thought was a particularly effective TV spot. In a sunlit kitchen, two attractive Japanese housewives were shown preparing tea. In front of each sat a clear pitcher of water, until the ladies introduced green tea. One woman then poured a small amount of powdered green tea into the enticing pitcher and the camera showed the container as it turned an alluring deep-green color. The conversation then turned to the supposed healthful qualities of green tea. Those qualities may or may not be inherent in green tea, but the claim was the same as Yōsai made eight hundred years ago in his *Drink Tea and Prolong Your Life.*

For diverse reasons, green tea is still a product with appeal inside Japan and out. Fukujuen, the tea retailer working with Suntory on the Iemon project, has an up-market store in downtown Kyoto. In the basement, young women serve customers tea. What is notable about the shop is that it has on hand teas produced all over Japan. The consumer can try Ureshino stir-roasted tea or some powdered tea from Uji. Customers are also encouraged to mix different teas to find the flavor that fits their discerning taste buds. The store is only one way in which green tea has tried to meet the challenge of an advanced consumer society. Green-tea candy, ice cream, and even cosmetics comprise other attempts to access the market.

Competition among producers to sell their teas to retailers is therefore keen. Every year in Shizuoka and all around the country producers gather to compete in regional auctions. In the Kanto Auction, tea farmers hailing from all prefectures north of Shizuoka who want to sell their raw tea (*aracha*) submit their finest products from that year. The teas are judged and ranked on their appearance, flavor, and other qualities in an auction lasting from 10:00 a.m. to 3:00 p.m. one day every spring. As judges inspect the products, conversations and greetings are exchanged among those who know each other. The best teas are awarded points, and it is possible for producers to receive all the points. Teas are also singled out for prizes. For example, one tea producer garnered 193 of 200 points and placed seventh, winning a silver medal. The final bid for one kilogram of his tea was over 35,000 yen (about US$360 at the time). Other teas sell for as much as 181,000 yen, or about US$1,800, for a kilogram. Sellers are allowed to state before the auction that they will not sell their tea for less than a certain amount, such as 5,000 yen per kilogram. New information on cultivation and processing methods is also discussed.[60]

According to information supplied to me by an official at Itoen, there were 102 tea retailers in Japan as of 2014.[61] Itoen, the biggest tea company in Japan, had the largest share of the market at 6.6 percent in 2008. In 2000, the last year for which I was able to retrieve sales information for all companies, most retailers were small; some had annual sales of about 500,000,000 yen, or about five million US dollars. To put this in perspective, in 2008, total tea sales in Japan amounted to 317 billion yen, and Itoen's share was 21 billion yen. In this sense, Japan has remained a land of many small tea producers and retailers marketing teas for individual tastes.

During 2010–2011 and again in 2014, I traveled to many tea-producing regions and saw many fields and factories. There were all types of enterprises, from small family concerns producing powdered tea and *gyokuro* in Uji to the huge modern facility of Itoen located in Shizuoka. At Yoshidaen in Uji, the small family-owned company possesses its own tea fields and handles tea from growing through processing to retailing, all within the same location. Machines are used, but there is much labor, especially the rolling, which is done by hand. Powdered tea was even ground on a stone grinder. Marukyū Koyamaen, also in Uji, is larger than Yoshidaen. At Marukyū, the main product is powdered tea sold to Urasenke, Japan's largest organization for the tea ceremony. At Itoen, on the other hand, scientists in spotless laboratories tested the product in hundreds of ways to mass-produce just the right bottled and bagged tea. Computers handle much of the processing. Itoen even has a subsidiary in Hawaii, where customers may buy green-tea bags in convenient boxes. The tea on the menus in St. Louis and Cape Town could well have come from an Itoen factory somewhere in the world or even Japan.

There has been a recent challenge for Japan's tea industry. On March 11, 2011, a massive earthquake took place deep in the ocean off northeastern Japan, causing a giant tsunami. These natural phenomena would have had little impact on tea producers, except that the tsunami triggered several meltdowns in nuclear reactors in Fukushima. Radioactive materials rode the winds to the south, irradiating tea crops in the Kanto and other areas. France and several other European countries therefore refused to buy Japanese green tea for the foreseeable future. How the tea industry will deal with this problem is yet to be determined, but it has had little effect on Japanese consumers.

Previously, I noted that green-tea ads usually feature traditional characters dressed in kimono and placed in historical scenes. Certainly, Japanese tea utilizes its appeal to old-fashioned Japanese values, although coffee has also gained a reputation as a sociable drink to rival tea. Furthermore, the idea of what constitutes "old-fashioned" values is increasingly open to interpretation. In this light, it is interesting to note the appearance of the awarding-winning anime, comic book, and TV series featuring a character known as "Hyōgemono."[62] Each tracks the story of Furuta Oribe, a samurai general and central figure in the world of the tea ceremony during the Warring States period about five hundred years ago. Furuta was known for his asymmetrical, even warped tea utensils and unusual sense of beauty. His appellation "Hyōgemono" refers to someone who plays the fool or makes jokes. Far from the prior association with hospitality, a figure from tea has become a heroic individual—his own man. Ways to appeal to the past are unending.

This book has stressed three themes concerning tea as a commodity in Japanese history. The modern period witnessed further developments in all three: tea farming, the drink's effects on health and worker productivity, and tea's place in Japan's consumer revolution. In agriculture, the period from 1868 to the present has contained the rationalization and mechanization of tea enterprises. Until 1925, improvements in tea farming were driven by the desire to export the product. While land under cultivation increased, fields came to occupy flatter areas than during the time before the Meiji Restoration. Productivity of these fields, concentrated in far fewer regions than before, grew by leaps and bounds thanks to better cultivation methods and the mentoring of "old farmers." The first modern unified system of production, arising after 1860, required a large labor force, mostly female, for plucking and rolling the leaves. After 1925, botanical knowledge and mechanization applied to harvesting through the final processing reduced costs by eliminating most of the workforce. The industry, however, remained splintered into innumerable small enterprises producing for local and niche markets.

Concerning health benefits, the impact may not be so obvious, as the "industrious revolution" had ended by the mid-nineteenth century. The populace, which was consuming tea almost universally by 1900, probably continued to derive benefits in longevity and general health when compared with other regions of the world. Then, too, during the twentieth century, a major advertising strategy for tea companies was to note the health benefits, especially to tout the role of vitamin C. Given the prominent place of tea in the workplace from 1890 to 1970, it probably encouraged office labor to be more diligent too.

Tea played an interesting role in the development of Japan's consumer society after 1850. Consumption of tea in Japan was pervasive during 1850–1960 in the rising consumer society of that era. However, as Japan became increasingly urban and affluent beginning in the 1960s, imported coffee began to take customers away from tea. Until 1980, growing population and per capita incomes allowed companies to increase tea sales. The effective use of advertising also helped fend off decline. Since 1980, tea consumption has declined as coffee became even more popular and Japan's "economic miracle" came to an end. To combat this trend, tea adapted to a world where convenience stores and vending machines played an important role by selling the beverage in PET bottles. As a result, the tea industry is a highly competitive and lively one; Japanese still find a place for green tea at home, in the office, and in restaurants.

I have come to the end of the nearly thirteen-hundred-year-long journey of tea in Japan and tried to show how Japanese green tea could have been on the menu in locations as diverse as St. Louis, Missouri, and Cape Town, South Africa. It remains to draw some conclusions about the beverage and its varied roles in Japanese history.

# Conclusion

This book has traced the history of Japanese tea from earliest times to the present, in a four-step chronology. The first phase, lasting roughly from 750 to 1250, might be termed the "prehistory of the tea industry," because cultivation, processing, exchange, and the cultural cachet attached to the herb demarcate it from following periods. Buddhist monks introduced *Camellia sinensis* to the Japanese archipelago from Tang China, and they tended the first bushes at their temples. With demand outrunning supply, Japanese tea was consumed primarily for its medicinal value and utilized in ceremonies performed to protect the state and the body of the divine sovereign. Eventually, civil aristocrats learned of the wonders of this plant and consumed it for their health and well-being, too.

Early tea cultivation was rude and spotty, and processing on the druggist's mortar yielded a brownish liquid that was quite unappetizing and bitter to the taste. Yōsai imparted his knowledge of this tea in his seminal health tract *Drink Tea and Prolong Your Life*. Members of the ruling elite exchanged tea in small amounts as gifts, the primary way in which the leaves changed hands. This system of "gift economy" did not just bind Japanese civil aristocrats, Buddhist prelates, and eventually even some warriors into a network but knitted the East Asian states of China, Korea, and Japan together in horizontal ways in the Buddhist world of the time.[1] The beverage seemed to transport clerics and aristocrats to "another world" of poetic inspiration, among other activities. In the first stage, poetry was always written in Chinese, symbolizing the foreignness and immense cultural cachet attached to the commodity.

During the 1200s, subtle changes were visible in the world of tea. Toganoo tea received a reputation as the best in Japan, becoming the first tea "brand." Buddhist monks helped to spread the custom of drinking tea to the Kanto, where warriors avidly took to it. There are also signs that tea was exchanged as a tax item in the estate system and as a commodity for trade. A trade network evolved between production centers at Nara and Kyoto and consumers in Kamakura.

Between 1300 and 1600, the production, exchange, and consumption of tea in Japan began to undergo a thorough transformation, constituting the second stage in tea history. Cultivation of the plant grew by leaps and bounds. Tea farming spread to all regions of Japan suited climatically for the plant, from the northern Kanto south and west. Farming of the tea bush remained relatively simple however. Zen monks who had business in southern China imported a new strain of tea from that land. Tea fields were located on all sorts of topography, from mountain patches to border plots. Fields were also bought, sold, transferred, and inherited. Production grew by an order of magnitude, as suggested by units of consumption. Peasants were hired as tea producers, and Gion Shrine and other employers supervised (and mistreated) their workforces.

Tea processing also improved. During the late 1200s, Japanese clerics imported the stone grinder and the whisk to the islands from Song China, where they had been invented. These two instruments produced much finer granules of powdered tea than the druggist's mortar had and opened the way for greater consumption, gift giving, and lavish tea gatherings. Powdered tea was hardly the only beverage made from the plant, as peasants who had no grinders continued to drink all sorts of teas, many of them oxidized.

As Japan splintered into economic blocs, regions as diverse as Nara and Musashi became famous for their tea brands. Tea was still given as a gift, but was increasingly taxed and traded. Most important, tea shops opened, and commoners visiting Nara and Kyoto could buy a "bowl for a coin." Some peddlers may have served powdered tea, but a cheap brand of steeped tea was the main item for sale. As the consumption of tea became a widespread habit, merchants who boiled the water unwittingly contributed to the overall health of the populace.

Tea played a major role in the economy of Zen monasteries, where poets sang its praises in Chinese verse. In other words, the drink maintained its strong associations with China, foreignness, and solitude up to 1300. By the 1400s and 1500s, however, artistic renderings and literary pieces suggest that the beverage was becoming naturalized to its Japanese surroundings, adopted as "something native," at the same time that it worked its way down the social pyramid and throughout most of the islands.

In the late 1500s, two more developments accelerated the spread of tea in Japan. First, in Ureshino, Chinese immigrants showed the Japanese how to make stir-roasted steeped tea. This type of tea not only tasted better, it was cheaper too. Then, in Uji, tea producers learned to build roofs over their fields with straw and other thatch. The resulting tea was sweeter, and the roof protected against frost and cold in the late spring. With this development, Uji tea outstripped Toganoo as the premier "brand" in Japan. Uji produced powdered tea, and with the development of the roof-over method of cultivation and an even better grinder, Sen Rikyū and others turned the serving of tea into a fine art.[2]

The third stage, the Edo period, witnessed the triumph of tea in Japan's economy and society. Early on, merchants helped to incorporate northeastern Japan into the tea world. Throughout the 1600s, merchants shipped truly daunting amounts of the herb northward through the towns of Tsuruga and Obama. Eventually, the tea habit caught on so strongly in northeastern Honshu that the region began to produce its own teas in a kind of substitution for import.

About 1740, Nagatani Yoshihiro invented genuine steamed steeped leaf tea (*sencha*) in Uji. Nagatani's contribution was to roll tea leaves on top of a hot roaster, resulting in the creation of a sweeter, green beverage. Steeped tea grew rapidly in popularity in Japan and easily outweighed powdered tea as the drink of the common person. Toward the end of the Tokugawa period, "jeweled dew" became the preferred beverage of the upper classes. Authors such as Hitomi Hitsudai, Miyazaki Yasusada, and Ōkura Nagatsune wrote in great detail about the cultivation and processing of a veritable plethora of Japanese teas. By the early 1800s, Japan appears to have been awash in teas of every conceivable kind.

Historians are unsure how widely tea was consumed in Japan during the late Edo period, but two available measures suggest that consumption was widespread in an incipient consumer society. First, local records reveal that diverse brands of tea were grown all over Japan from southern Kyushu to the cold Tohoku. A three-pronged system for dealing in tea connected the islands in a commercial tea network. Second, tea was ubiquitous in Edo culture by the early 1800s, indicating that the drink was naturalized to Japan and available almost everywhere. The beverage appeared in fiction, Japanese poetry, woodblock prints, and even advertisements. The teahouse was a common feature of life in the islands. The delicious liquid was an essential element of Edo society by 1800.

Finally, in 1824, a thirty-three-year-long conflict broke out between tea producers in Shizuoka and tea merchants in Sunpu and Edo, throwing into graphic relief the conditions of all parties. Over one hundred villages participated in a lawsuit to end expensive and unnecessary handling fees on the trading of tea. Producers in Shizuoka were so poor that typically they took advances on the year's tea crop in order to pay their taxes and buy living essentials from merchants. The long-running incident underlines the solidarity of the tea producers in the face of abuses by merchants and the indifference and indecision of the *bakufu*.

The modern era beginning in 1858 comprises the final stage of the commodity's history in Japan. Japanese green tea had been shipped to Europe for the first time in the early 1600s, and exporting tea between 1860 and 1925 drove the need for major changes in Japan's tea industry. While tea acreage grew somewhat, more remarkable was the shifting of production to flatter areas that were concentrated in far fewer regions of Japan. Standardization all but wiped out many Edo brands of tea not suited for export. The work was labor-intensive in the first phase to 1925, as a mobile female tea working class was hired to pluck and roll the leaves.

A prewar survey indicates that tea consumption was ubiquitous in the islands at that time. Most of the tea drunk in Japan was the homegrown coarse variety (*bancha*) for a largely rural populace. To compensate for declining exports after 1925, tea retailers produced their first advertisements and utilized mail-order services. Tea was commonly alluded to in Japanese literature, particularly as a symbol of sociability and hospitality (or the lack thereof) or as a nostalgic reminder of traditional Japan.

Mechanization and botanical experimentation has yielded a unified system without the high labor costs during the postwar era. Try as they might, however, producers could not rationalize green tea into the efficient plantation and factory systems that already existed for black tea in India and Sri Lanka, and for coffee, chocolate, and sugar in other parts of the world. Steeped leaf tea for home consumption garnered all the attention and investment. Despite the gradual end to the export market, annual green-tea production grew to 100,000 tons by 1980. A survey of the late 1980s showed that tea was imbibed and used for special dishes throughout the archipelago.

Commencing in the 1960s, Japan joined the rest of the world in undergoing a dietary transformation. The development of instant coffee and the rise of that drink's consumption in Japan to amounts much greater by weight than Japanese tea presented a crisis for the "native" beverage. Tea growers and retailers have fended off this challenge with increasing difficulty since 1980. Up-market teas appealed to urban consumers with growing incomes. Advertisements on TV and radio evoked a sense of "Japaneseness" associated with tea.

The market for both tea and coffee could expand together only so long as Japan's population continued to grow and the "economic miracle" was under way. Beginning in 1980, tea production and consumption declined, and then stabilized. Commencing in 1990, retailers used the PET bottle sold in convenience stores and vending machines to combat decline. This strategy, along with effective TV ads emphasizing tea's traditional appeal, supposed value to good health, and relaxing qualities, helped the drink to retain a lower-profile place. The contemporary tea industry is highly competitive, both for producers and for retailers. In literature and comics, tea still symbolizes hospitality and sociability, but some references to the past stress tea as the drink of unique individuals. Retailers look increasingly to the small but dynamic export market, as witnessed by my experiences in St. Louis, United States, and Cape Town, South Africa.

The history of tea may speak to many different issues, but in my introduction I raised three questions that are of particular moment. The first issue concerns the collective health and work ethic of a populace that consumed a stimulative beverage such as tea. To elaborate, Hayami Akira has spoken of an "industrious revolution" in Japan during the Edo period.[3] For Hayami, this revolution described a great transition occurring during the sixteenth and seventeenth centuries. Samurai became the leading elite and the house of Tokugawa took control of the polity. While the economy had used currency for land-tax payments from the 1300s, the 1500s witnessed the advent of land surveys and a unified coinage. Agriculture became more efficient and yields rose. Living standards also improved. The creation of innumerable stem households encouraged these trends.

In this vein, it is interesting to observe the prominent place of tea in this "industrious society." By 1700, even housewives in Edo enjoyed their morning bowls of tea. While tea does not contain as much caffeine as coffee, imbibing repeated bowls of the drink undoubtedly stimulates the nervous system and focuses the mind. Was the widespread popularity of tea, which not only promotes good health but also gives drinkers an "energy boost," partially responsible for the growing productivity of Japanese workers and farmers from the late 1500s to 1868? There is no way to be sure about this correlation between drinking tea and Japan's general economic development, but it is a compelling idea worthy of full consideration.

Throughout the text of this book, reference has been made to Francks' demand-pull "virtuous circle" and the degree to which Japanese tea producers participated in such a consumption-production feedback loop. Jan de Vries is a European historian who also proposed the existence of an industrious revolution. For him, its cause had two essential parts: a reduction in leisure time and increase in the utility of money; and a change of focus for labor from goods and services produced in the household to marketable goods. De Vries' second point is crucial here and, as mentioned earlier, was repeated in chapters 2 and 3 in the form of Francks' demand-pull "virtuous circle." Turning the focus from Europe to Japan, one can see both of De Vries' transformations under way in Tokugawa Japan after 1700 in the economy as a whole.

Concentrating on tea with regard to each of these two changes leads to clearer answers. First, the numerous, detailed writings on tea cultivation and processing in the Edo era emphasize a concern for intense, meticulous work, often leading to tea sales on the market to boost peasant incomes. When the agricultural expert Miyazaki Yasusada wrote in 1697 that those farmers who followed his advice would attain wealth and property for the extra time they expended, he was in fact stating a textbook case of De Vries' two characteristics of an "industrious revolution."

Regarding the movement of labor from producing goods and services within the household to crafting them for the market, however, the answer is somewhat more mixed than Miyazaki's advice implies. Certainly, a goodly proportion of tea production in the Edo period took place for sale to consumers. The huge trade to northeastern Japan in the 1600s should suffice to make this point. Interestingly, though, the result of all that trade up north was to allow residents to grow their own tea for home consumption. Indeed, Tokugawa peasants produced some large—ultimately unknowable—proportion of their tea for their own family members to drink. De Vries' second characteristic therefore has a more limited application in the case of Tokugawa Japan. I shall return to this point later.

There is one other point about Japan's "industrious revolution." According to Hayami and De Vries, this important transformation took place during the early modern period beginning in the seventeenth century. Japanese tea, however, had become a drink with commoner appeal much earlier, around 1400. It is interesting to note that Japan's population apparently began a sustained spurt in growth at about the same time.[4] Undoubtedly, as William McNeill has suggested, boiling water for drinking tea and thereby killing parasites played some role in the advancing health of Japan's populace.

During the centuries from 1400 to 1700, agriculture began to improve, and commerce and industry underwent marked expansion too. Should the date for the advent of Japan's industrious revolution be pushed back to an earlier time? Of course, data are sparse and there are critics of the concept of the industrious revolution.[5] Such critics, however, often try to show that there were medieval roots for European production methods between the fifteenth and seventeenth centuries, reinforcing the idea of an analogous continuity for the same period in Japan. Of course, Europeans did not consume tea widely at that early date, unlike the peoples of East Asia.

This discussion of the purported industrious revolution in Japan and Europe is related to the second and third issues mentioned in the introduction. The second issue is the relationship between tea cultivation and the advent of advanced agriculture in Japan. As it seems now, Japan's agriculture until 1300 or so was extensive; fields were farmed in a hit-or-miss way. Between the 1300s and 1700, Japan's agrarian world underwent an important transition as cultivation stabilized and then expanded, yields rose, and famine became less pervasive. During 1700–1900, agriculture became even more intensive, with the application of fertilization and high labor inputs. Agrarian treatises helped spread the best practices. During the late 1800s, the Meiji land tax was the government's primary source of revenue. After 1900, Japanese agriculture became even more productive, mechanized, and even industrialized.

The story of tea farming fits perfectly—perhaps too perfectly—into this general pattern. Until the 1300s, little attention was paid to tea cultivation, and much of it was undoubtedly swidden cropping. Between the 1300s and 1700, however, tea cultivation intensified, yields rose, and tea patches came to cover many of Japan's regions that were climatically suited to the plant. Even northeastern Japan played a belated role in this story. During 1700–1900, fertilizer was applied systematically for the first time and literate farmers learned in great detail how to cultivate and process their crops through informative treatises. The twentieth and twenty-first centuries have witnessed a jump in productivity, the mechanization of the industry, the use of botany to improve the health of the tea plant, and eventually the utilization of computers to orchestrate tea farming and processing. Therefore, historians can assert that tea farming formed an invaluable sector of Japan's overall agricultural enterprise, an occupation that provided a foundation for Japan's industrialization.

At first glance, discussion of the third issue, the relationship between tea and the rise of consumer society, seems almost as straightforward as that of tea and farming. Until 1300, the main consumers of Japanese tea were a tiny elite of clerics, warriors, and civil aristocrats. There was nothing like a "consumer society." Beginning in 1400, however, as the productivity of tea gained for many reasons, the consumption of tea spread geographically and down the social pyramid. It reached one milestone in 1700, when tea was consumed throughout what was considered the Tokugawa realm, including northeastern Japan. With the invention of genuine *sencha* and other tasty teas, the increase and spread of urbanization, and a probable per capita rise in incomes and living standards for many, however, Japanese green tea became the drink of choice for a large proportion of the populace.[6] This trend was especially marked after 1800, and tea certainly can be said to have assisted in the development of a nascent consumer society at that time.

As Japan took off industrially after 1900, tea increasingly assumed the role of the major beverage consumed by the Japanese. To be sure, much of it was homegrown in prewar Japan, but the alternative (coffee) was not that important, except symbolically. With the coming of the dietary transformation after 1960, tea and coffee became true competitors. At first, Japan's increasing population and "economic miracle" allowed tea to remain the best-known drink in Japan's consumer society. After 1980, however, coffee was the most frequent choice, and only the invention of PET bottles saved tea from precipitous decline. Yet, even today, Japanese green tea appeals to consumer tastes in many ways. Therefore, historians can assert that tea in Japan was from the beginning, and still is today, a significant commodity in Japan's consumer society.

A closer examination of the data suggests more precisely what role Japanese green tea played in the evolution of consumer society in Japan during the last century. The data on exports and total production are exact, whereas those on tea produced for home consumption and that processed for domestic sale are best-guess estimates. Table 8 suggests, in however general terms, that figures for total production, or even total production minus exports, *overestimates* the role that tea played in the evolution of consumer society in Japan, especially initially. This generalization about production numbers would, to my mind, hold true for Edo Japan too.

**Table 8** The relative place of tea in the Japanese home market, 1925–2013

| *Year* | *Tea production* | *Exports* | *Domestic market* | *Homegrown* |
|---|---|---|---|---|
| 1925 | 36,000 | 12,000 | 12,000 | 12,000 |
| 1960 | 75,000 | 9,750 | 42,750 | 22,500 |
| 1980 | 102,000 | 3,150 | 88,450 | 10,400 |
| 2013 | 86,000 | 2,150 | 79,550 | 4,300 |

*Note:* All amounts are given in tons.

Comparison with tea consumption in Great Britain makes my point even more clearly. Tea was first imported into Great Britain in quantity in the late 1600s. By the 1700s, tea was "increasingly available" in grocers' shops and other retail operations, and by 1800, "no longer was the question whether someone drank tea, but the quantity and quality she (or he) partook."[7] The difference between Great Britain and Japan is that, in the former country, all tea had to be imported and purchased in a store and therefore indicated quite well how far consumer society had developed. By contrast, in Japan, until relatively recently rural folks could produce their tea at home, so that the commodity never went on the market. Therefore, it seems fair to assert that, insofar as tea in Japanese economic history is concerned, the beverage played a smaller role in the creation of a consumer society that evolved later than was the case in Great Britain. Both countries are famous tea-loving nations and each had created an incipient consumer society as early as 1800, as evidenced by the function of tea, but Japan's consumerism apparently developed later and over a shorter period of time.[8]

Be that as it may, there is one other point worth making, obvious as it may be. The centuries-long transformation of tea is usually read as a success story and as one element in the continuing progress of Japanese, and even world, civilization. I wonder, however, whether the mere production of more and more standardized bottles of green tea should really be read as "success." In the present era, when industrialized agriculture raises so many problems, the development of the modern tea industry evinces the same thoughts. The "golden age" for tea consumers was probably the Edo era, before the drive for tea exports wiped out all those uncounted varieties of tea. This comparison reminds us that the bottom line should be the health and happiness of the population, not simply more profits for large corporate "farms."

As with industrialized farming and processing, I also have my doubts about the wisdom of an ever-expanding consumer society. Japan and the rest of the world face an ecological crisis because of the ideology that "growth is good," associated with mindless consumption on a larger and larger scale. Was the Industrial Revolution a good idea, or one of the worst mistakes that humanity has ever made? As was the case for tea farming, I would argue that the period of most delicious and variegated tea consumption in Japan was around 1800, when drinkers could choose from countless brands of the beverage and before the invention of items such as tea ice cream, candy, and cosmetics.

Having written a history of Japanese green tea, I think it behooves me to ask: What is the future of tea in Japan? Relevant factors include the shrinkage and ageing of Japan's population, the low growth levels of Japan's domestic and the world's economy, and increasing competition from other beverages. Given these constraints, I think that Japanese green tea faces a future of slowly declining consumption at home, while the world market looks more favorable. At home, everything depends upon how much the younger generation adopts the tea habit. Abroad, appeals to the exoticism and supposed health benefits are leading to estimates that demand for Japanese green tea will grow by 7 percent by 2023. Japanese tea has been around for almost thirteen hundred years, and I think it will remain with us for a while yet.

# Notes

*Abbreviations*

| | |
|---|---|
| *KBK* | *Kanezawa bunko komonjo.* Vols. 1–12. Yokohama: Kanagawa kenritsu Kanezawa bunko, 1964. |
| *KI* | *Kamakura ibun.* Vols. 1–44. Tokyo dō, 1973–1997. |
| *SZKT* | *Shintei zōho kokushi taikei.* |

## *Introduction*

1. To list all the outstanding works examining *chanoyu* from an artistic or cultural point of view would take many pages. A few examples in English would include Louise Cort, *Shigaraki, Potter's Valley;* Paul Varley and Kumakura Isao, eds., *Tea in Japan: Essays on the History of Chanoyu;* Morgan Pitelka's *Japanese Tea Culture: Art, History, and Practice,* and also by Pitelka, *Handmade Culture: Raku Potters, Patrons, and Tea Practitioners,* and his *Spectacular Accumulation: Material Culture, Tokugawa Ieyasu, and Samurai Sociability;* and Kristen Surak, *Making Tea, Making Japan: Cultural Nationalism in Practice.* In Japanese, the scholarly journals and series *Chanoyu bunka gaku, Nomura bijutsukan kenkyū kiyō, Sadō gaku taikei, Sadō zenshū, Sadō koten zenshū,* and *Sadō shūkin* would be at the head of the artistic list.

2. Some examples include Kumakura Isao, *Chanoyu no rekishi: Sen Rikyū made;* Murai Yasuhiko, *Cha no bunka shi;* Kōzu Asao, *Chanoyu no rekishi;* and Varley and Kumakura, *Tea in Japan.*

3. Literature on a proposed "industrious revolution" for both Japan and Western Europe is plentiful. See especially Hayami Akira, *Japan's Industrious Revolution: Economic and Social Transformations in the Early Modern Period* (London and Tokyo: Springer, 2015). Several historians of early modern Japan have also invoked the industrious revolution. Note especially David Howell, *Capitalism from Within: Economy, Society, and the State in a Japanese Fishery* (Berkeley and Los Angeles: University of California Press, 1995), p. 6; Kären Wigen, *The Making of a Japanese Periphery, 1750–1920* (Berkeley and Los Angeles: University of California Press, 1995), p. 290. Penelope Francks discusses the issue in "Rural Industry, Growth Linkages, and Economic Development in Nineteenth-Century Japan," *The Journal of Asian Studies* 61 (February 2002): 35. For Western Europe, see Jan de Vries, *The Industrious*

*Revolution: Consumer Behavior and the Household Economy, 1650 to the Present* (New York: Cambridge University Press, 2008). This issue will be discussed in more detail in chapters 2, 3, and the conclusion.

4. The number of books dealing with "commodity history" and the creation of consumerism is long, beginning with Sidney Mintz, *Sweetness and Power* (New York: Penguin Books, 1985). Almost all the items studied have addictive properties, including tobacco, coffee, tea, and chocolate. On tea, see especially Markman Ellis, Richard Coulton, and Matthew Mauger, *Empire of Tea: The Asian Leaf that Conquered the World* (London: Reaktion Books, 2015). Two examples for East Asia include Carol Benedict, *Golden-Silk Smoke,* and Merry White, *Coffee Life in Japan* (Berkeley and Los Angeles: University of California Press, 2012). On line, see www.hcs.harvard.edu/tempus/Book_Reviews_files/xii_2_feature.pdf for just a few illustrations of ongoing work in this field.

5. The Japanese word *sencha* and its English equivalents—"steeped," "boiled," or "brewed" green leaf tea—is a vague and troublesome term. In its broadest sense, both the Japanese and the English words refer to leaf tea that has been placed in or inundated with hot water to produce a beverage. For much of Japanese history, it is not clear that this "steeped" tea was even green. Japanese authors often utilize the word *senjicha* for this more general meaning. In its narrow and most precise definition, *sencha* describes a type of green tea in Japan that is processed by boiling the leaves to stop oxidation and then drying those leaves while rolling them by hand or machine on a thin platform through which heat passes. This particular method was not invented until around 1740 in Uji, as explained in chapter 3. In this book, I shall use the words "steeped tea" to refer to the general sense, and *sencha* for its precise modern definition.

6. According to Vaclav Smil and Kazuhiko Kobayashi in *Japan's Dietary Transition and Its Impacts* (Cambridge, MA, and London: MIT Press, 2012), pp. 118–119, all presumed benefits of green tea with regard to cancer are doubtful. On Alzheimer's disease, see "Remember to Drink Your Tea," in *Tufts University Health & Nutrition Letter* 22 (January 2005): 6.

7. This brief introduction to tea farming owes much to Kida Taiichi, "Science of Tea—Part II," *Chanoyu Quarterly* (Autumn 1970), pp. 51–53.

### *Chapter One: The Prehistory of Japan's Tea Industry, 750–1300*

1. On the early history of tea in China, see James Benn, *Tea in China: A Religious and Cultural History* (Honolulu: University of Hawai'i Press, 2015), pp. 21–41. Also note Bret Hinsch, *The Rise of Tea Culture in China* (Lanham, Boulder, New York, and London: Rowman and Littlefield, 2016).

2. Victor Mair and Ehrling Hoh, *The True History of Tea* (London: Thames and Hudson, 2009), p. 42

3. Ibid., p. 48.

4. I follow the reasoning of Kōzu Asao, *Chanoyu no rekishi* (Kadokawa sensho, 2009), pp. 34–37.

5. Yamaguchi Satoshi, "Identeki tayōsei kara mita Nihon rokucha no kigen ni tsuite," *Cha no bunka* 5 (2004): 104–110.

6. Suk Yong-un, "History and Philosophy of the Korean Tea Art," *Koreana : Korean Art and Culture: Tea and Tea Culture* 11 (Winter 1997): 4–6, writes that the Silla king offered tea for the memorial services of elite Buddhist monks and that monks used tea in religious ceremonies.

7. Kōzu, *Chanoyu no rekishi,* pp. 48–49; Ono Yoshihiro, "Saga chō no Owari ni okeru rokuyū tōki seisan to sono haikei," *Kodai bunka* 54 (October 2002): 27–36; Takahashi Akihito, "Shiki chawan kubote yōki kō," *Kokuritsu rekishi minzoku hakubutsu kan kenkyū hōkoku* 71 (March 1997): 531–587.

8. Ono, "Saga chō no Owari ni okeru rokuyū tōki seisan to sono haikei."

9. Kōzu, *Chanoyu no rekishi,* pp. 38–39.

10. Terada Takashige, "Nara ken ni okeru shoki chagyō no tenkai ni tsuite," *Nara gaku kenkyū* 7 (March 2004): 17–25.

11. The argument concerning these two famous clerics and their relationship to tea follows Kōzu, *Chanoyu no rekishi,* pp. 40–41. See also Hashimoto Motoko, "Heian Kamakura no kissa bunka," *Kōza Nihon chanoyu zenshi* (Kyoto: Shibunkaku shuppan, 2013), pp. 27–31.

12. Fukuchi Shōsuke, *Heian jidai no cha* (Kadokawa shoten, 2006), pp. 55–56. Fuyutsugu was governor first of Kawachi and then of Ōmi.

13. Murai Yasuhiko, *Cha no bunka shi* (Iwanami shinsho, 1979), pp. 29–30.

14. Some of my analysis is drawn from Katherine Rupp, *Gift-Giving in Japan* (Stanford, CA: Stanford University Press, 2003), pp. 179–197.

15. Ōtsuki Yōko, "Kyūseiki shotō no Tōfū bunka to cha," *Shoku Nihongi kenkyū* 363 (August 2008): 19–20; on Saichō's tea field, see Kōzu, *Chanoyu no rekishi* , p. 45.

16. Ōtsuki, "Kyūseiki shotō," pp. 22–23.

17. Ibid., p. 27.

18. Ōtsuki Yōko, "Tōsō Gikū ni tsuite no shohoteki kōsatsu," *Higashi Ajia bunka kōshō kenkyū* 1 (2010): 129–140. Also note Takagi Shingen, "Tōsō Gikū no raichō o meguru shomondai," *Kōyasan daigaku ronsō* 16 (February 1981): 55–90; and Tanaka Fumio, "Tōjin no taiNichi kōeki," *Keizai kei* 229 (October 2006): 11–23.

19. Fukuchi, *Heian jidai no cha,* pp. 57–60.

20. Ibid., pp. 87–94.

21. On Anshōji in Heian, see ibid., pp. 77–80.

22. *Shintei zōho kokushi taikei, Shoku Nihongi,* Tenpyō 9/4/8, p. 143.

23. M. W. De Visser, *Ancient Buddhism in Japan* (Leiden: E. J. Brill, 1935), pp. 494–497.

24. Ōtsuki Yōko, "Ki no midokkyō no hikicha," *Kodaishi no kenkyū* 13 (December 2006): 17–27. I follow Ōtsuki throughout this discussion. For another recent treatment of this topic, see Sōma Noriko, "Ki no midokkyō ni okeru hikicha ni tsuite," *Geinōshi kenkyū* 169 (April 2005): 1–15. The classic discussion of this ritual and its history is Kurabayashi Masatsugu, *Kyōen no kenkyū:saiji sakuin hen* (Ōfū sha, 1980), pp. 268–300.

25. Ōtsuki, "Ki no midokkyō," pp. 29–31.

26. The best book on tea as medicine in both China and Japan is Iwama Machiko, *Cha no iyaku shi* (Kyoto: Shibunkaku, 2009).

27. Ibid., pp. 121–122.

28. Ōtsuki, "Ki no midokkyō," pp. 29–30, contains the text of this fragment from the *Kurōdo shiki.* Ōtsuki's position on this issue in unclear. See Zhang Jian-li, *Sadō to chanoyu* (Kyoto: Tankō sha, 2004), pp. 72–75, for a supporter of leaf tea. Also note Zhang's "Heian jidai kara Kamakura jidai ni okeru seicha," *Geinōshi kenkyū* 155 (2001): 1–19.

29. See Fukuchi, *Heian jidai no cha,* pp. 107–108. The encyclopedia is the *Wamyō ruiju shō.* Also note Iwama, *Cha no iyaku shi,* pp. 126–128.

30. This argument about the druggist's grinder and early tea may be found in Sawamura Shin'ichi, "Chūsei izen no matcha no ryūdo to aji," *Nihon chori kagakkai shi* 44 (March 2011): 40, 42–44. As noted in the text, Itoen performed experiments with the druggist's mortar and the tea grinder and compared the two beverages. That which was ground on the druggist's mortar was bitter and unappetizing and bore little resemblance to modern Japanese green tea in color, texture, or taste.

31. Fukuchi, *Heian jidai no cha,* p. 166. These books of medicine are, of course, the *Honzō wamyō* and *Ishinpō.* See Iwama, *Cha no iyaku shi,* pp. 122–126 and 436–447 for discussion.

32. Iwama, *Cha no iyaku shi,* p. 131.

33. Fukuchi, *Heian jidai no cha,* pp. 179–181.

34. Ibid., p. 194. The original passage may be found in *Dai Nihon kokiroku Shōyūki* Chōwa 5/5/11, pp. 187–188.

35. Ibid., pp. 260–261; *Shin Nihon koten bungaku taikei, 36 Konjaku monogatari shū* (Iwanami shoten, 1994), pp. 396–399. See the translation by Yoshiko Dykstra in *The Konjaku Tales Japanese Section* (II) *from a Medieval Japanese Collection* (Osaka: Kansai Gaidai University, 2001), pp. 288–291.

36. In these diaries, tea bowls are usually mentioned in combination with other unnamed utensils. Then, too, it is unclear why civil aristocrats would have had their ashes interred in a tea bowl or used the bowl as a lid. Was the bowl tied to personal use? Was it related to tea's supposed medicinal properties? It was apparently a Shingon custom.

37. The mention of Tadazane and Yorinaga raises an interesting question. These Fujiwara kinsmen are famous for constructing and living in the beautiful villa at the Byōdōin in Uji. Uji, of course, has been a renowned center of tea production for centuries. Were the Fujiwara raising and processing tea at the Byōdōin? Given what is known of tea in later periods, it is rather unlikely that Uji was a prominent tea production center in the 1100s, but one cannot be certain. Archaeologists are recovering evidence of other garden plants there on a regular basis, so one cannot rule out the possibility that the Fujiwara drank tea produced at this famous estate. The retired emperor GoShirakawa made several trips to Uji, possibly to enjoy tea there.

38. Fukuchi, *Heian jidai no cha*, pp. 333–342. Yukinari's diary is called *Gonki* and Tsuneyori's *Sakeiki*.

39. This according to *Daikyō zōji*, found in ibid., pp. 344–346.

40. *Honchō mudai shi*, cited in ibid., pp. 322–323.

41. As the reader may apprehend, much of this tea was consumed in Buddhist court ceremonies. Nagai Susumu, "Sōron: buke no miyako Kamakura no cha," in *Kikaku ten: Buke no miyako Kamakura no cha* (Yokohama: Kanezawa bunko, 2010), p. 6, lists the rite for the Indian protective deity Mahakala (Daikokuten), the Buddha's birthday ritual, and the ceremony for various enlightened beings called arhats as being among those most frequently noted in the sources.

42. I made this tabulation from Fukuchi, *Heian jidai no cha*, pp. 9–364.

43. From *Ryōunshū*, in ibid., p. 11

44. From *Honchō monzui*, in ibid., p. 197

45. From *Shinsen rōeishū*, in ibid., p. 270.

46. For more on the ties between Buddhism and tea, see *Sanbō ekotoba*, in ibid., p. 162; *Nihon ōjō gokuraku ki*, in ibid., pp. 168–169; *Honchō hokke genki* in ibid., pp. 195–197; and *Daibiroshana jōbutsu kyō-so*, in ibid., pp. 233–234.

47. Ibid., pp. 203–214.

48. Meanwhile, tea was increasing in popularity in Korea. While scholars have no evidence of Japanese emissaries visiting the new Koryŏ dynasty (935–1259) to imbibe tea, well-traveled Song ambassadors did. When they came, they brought their custom of drinking powdered tea with them. Brick tea was also popular as a medicine at the Koryŏ court. During the twelfth century, the Koryŏ court maintained a "tea pavilion" where aristocrats and their visitors enjoyed the beverage. Given the friendly relations between the Kyoto and Koryŏ courts, it would not be surprising to find that they visited each others' capitals and donated gifts of tea to each other. Kim Pa-Mang, "Kōrai Richō no kissa bunka to rekishi," *Sadō taikei 7 Tōyō no cha* (Kyoto: Tankō sha, 2000), pp. 183–224; Kam Sung-hi, *Hanguk cha saenghwol jangsho* (Seoul: Hanguk cha saeng hwal mun hwayon, 1994), pp. 32–40.

49. See *Jōshōji nenchū aiorichō* and *Fusō ryakki*, cited in Fukuchi, *Heian jidai no cha*, pp. 295–296 and 223–230.

50. See *Genkyū shi utaai*, cited in ibid., pp. 364–366.

51. See *Honchō zoku monzui*, cited in ibid., pp. 297–309.

52. See *Honchō monzui* cited in ibid., p. 197. Iwama, *Cha no iyaku shi*, p. 121, uses this citation to bolster her belief that tea's first function was as a medicine. She ties the first

character of the temple's name meaning "medicine" to the existence of the tea field to draw this conclusion.

53. Books and articles exploding the cultural myths surrounding Yōsai are legion. See Kōzu, *Chanoyu no rekishi*, pp. 54–65; Yoneda Mariko, "Chaso Yōsai zō no saikentō," *Geinōshi kenkyū* 177 (April 2007): 1–16. On Yōsai, also see Takahashi Shūei, "Kamakura jidai no mikkyōsho ni miru cha," *Kanezawa bunko kenkyū* 315 (October 2005): 1–9; Nagashima Fukutarō, "Yōsai zenshi to nanto no cha," *Nanto bukkyō* 16 (1965): 41–50; Nakamura Shūya, "Yōsai izen no cha," in Tanihashi Akio, ed., *Sadō gaku taikei 2 Sadō no rekishi* (Kyoto: Tankō sha, 2000), pp. 351–377; Hashimoto, "Heian Kamakura no kissa bunka," pp. 33–37. Also note Andrew Goble, *Confluences of Medicine in Medieval Japan* (Honolulu: University of Hawai'i Press, 2011), pp. 8–10. My interpretation of Yōsai's role in the history of Japan differs substantially from Goble's.

54. Kōzu, *Chanoyu no rekishi*, pp. 54–56.

55. See Yasuda Motohisa, *Nihon no rekishi 7 Insei to Heishi* (Yoshikawa kōbunkan, 1974), pp. 161–163.

56. Ethan Segal, *Coins, Markets, and the State: Economic Growth in Early Medieval Japan* (Cambridge, MA: Harvard University Press, 2011), pp. 23–65; W. Wayne Farris, "Shipbuilding and Nautical Technology in Japanese Maritime History: Origins to 1600," *The Mariner's Mirror* 95 (August 2009): 260–284.

57. Kawazoe Shōji, "Kamakura chūki no taigai kankei to Hakata," *Kyushu shigaku* 88–90 (1988): 132; on Yōsai's time in Imazu, see Kawazoe Shōji, "Yōsai to Imazu Seiganji," *Nihon rekishi* 332 (January 1976): 10–25. Chinese fleet captains were apparently often of assistance to Japanese clergy. Consider the slightly later example of another of these Song fleet captains, Xie Guo-ming (?–1252); Kawazoe, "Kamakura chūki no taigai kankei to Hakata," pp. 143–149. On Xie, see also Goble, *Confluences of Medicine in Medieval Japan*, p. 10. Xie based his trading operations in Hakata and spent his time going back and forth to south China, where he also undoubtedly had a home. Xie, who had married a Kyushu woman, was quite wealthy. He came to know the monk Enni (1202–1280), who was a late contemporary of Yōsai. When Enni reached Hakata en route to Song China, Xie provided economic support for Enni's passage to and stay in China. On his return, Enni wanted to build a new temple to be called Shōtenji, and his friendship with Xie and other Song captains based in Hakata paid off handsomely. Xie donated a large plot of land for the site of the temple, and through his knowledge of Song temple architecture probably paid for Chinese artisans to come to northern Kyushu and work there. He oversaw the transportation of some 530 pieces of lumber from Kiangsu in China to northern Kyushu in several large ships. Then he donated another large parcel of land for the maintenance of Shōtenji. In 1248 when the temple burned, he rushed Enni from Kyoto to Hakata and within one year had had the temple rebuilt. Of course, Xie became the temple's patron (*dan'ochi*), and Enni its first head. Xie was also associated with the shrines at Hakozaki and Munakata. Note *Kamakura ibun*, 10:323 and 359.

58. Kawazoe, "Kamakura chūki no taigai kankei to Hakata," p. 148.

59. Kōzu, *Chanoyu no rekishi*, p. 57. Also on Hakata, see Horimoto Kazushige, "Chanoyu kara mita Hakata," in Tanihashi Akio, ed., *Sadō gaku taikei 2 Sadō no rekishi* (Kyoto: Tankō sha, 2000), pp. 297–327.

60. Another related question is: Did Yōsai learn of powdered green tea during his visits to China (1168–69; 1187–92)? The timing fits, but there is little evidence on this issue. Sawamura Shin'ichi, "Chusei izen no matcha no ryūdo to aji," *Nihon chōri kagakkai shi* 44 (March 2011): 44, argues persuasively that Yōsai never drank powdered tea in Song China. Also see Sawamura's "Rikyū jidai izen no matcha no ryūdo ni kansuru kōsatsu," *Chanoyu bunka kagaku* 17 (February 2010): 30–31.

61. *SZKT, Azuma kagami*, Kenpo 2/2, pp. 709–710 (italics mine).

62. Kōzu, *Chanoyu no rekishi,* pp. 58–59.

63. *SZKT, Azuma kagami,* Kenpo 2/2, pp. 709–710.

64. On this text, see *Yōsai 'Kissa yōjōki' no kenkyū* (Kyoto: Kyūtai shuppan sha, 2014). Also note James Benn's handy translation of the text in *Tea in China,* pp. 145–171. To be sure, the text that has come down to later centuries is composed of two chapters, while that offered to Sanetomo consisted of only one. The first chapter of the modern text discusses the names for tea, its physical effects, and the method for processing tea; the second chapter expounds upon mulberry leaves as a medicinal treatment, telling of the ways to drink those leaves. It seems likely that the original *Drink Tea and Prolong Your Life* may have been composed of only one chapter—the first. See Kōzu, *Chanoyu no rekishi,* p. 59.

65. This summary and all quotations are drawn from volume 1 of the *Kissa yōjōki* as found in Sen Sōshitsu et al., eds., *Sadō koten zenshū* (Kyoto: Tankō sha, 1956), 2:4–14.

66. Sen Sōshitsu, *The Japanese Way of Tea* (Honolulu: University of Hawai'i Press, 1998), p. 69. Sen wonders why Yōsai, the founder of Rinzai Zen Buddhism in Japan, should have preferred Shingon doctrine, but as I showed above, Yōsai was eclectic in his religious beliefs.

67. *Kissa yojōki,* cited in Yoshimura Tōru, "Chūsei no cha: chōsei to chagyō," *Kyoto bunka tanki daigaku kiyō* 3 (January 1985): 111.

68. Ibid., p. 3. It is interesting that Yōsai concluded this passage by describing the plucking of tea leaves in more detail: "When you want to pluck [some tea leaves], allot many workers, as well as much food and firewood for charcoal, and then simply pick some."

69. Hashimoto Motoko, "Chūsei ni okeru cha no seisan ni tsuite," *Cha no bunka* 9 (2010): 70.

70. Kōzu, *Chanoyu no rekishi,* pp. 63–64.

71. Ibid., p. 64.

72. For some examples of tea as a gift, see *KI,* 16:391, 23:253, and 44:98.

73. *KI,* 43:204.

74. *KI,* 5:334.

75. *KI,* 14:128–129.

76. *KI,* 23:27. Eison is reputed to have been the founder of the Buddhist tea ritual (*ōchamori*) held at Saidaiji from 1264. While tea utensils are listed among the possessions of Saidaiji in the report *Saidaiji kōmyō Shingon-e no chōsa hōkokusho* (Nara: Gangōji bunka zai kenkyūjo, 1982), pp. 1–37, the idea that this ceremony developed in response to the victory over the Mongols is probably another myth constructed after the fact. No other contemporary evidence confirms this story. For an alternative view, see Sen, *The Japanese Way of Tea,* pp. 80–81.

77. *KI,* 22:240.

78. *KI,* 4:163.

79. Yoshimura, "Chūsei no cha—chōsei to chagyō," pp. 113–114; *KI,* 11:158–161.

80. Hashimoto Motoko, "Kamakura jidai ni okeru Sōshiki kissa bunka no juyō to tenkai ni tsuite," *Nara shien* 46 (March 2001): 29–30. Hashimoto has updated this essay in "Heian Kamakura no kissa bunka," pp. 37–41. To be sure, the Sōtō Zen master Dōgen wrote his *Eihei shingi* (Precepts for Everlasting Peace) during the mid-thirteenth century, but as Murai Yasuhiko, *Cha no bunka shi* (Iwanami shoten, 1979), pp. 78–80, and others have noted, the most important and detailed of these behavioral guidelines for Zen monks were not compiled until the fourteenth century. For an alternative view, see Sen, *The Japanese Way of Tea,* pp. 77–80.

81. Kōzu, *Chanoyu no rekishi,* pp. 60–62.

82. See Yoshimura Tōru, "Chūsei no cha—chōsei to chagyō," *Kyoto bunka tanki daigaku kiyō* 3 (January 1985): 112.

83. The text of this letter is found in Yamada Tetsuya, "'Shōgetsu shōnin ate Kōben shojō' ni tsuite," *Chanoyu bunkagaku* 3 (March 1996): 67–69.

84. See Nagai Susumu, "Sōron: buke no miyako Kamakura no cha," in *Kikaku ten: buke no miyako Kamakura no cha* (Yokohama: Kanezawa bunko, 2010), p. 7. The text of *Kantō ōgenki* may be found in Shōkai, *Kantō ōgenki*, ed. Hosokawa Ryōichi (Heibon sha Tōyō bunko, 2011).

85. This summarizes the argument of Ishida Masahiko, "'*Kantō ōgenki*' ni iu 'chocha' ni tsuite," *Chatō* 17 (1981): 13–30.

86. See Yoshimura, "Chūsei no cha—chōsei to chagyō," pp. 112–113. Also note *Kamakura ibun* 10:130. On Son'ei and Kōfukuji tea, see Tanaka Minoru, *Chūsei shiryō ronkō* (Yoshikawa kōbunkan, 1994), p. 238.

87. See Yoshimura, "Chūsei no cha—chōsei to chagyō," p. 113; *KI*, 11:8.

88. Yoshimura, "Chūsei no cha—chōsei to chagyō," pp. 114–115; *KI*, 11:9. Also note Yoshimura, p. 114, where Son'ei writes: "At your convenience, when you come to Kamakura this time, please bring some Nara tea for us."

89. I am grateful to Nagai Susumu of the Kanezawa Library and Museum for suggesting this idea to me during a conversation in June 2011.

90. See *KI*, 1: 413.

91. *KI*, 26:333; *Kanezawa bunko komonjo*, 5:37–38.

## *Chapter Two: Tea Becomes a Beverage for a Wider Market, 1300–1600*

1. For the following summary, I have relied on Nagai Susumu, *Kanezawa Sadaaki* (Yoshikawa kōbunkan, 2003), pp. 1–16. For detailed work on the Kanezawa Hōjō, also note Nagai Susumu, *Kanezawa Hōjō shi no kenkyū* (Yagi shoten, 2006); and Fukushima Kaneharu, *Kanezawa Hōjō shi to Shōmyōji* (Yoshikawa kōbunkan, 1997).

2. Nagai, *Kanezawa Sadaaki*, pp. 23–30. On the Kanezawa, also note Goble, *Confluences of Medicine in Medieval Japan*, pp. 17–22.

3. For this discussion of tea in the Kanezawa collection, I have relied upon Fukushima Kaneharu, "Kamakura to tōgoku no cha," in *Kamakura jidai no cha* (Yokohama: Kanagawa kenritsu Kanezawa bunko, 1998), pp. 36–39; Fukushima Kaneharu, "Kamakura kōki no Kamakura Kyoto no kōryū," in *Kamakura jidai no kissa bunka* (Kyoto: Sadō shiryōkan, 2008), pp. 117–129; Hashimoto Motoko, "Kamakura jidai ni okeru Sōshiki kissa bunka no juyō to tenkai ni tsuite," *Nara shien* 46 (2001): 18–35; and most especially Nagai Susumu, "Sōron: buke no miyako Kamakura no cha," in *Buke no miyako Kamakura no cha* (Yokohama: Kanagawa kenritsu Kanezawa bunko, 2010), pp. 5–10. See also Hashimoto Motoko, "Heian Kamakura no kissa bunka," in *Kōza Nihon chanoyu zenshi* (Kyoto: shibunkaku shuppan), pp. 36–51. Please note that many documents are fragmentary and lack an exact date and the names of the correspondents. I have used the utmost care in citing only those documents that come from the relevant years, that is, 1300–1333.

4. *KBK*, vol. 3, no. 1842, p. 44; vol. 3, no. 2179, p. 162. On *tsutsumi*, see Kōzu, *Chanoyu no rekishi*, p. 68. According to Kōzu, these *tsutsumi* may have usually held good leaves of tea that had been separated from the bad. Once the bag(s) arrived, then the tea might have been consumed as leaf tea or ground and imbibed as powdered tea.

The reader should note that the leaf tea (*hacha; cha no ha*) mentioned throughout the Kanezawa documents is not what is known today as "steeped green tea" (*sencha*). The term is not even used in these records. According to Kōzu, *Chanoyu no rekishi*, p. 64, the leaf tea noted here is close to what is known in China as *sancha*, a steamed and roasted tea either ground or placed directly in hot water and imbibed. True steeped tea (*sencha*) as consumers know it today did not become available until the eighteenth century.

5. *KBK*, vol. 2, no. 2014, p. 99.

6. Yoshimura Tōru, "Chūsei no cha—chōsei to chagyō," *Kyoto bunka tanki daigaku kiyō* 3:125 and 128 (January 1985). See *KBK,* vol. 2, nos. 840 and 841, pp. 3–4, and *KBK,* vol. 5, no. 3468, pp. 64–65.

7. See *KI,* 40:134. Yet he had received a small gift of tea earlier in the year, probably from the harvest of the previous year. See *KI,* 40:133. The monk lived in Tōzenji.

8. *KBK,* vol. 2., no. 1516, p. 243.

9. *KBK,* vol. 6., no. 5111, p. 365.

10. *KBK,* vol. 5, no. 3579, p. 98.

11. *KBK,* vol. 3, no. 1892, pp. 59–60.

12. *KBK,* vol. 6., no. 4375, p. 213. In *KBK,* vol. 5, no. 3758, pp. 158–159, an unknown person makes a gift of three *kin* (1,800 grams) of tea from the first picking (*ichibancha*).

13. *KBK,* vol, 4., no. 2642, p. 25; and vol. 2, no. 1142, p. 112.

14. *KBK,* vol. 6, no. 4555, p. 134; and no. 5141, pp. 378–379. Also see *KI,* vol. 35, p. 193, for Sadaaki's comment in 1319 that the color of some tea given to him as a gift was poor. On praise for sweet-smelling tea, see Yoshimura, "Chūsei no cha—chōsei to chagyō," pp. 126–127. *KBK,* vol. 4, no. 2642, p. 25.

15. Note *KI,* 34:84, where a tea patch, including the remainder of a grove, is listed as only .6 acre. Also note Ōhashi Toshio, "Chūsei Kamakura no chaen," *Sadō geppō* 471 (October 1951): 8–10; and Hashimoto Motoko, "Chūsei ni okeru cha no seisan ni tsuite," *Cha no bunka* 9 (2010): 70–79.

16. *KBK,* vol. 2, no. 991, p. 60; a tea field is mentioned in a document dated to 1317. See *KI,* 34: 275.

17. *KBK,* vol. 2, no. 974, p. 54.

18. Nagai, "Sōron: buke no miyako Kamakura no cha," p. 7.

19. *KBK,* vol. 5, no. 3415, p. 49; vol. 5, no. 3390, p. 40.

20. *KBK,* vol. 3, no. 1820, p. 36.

21. *KI,* 28:282, dated to 1303.

22. *KBK,* vol. 6, no. 5090, pp. 354–355.

23. Sawamura Shin'ichi, "Chūsei izen no matcha no ryūdo to aji," *Nihon chōri kagaku kaishi* 44 (2011): 39–45, has done the scientific work on this problem. For a generally concurring opinion, see Nagai, "Sōron: buke no miyako Kamakura no cha," pp. 8–10. On the stone grinder itself, see Miwa Shigeo, *Mono to ningen no bunka shi* 25 *Usu* (Hōsei daigaku shuppan kyoku, 1978), pp. 125–126; 230–292. The earliest reference to the stone grinder in China is 1079; for Korea, the implement is thought to have become available from Song China around 1190. On Korea, see Kumakura Isao, *Chanoyu no rekishi—Sen Rikyū made* (Asahi sensho, 1990), pp. 47–49.

24. *KBK,* vol. 1, no. 127, p. 36. Also note *KBK,* vol. 2, no. 1156, p. 120. For a complaint about tea that was ground too coarsely, see *KBK,* vol. 5, no. 371 8, p. 141.

25. See, for example, a woman's request to borrow the grinder in *KBK,* vol. 4, no. 3182, p. 278: or *KBK,* vol. 5, no. 4152, pp. 298–299. Also note *KBK,* vol. 4, no. 3189, p. 281, for the mention of a stone tea grinder.

26. According to Kōzu, *Chanoyu no rekishi,* pp. 73–74, the first appearance of the whisk in Song literature dates to 1110. Also see Kōzu's discussion of the other less important tea utensils of the Kanezawa in ibid., pp. 68–73. These include bowls, powdered tea containers (*chatō*), and ladles (*saji*). On the whisk, see also Sawamura, "Rikyu jidai izen no matcha," pp. 34–36.

27. *KBK,* vol. 1, no. 164, p. 48.

28. *KBK,* vol. 2, no. 1418, p. 209. Also note *KBK,* vol. 4., no. 2556, p. 293; vol. 5, no. 4159, p. 302.

29. *KBK,* vol. 1, no. 619, p. 206.

30. Nagai Susumu, "Sōron: Buke no miyako Kamakura no cha," in *Buke no miyako Kamakura no cha* (Yokohama: Kanezawa bunko, 2010), pp. 7–8.

31. *KBK*, vol. 4, no. 3207, p. 287.

32. Hashimoto Motoko, "Shimo Kawabe no shō ni okeru kissa bunka," *Kanezawa Hōjō shi Shimōsa no kuni Shimo Kawabe no shō no sōgōteki kenkyū* (Yokohama: Kanagawa kenritsu Kanezawa bunko, 2010), p. 48. One document suggests that the harvest from the fields at Akaiwa could be as much as ten *kin* (6,000 grams). See Yoshimura, "Chūsei no cha—chōsei to chagyō," p. 127. One small mystery is why Shōmyōji would have chosen swampy lands when proper drainage was so important to the health of the shrubs.

33. On Tōzenji, see *KBK*, vol. 3, no. 1902, p. 62; on Eikōji, see *KBK*, vol. 3, no. 2571, pp. 298–299. One record states that Tōzenji sent 3 *kin* (1,800 grams) of its first picking (*ichibancha*) to Shōmyōji. See *KBK*, vol. 5, no. 3758, pp. 158–159.

34. In 1316, "evil bands" (*akutō*) are recorded as burning a tea field located near Saidaiji. See Yoshimura Tōru, "Chūsei no cha—chōsei to chagyō," p. 115.

35. For an example, see Yoshimura Tōru, "Chūsei no cha—chōsei to chagyō," p. 128. *KBK*, vol. 5, no. 3546, p. 89.

36. *KBK*, vol. 3, no. 2379, p. 240. In this regard, note the tea implements owned by two nearby temples, Tōfukuji in Kyoto and Kongōji in Kawachi Province, seen in *KI*, 33:347 (1316) and *KI*, 36:331 (1323).

37. *KBK*, vol. 1, no. 118, p. 34.

38. Ibid., no. 619, p. 206; *KI*, 30:150, dated to 1308.

39. *KBK*, vol. 1, no. 212, p. 65.

40. Ibid., no. 192, p. 57.

41. Ibid., no. 560, p. 188; *KI*, 33:126, dated to 1315.

42. For one such occasion, see Yoshimura Tōru, "Chūsei no cha—chōsei to chagyō," pp. 116 and 119. See *KBK*, vol. 1, no. 560, p. 188; *KBK*, vol. 1, no. 125, p. 36. For the record, in the first case the warrior wrote that he would make up the difference with other "various kinds" of tea.

43. For one example dating to 1321, see *KI*, vol. 36, p. 81. For an example of Sadaaki sending tea from Kyoto to Shōmyōji, see *KI*, vol. 38, p. 46.

44. See *KI*, vol. 38, p. 147, for use of this term.

45. *KBK*, vol. 1, no. 417, pp. 137–138.

46. *KBK*, vol. 1, no. 206, pp. 61–62.

47. Fukushima, "Kamakura to tōgoku no cha," pp. 38–39.

48. *KI*, vol. 41, p. 4.

49. *KBK*, vol. 6, no. 4656, p. 18.

50. *KBK*, vol. 2, no. 1256, p. 152.

51. *KBK*, vol. 5, n. 3750, p. 156.

52. *KBK*, vol. 1, no. 411, pp. 134–135; *KBK*, vol. 1, no. 401, pp. 129–130.

53. *KI*, vol. 31, p. 240.

54. *KBK*, vol. 1, no. 289, p. 88.

55. *KBK*, vol. 1, no. 170, pp. 50–51. For other ceremonial uses of tea, note Hashimoto, "Kamakura jidai ni okeru Sōshiki kissa bunka no juyō to tenkai ni tsuite," pp. 22–24.

56. On Shōmyōji and tea, see also Takahashi Shūei, "Kanezawa bunko shiryō ni miru Kamakura jidai no cha," in Ōsumi Kazuo, ed., *Chūsei bukkyō to sono shūhen* (Yoshikawa kōbunkan, 2000), pp. 150–163; Nagai Susumu, "Chūsei tōgoku no ritsuin no cha," *Kamakura* 107 (2009) 27–41.

57. *KI*, 34:274.

58. *KBK*, vol. 1, no. 329, p. 99; *KI*, 43:137.

59. *KBK*, vol. 1, no. 285, p. 87.

60. For other tea gatherings, note *KBK*, vol. 3, no. 1755, p. 16.

61. *Isei teikin ōrai* cited in Yoshimura, "Chūsei no cha—chōsei to chagyō," pp. 150–151. *Yūgaku ōrai*, a source dated to about the same time period, adds Mount Hiei (Enryakuji) and Ishiyamadera in Ōmi and Oyamadera in Ise.

62. A point of interest: one entry for Uji indicates that on 5/4/1374 at least seven *kin* (4,200 grams) of tea arrived as a present. This is the earliest known mention of Uji tea. See *Shinshū ki*, ibid., p. 150. (*Shinshū ki* is the diary of *gagaku* performer named Toyohara Akinobu, a court aristocrat.)

63. *Gion sha shamu shikkō Hōjūin Kenshin shojō*, cited in Yoshimura Atsuru, "Chūsei no cha—chōsei to chagyō," p. 140.

64. *KBK*, vol. 4, no. 2995, p. 212. In Great Britain, thefts of tea were also a sign of the value of the commodity as early as fifty years after its introduction. See Markman Ellis, Richard Coulton, and Matthew Mauger, *Empire of Tea: The Asian Leaf that Conquered the World*, pp. 115, 120–122, and 131–132.

65. *KBK*, vol. 3, no. 2571, pp. 298–299. On tea in Zen life, also see Tsutsui Kōichi, "Dōjō kara shichū no sankyo e," *Rekishi kōron* 3 (September 1977): 80–88.

66. For these various documents, see Yoshimura Tōru, "Chūsei no cha—chōsei to chagyō," pp. 134–158, passim. It should be noted that one field in Murasakino (Kyoto, 1391) lists "seasonal tea" (*setsucha*) at a value of 200 coins (p. 156).

67. See *Kodai chūsei toshi seikatsu shi (bukka) deeta beesu*. http://www.rekihaku.ac.jp/up-cgi/searchrd.pl (accessed June 15, 2011).

68. *KBK*, vol. 7, no. 5589, p. 279.

69. Ibid., no. 5483, pp. 207–208.

70. *KBK*, vol. 6, no. 4735, p. 313.

71. *KBK*, vol. 7, no. 5536, p. 244. Shōmyōji also tried to buy tea during the upheavals of the late 1300s, but a widespread famine apparently made it nearly impossible to trade in tea during one unspecified year. *KBK*, vol. 3, no. 2171, p. 159.

72. *Gion sha shake kiroku*, cited in Yoshimura Atsuru, "Chūsei no cha—chōsei to chagyō," pp. 138–139. Also note the two letters from Gion officials printed on the same pages.

73. *Gion sha shake kiroku*, cited in ibid., p. 141. These two types of shrine workers also served the beverage to passersby. See Nyūnoya Tetsukazu, "Ippuku issen cha shōkō," *Ritsumeikan bungaku* 509 (December 1988): 207–212.

74. See the letter sent by the head of the shrine cited in Yoshimura Tōru, "Chūsei no cha—chōsei to chagyō," p. 141.

75. *Suda Hachiman gūsha rensho mōshijō an*, cited in ibid., pp. 142–143.

76. *Gion sha shake kiroku*, cited in ibid., p. 135.

77. Ibid., p. 138.

78. Ibid. The reading *kuronicha* is speculative.

79. Zhang Jian li, *Sadō to chanoyu*, pp. 184–187.

80. One possibility for the *kuronicha* is that it was processed as follows. During the end of the picking season, in June and July, tea gatherers took both the tea leaves and the stems. These were then boiled and placed in a covered container for a week. As oxidation began, the container was opened and the contents were allowed to dry. This eventually produced a black tea that was whisked until the bowl of tea was filled with bubbles, and salt or other condiments were added. It is notable that such a concoction would have been nourishing for a populace suffering from malnutrition. The preceding description fits well with the units of measurement used, that is, first *ren* (for long items) and then *koku* (for more solid foods). On this and other types of tea, see Nakamura Yōichirō, *Bancha to Nihonjin*, pp. 41–91.

81. The steps followed for Nakahara's processing of tea are never delineated, but assuming that he was consuming powdered green tea, then the process would have probably been the same as that outlined by Yōsai in *Drink Tea and Prolong Your Life*. In other words, the plucked leaves would have been steamed, dried, ground, and then mixed with hot water for a drink. For more on Nakahara, see Lori Meeks, *Hokkeji and the Reemergence of*

*Female Monastic Orders in Premodern Japan* (Honolulu: University of Hawai'i Press, 2010), pp. 247–248.

82. *Moromori ki,* cited in Yoshimura Tōru, "Chūsei no cha—chōsei to chagyō," p. 131.

83. Ibid.

84. Ibid., p. 136.

85. Ibid., p. 145.

86. Ibid., p. 147.

87. See, for example, Nezu Munenobu, "*Daikan shingi* to gozan bungaku ni okeru kissa no shokeitai," *Nagano kenritsu rekishikan kenkyū kiyō* 9 (March 2003): 30–45. The information on *yotsugashira charei* comes from Kōzu, *Chanoyu no rekishi,* pp. 74–75.

88. On this general point, see Gorai Shigeru, *Shomin shingyō no shosō* (Kadokawa shoten, 1995), pp. 154–165.

89. Tsuji Nobuo, "Kazari to furo to cha," *Kazari to Nihon bunka* (Kadokawa shoten, 1998), pp. 146–150. Some scholars think that Zen prelates may also have been the first to introduce the Chinese custom of drinking steeped tea to Japan. If so, the tea would have likely been the stir-roasted variety (*kamairicha*), explained below. On this minority view, see Kōzu, *Chanoyu no rekishi,* pp. 242–243.

90. This paragraph owes much to the work of Kumahara Masao, *Kamakura no cha* (Kawahara shoten, 1948), pp. 97–159.

91. These three poems come from ibid., pp. 99, 112, and 149, from three collections dating from the late thirteenth and fourteenth centuries. Respectively, they are the *Tōkishū, Kanrinshū,* and *Ungakuonkin.*

92. See Zhang, *Sadō to chanoyu,* pp. 131–134; Hashimoto Motoko, "Muromachi jidai nōson ni okeru Sōshiki kissa bunka no juyō ni tsuite," pp. 103–106 (2002).

93. All these amounts may be found in Yoshimura Tōru, "Chūsei no cha—chōsei to chagyō," pp. 159 (*Kiyomizudera monjo*), 161–162 (*Kyōgen kyōki*), 164 (*Yamashina ke raiki*), 174–176 (*Kanmon gyoki; Katsuragawa myōōin shiryō; Hōkyōji monjo; Sūzenji monjo,* 184 (*Yamashina ke raiki*), 186–187 (*Daijōin jishazōjiki*), and 199 (*Tōji monjo*). Hashimoto has noted some of the same examples in "Muromachi jidai nōson ni okeru Sōshiki kissa bunka no juyō ni tsuite," pp. 103–106.

94. Zhang Jian-li, "Muromachi jidai ni okeru chaen to seicha," *Ritsumeikan bungaku* 574: 808–816 (March 2002); Zhang, *Sadō to chanoyu* (Kyoto: Tankō sha, 2004), pp. 122–130.

95. Zhang, *Sadō to chanoyu,* pp. 126–127.

96. Yoshimura Tōru, "Chūsei no cha—chōsei to chagyō," p. 192 (*Daijōin jisha zōjiki*).

97. About sixty-three excavations dating from the fourteenth through the seventeenth centuries have yielded utensils used in tea consumption. See Niigaki Tsutomu, "Okinawa ni okeru chanoyu no fukyū to sono eikyō," *Nantō kōko* 26 (2007): 209–220.

98. For these trends, see Farris, *Japan's Medieval Population,* pp. 128–163; 221–261.

99. Yamaguchi Satoshi, "Identeki tayōsei kara mita Nihon rokucha no kigen ni tsuite," *Cha no bunka* 5 (2004): 104–110.

100. Hashimoto Motoko, "Chūsei chaen ni tsuite," *Nenpō chūsei shi kenkyū* 31 (2006): 159–182.

101. Itō Toshikazu, "Chūsei kōki ni okeru Tōdaiji ryō Yamato no kuni Kawakami no shō no yakibata keiei to cha saibai," *Nihon joshi daigaku bungaku bu kiyō* 48 (1999): 29–47; *Yamanashi ken shi minzoku chōsa hōkokusho 2 Fukushi no minzoku* (Kōfu: Yamanashi ken, 1995), pp. 157–168.

102. Hashimoto Motoko, "Chūsei chaen ni tsuite," pp. 166–173.

103. Yoshimura, "Chūsei no cha—chōsei to chagyō," p. 178 (*Kyōgaku shiyōshō*). On this topic, also see Hashimoto Motoko, "Chūsei ni okeru cha no seisan to ryūtsū," in Nishimura Keiko, ed., *Nihon kinsei kokka no shosō,* pp. 184–188; and Hashimoto, "Muromachi jidai nōson ni okeru Sōshiki kissa bunka no juyō ni tsuite," *Nenpō chūsei shi kenkyū* 27 (2002): 108–109.

104. Yoshimura, "Chūsei no cha—chōsei to chagyō," p. 187 (*Harutomi sukune no ki*).

105. Ibid., pp. 188–189 (*GoHōkōin zatsuji yōroku; Yamashina ke raiki*). An interesting document from 1413 shows that a tea field in Ōmi Province was located in an inlet near Lake Biwa.

106. On these religious sites and tea processing at Imabori and Suganoura, see Hashimoto, "Muromachi jidai nōson ni okeru Sōshiki kissa bunka no juyō ni tsuite," pp. 108–109.

107. Yoshimura, "Chūsei no cha—chōsei to chagyō," pp. 164–207.

108. Zhang, *Sadō to chanoyu*, pp. 142–143.

109. Yoshimura, "Chūsei no cha—chōsei to chagyō," p. 207 (*Morimitsu kōki*).

110. Futaki Ken'ichi, *Chūsei buke shakai no sahō* (Yoshikawa kōbunkan, 1999), pp. 142–149.

111. Yoshimura Tōru, "Chūsei no cha—chōsei to chagyō," p. 179, lists tea provided to twenty-four local samurai (probably residing in Kii Province) in the mid-fifteenth century, probably for *bakufu* ceremonies (*Katsuhara monjo*).

112. Nakano Yasuhide, *Shūgi, kissho, jufu* (Yoshikawa kōbunkan, 1988), pp. 24–74.

113. Kim Pa Mang, "Kōrai Richō no kissa bunka to rekishi," in Takahashi Tadahiko, ed., *Sadō gaku taikei 7 Tōyō no cha* (Kyoto: Tankō sha, 2000), pp. 209–224.

114. Sŏng Hui-gyŏng, *Nongsangdang Ilbon hangnok*, annotated by Murai Shōsuke (Iwanami shoten, 1987), p. 67. The text says simply "steeped tea" (*sencha*), but I concur with Kōzu, *Chanoyu no rekishi*, p. 243, in interpreting the term as stir-roasted tea.

115. To mention a few more examples, Hiyoshi Shrine made a regular spiritual offering of tea made from leaves plucked from the shrine's own bushes. See Hasegawa Yoshikazu, "Hiyoshi sannō matsuri no gokū kennō," *Kikan kokoku to bunka* 87 (June 1999): 102–103. Yakushiji served meals in Nara at which tea was included. See Yamagishi Tsuneto, "Hōe no hensen to 'ba' no yakuwari," *Girei ni miru Nihon bukkyō* (Kyoto: Hōzōkan, 2001), pp. 199–241. The diaries of several nobles record numerous tea rites in which clerics officiated for the court during the fifteenth century. For more specific details, see Nagata Naoki, "Kokiroku ni miru Muromachi jidai no charei in tsuite," *Geinōshi kenkyū* 134 (May 1996): 17–37. For the record, the diaries include *Kanmon gyoki* of Fushiminomiya Sadafusa, the *Kyōgen nikki* of Yamashina Akikoto, and the *Kennaiki* of Marinokōji Tokifusa—all of the early and mid-fifteenth century. Also note Chiba Noritaka, "Honganji to chanoyu," in *Rekishi to bukkyō no ronshū* (Kyoto: Jishōsha, 2000), pp. 15–28.

116. Yoshimura, "Chūsei no cha—chōsei to chagyō," pp. 158–206.

117. See Hashimoto, "Muromachi jidai nōson ni okeru Sōshiki kissa bunka no juyō ni tsuite," pp. 103–110.

118. Yoshimura, "Chūsei no cha—chōsei to chagyō," pp. 161–201.

119. Ibid., p. 161 (*Kyōgen kyōki*).

120. Ibid., p. 187 (*Daijōin zōjiki*).

121. Ibid., p. 186 (*Yamashina ke raiki*). The value of a *hiki* is unclear here. Otowa hut likely was a small temple in an estate serving as the shipping point for the tea tax. On the Yamashina and tea, see Inagaki Hiroaki, "Chūsei kuge no cha," in Tanihashi Akio, ed., *Sadō no rekishi: Sadōgaku taikei* (Kyoto: Tankō sha, 1999), pp. 53–90.

122. See *Kodai chūsei toshi seikatsu shi (bukka) deetabeesu*. http://www.rekihaku.ac.jp/up-cgi/searchrd.pl (accessed June 15, 2011).

123. Yoshimura, "Chūsei no cha—chōsei to chagyō," pp. 162–210.

124. Ibid., p. 180 (*Yonera monjo*).

125. Ibid., p. 182 (*Daijōin jisha zōjiki*).

126. Ibid., p. 196 (*Daijōin jisha zōjiki*).

127. Ibid., pp. 203–204 (*Eishō nenchūki*).

128. Hashimoto Motoko, "Muromachi jidai nōson ni okeru Sōshiki kissa bunka no juyō ni tsuite," p. 110.

129. Articles on medieval tea shops are numerous. See Hashimoto Motoko, "Chūsei no chaya ni tsuite," *Rakuhoku shigaku* 11 (2009): 1–19; Koyama Kyōko, "Chūsei Kyoto ni okeru shomin no chaya," *Rakuhoku shigaku* 6 (2004): 102–117; Tanihashi Akio, "Kaisho no cha to ippuku issen no cha," *Tankō* (May 1993), pp. 90–99; Yoshimura Tōru, "'Ippuku issen' to monzen no chaya," *Chūsei chiiki shakai no rekishi zō* (Aun sha, 1997), pp. 273–290; Nishimura Masaru, *Seichi no sōzōryoku* (Hōzōkan, 1998); Iezuka Tomoko, "Chūsei chaya kō," *Ritsumeikan bungaku* 605 (March 2008): 44–58; Nyūnoya Tetsukazu, "Ippuku issen cha shōkō," *Ritsumeikan bungaku* 509 (December 1988): 207–212; Fujiwara Shigeo, "Kaya shōkō," *Emaki ni chūsei o yomu* (Yoshikawa kōbunkan, 1995), pp. 101–145; Sakurai Eiji, "Ichi ni toshi o miru," *Asahi hyakka Nihon no rekishi bessatsu 7 Rekishi o yominaosu: Chūsei no tate to toshi* (Asahi shinbun sha, 1994), pp. 60–69; Takahashi Yasuo, *Rakuchū rakugai* (Heibonsha, 1988); Kawashima Masao, "Chaten kō," *Tankō* (October 1975), 33–37; Takahashi Yasuo, "Chaya: Machishū bunka no ichidanmen," *Nihon toshi shi nyūmon 3 Hito* (Tokyo daigaku shuppan kai, 1990), pp. 238–239; Imatani Akira, *Kyoto 1547 nen* (Heibon sha, 1988); Nanbada Tetsu "Kaiga ni miru shomin no incha fūzoku—shaji sankei manjara zu o chūshin ni," *Sadō shukin 2 Chanoyu no seiritsu* (Shōgakkan, 1984), pp. 24–33.

130. On these "hospitality stations," see Miyazaki Enjun, *Chūsei bukkyō to shomin seikatsu* (Kyoto: Nagata bunshō dō, 1987), pp. 157–171; Aida Nirō, *Chūsei no sekisho* (Yoshikawa kōbunkan, 1943), pp. 364–400.

131. Hashimoto, "Chūsei chaya ni tsuite," pp. 2–4.

132. This document and the incident are usually cited as the first evidence of independent tea shops. The document may be found in several places, including Koyama Kyōko, "Chūsei Kyoto ni okeru shomin no chaya," *Rakuhoku shigaku* 6 (2006): 104, Nyūnoya, "Ippuku issen cha shō," pp. 217–219, and Imatani, *Kyoto 1547 nen*, p. 182. The record is from the *Tōji hyakugō monjo-ke.*

133. Kōzu, *Chanoyu no rekishi*, pp. 100–101.

134. Sin Suk-ju, writing in *Haedong jegukgi* as cited in Kōzu Asao, *Chanoyu no rekishi*, p. 94.

135. In addition to the previously noted *Jizō bosatsu reigenki-e*, the most famous examples include the *Shichijū ichiban shokunin utaawase, Uesugi bon Rakuchū rakugai zu byōbu*, the *Rokudō Chinnōji sankei manjara*, the *Buzen no kuni Usa Hachimangū massha wakan ukidono kedai ichi no zu*, and the *Gion Ōmandokoro ezu*. Also note Kanō Hideyori's *Takao kan pūzu byōbu* on the cover of Kōzu's *Chanoyu no rekishi* and discussed briefly on p. 96. For a complete set of these and other pictorial sources regarding tea, see *Chanoyu kaiga shiryō shūsei* (Heibonsha, 1992). For a discussion of the *Rokudō Chinnōji sankei manjara*, see Nishiyama Masaru, *Seichi no sōzōryoku*, pp. 59–61.

136. On the temporary hut in Japanese history, see Fujiwara Shigeo, "Kaya shōkō," pp. 101–145.

137. Kōzu, *Chanoyu no rekishi*, p. 96.

138. Much of the discussion in this paragraph follows Hashimoto, "Chūsei no chaya ni tsuite," pp. 5–13.

139. See Koyama, "Chūsei Kyoto ni okeru shomin no chaya," p. 110, and Kumakura Isao, *Chanoyu no rekishi—Sen Rikyū made* (Asahi sensho, 1990), pp. 86–90. Also note Nyūnoya, "Ippuku issen cha shō," 212–217. For more on low-grade steeped tea, see Nakamura Yōichirō, *Bancha to Nihonjin*. Nakamura deals with tea picking and processing on pp. 143–180. Also see his *Cha no minzokugaku* (Meicho shuppan, 1992), pp. 29–31, where the author implies that the frothy tea served to commoners at these tea shops might have contained grains or other food items and were meant to fill hungry bellies. Also in the same volume, Nakamura deals with ethnographic sources of value on the plucking of tea (pp. 83–126) and the processing of steeped tea of various grades, pp. 191–254 (*Cha no minzokugaku*).

140. Kōzu, *Chanoyu no rekishi*, pp. 98–99. These comedic presentations are called *kyōgen* in Japanese. Also see Kōzu's discussion of the skit "The Present Gods" (*Ima jinmei*), in

which an elderly couple go to Uji, where they try to sell whisked steeped tea that had been dried in the sun and not in a roaster. They fail because they charge the same price as if the tea were prepared like regular powdered tea; *Chanoyu no rekishi*, pp. 99–100. See also Patricia Graham, *Tea of the Sages: The Art of Sencha* (Honolulu: University of Hawai'i Press, 1998), p. 16. The reader is again cautioned that true steeped tea (*sencha*) as it is known today did not come into existence in Japan until the mid-1700s. On *kyōgen* featuring Uji tea, see Moriya Atsushi and Nakamura Yasuo, "Uji sarugaku no katsudō," in *Uji shi shi: 2 Chūsei no rekishi to keikan*, pp. 710–717. As noted in the text, the appearance of tea and tea shops in such popular literature surely signifies the complete naturalization of the beverage to Japanese society.

141. Koyama, "Chūsei Kyoto ni okeru shomin no chaya," pp. 110–112.

142. Kōzu Asao, *Chanoyu no rekishi*, pp. 94–95. The skit is "Satsuma no kami," in which a samurai tries to bilk the tea shop owner by only paying one coin for two bowls. One coin may also have been enough to buy one *gō* of inferior grade rice (85 cc).

143. Ibid., pp. 96–98.

144. Takahashi Yasuo, "Chaya—machishū bunka no ichidanmen," p. 238.

145. Imatani, *Kyoto 1547 nen*, pp. 183–186; Iezuka, "Chūsei chaya kō," pp. 53–55.

146. Yoshimura, "Chūsei no cha—chōsei to chagyō," pp. 191–192 (*Kyōō Gokokuji monjo*). The rent was 80 coins in 1473.

147. Hashimoto, "Muromachi jidai nōson ni okeru Sōshiki kissa bunka no juyō ni tsuite," pp. 110–116.

148. Ibid., 106–107. Of course, songs supply crucial evidence about the life of tea workers in the modern era as well. See Nakamura Yōichirō, *Cha no minzokugaku* (Meicho shuppan, 1992), pp. 307–343.

149. Hashimoto, "Chūsei chaen ni tsuite," p. 174.

150. Hashimoto, "Muromachi jidai nōson ni okeru Sōshiki kissa bunka no juyō ni tsuite," pp. 108–109, on tea grinders among peasants in village corporate communities (*sō*).

151. See the document date to 1450 in Ikeda Yoshinobu, ed., *Chūsei nōmin no seikatsu* (Kyoto: Kōraku dō, 1992), p. 7.

152. Ishibashi Kentarō, "Tōcha to monkō," *Kusado sengen* 235 (December 1996): 5–7.

153. Itō Tadamasa, "Imabori jūzenshi sha no dōan to miyaza," in Nakamura Ken, ed., *Yōkaichi shishi* 2 *Chūsei* (Yōkaichi: Yōkaichi shiyakusho, 1983), pp. 546–592.

154. Articles on this topic are legion. A good starting place is Hashimoto Motoko, "Chūsei kōki sōsai girei ni okeru kissa bunka ni tsuite," *Nara shien* 55 (2010): 1–16, who focuses on not only the ruling Ashikaga house but also funeral rites for commoners carried out at small village shrines and temples. Yoshimura Tōru has written voluminously on this topic for all rites of passage in "Nitchū chazoku no hikaku shakai shi kenkyū," in *Sadō bunka gakujutsu josei kenkyū* (Santoku an, 2001), pp. 7–14; "Nitchū chazoku no hikaku shakai shi kenkyū," in *Sadō bunka gakujutsu josei kenkyū* (Santoku an, 2002), pp. 1–8; "San'iku sōsō girei ni miru Nitchū chazoku no hikaku kenkyū," *Hikaku Nihon bunka kenkyū* 8 (2004): 35–61; and "Chatō ni miru mō hitotsu no cha bunka kenkyū," and "Sōgōteki na chabunka shi kenkyū o motomete," *Kyoto bunka tanki daigaku kiyō* 31/32 (1999): 3–12. Yoshimura also notes tea for use in the treatment of smallpox. Also see Tamamuro Taijō, "Sōshiki to butsuji," in Takeda Chōshū, ed., *Sōsō bosei kenkyū shūsei* 3 *Senzo kuyō* (Meicho shuppan, 1979), pp. 66–92, who deals with last rites as performed in various sects. Finally, see Nakamura Yōichirō, *Cha no minzokugaku* (Meicho shuppan, 1992), pp. 57–82; 127–190.

155. Evidence suggests that this was mostly an elite pastime, but see Tsuji Nobuo, "Kazari to furo to cha," *Kazari no Nihon bunka* (Kadokawa shoten, 1998), pp. 162–163; and Takemoto Chizu, "Sadō shi ni miru 'rinkan chanoyu' no ichizuke," in Futaki Ken'ichi, ed., *Sengoku shokuhō ki no shakai to girei* (Yoshikawa kōbunkan, 2006), pp. 417–435.

156. Yoshimura, "Chūsei no cha—chōsei to chagyō," p. 161 (*Kyōgen kyōki*).

157. Ibid., pp. 167–173 (*Kyōō Gokokuji monjo*).
158. Ibid., p. 176 (*Tansan jinja monjo*).
159. Ibid., pp. 191–192.
160. William McNeill, "The Historical Significance of the Way of Tea," in Paul Varley and Kumakura Isao, eds., *Tea in Japan* (Honolulu: University of Hawai'i Press, 1989), pp. 259–261.
161. Penelope Francks, "Rural Industry, Growth Linkages, and Economic Development in Nineteenth-Century Japan," p. 43. Francks' "virtuous circle" and the linkages derived from it are concepts derived from the experience of Third World countries in the Green Revolution. As noted in my conclusion, these ideas dovetail nicely with the work of the Europeanist Jan de Vries.
162. Ōishi, *Chagyō hattatsu shi*, pp. 232–235. Also see Kōzu, *Chanoyu no rekishi*, pp. 243–246.
163. On the origins of stir-roasted tea and the immigrant Ming Chinese, see Ōishi Sadao, *Nihon chagyō hattatsu shi* (Nōbun kyō, 2004), pp. 232–233.
164. Kōzu, *Chanoyu no rekishi*, p. 245.
165. See Yoshimura, "Chūsei no cha—chōsei to chagyō," p. 185 (*Sekiso ōrai*). On the Uji tea industry, also see Yoshimura Tōru, *Uji bunko* 4 *Uji cha no bunka shi* (Uji: Uji shi kyōiku iinkai, 1993), pp. 29–43; Kumakura Isao and Wakita Haruko, "Chagyō to shōhin ryūtsū no hatten," *Uji shi shi* 2 *Chūsei no rekishi to keikan* (Uji: Uji shiyakusho, 1974), pp. 431–460. The exposition in Yoshimura and Kumakura/Wakita differs somewhat from that of Hashimoto in her works.
166. The information in this paragraph comes largely from Hashimoto Motoko, "Nihon chūsei ni okeru Uji cha no rekishi," *Rokucha to kenkō* (Kyoto: Kyoto fu chagyō kai gisho, 2008), pp. 65–69. The information about Uji's ranking in 1383 also comes from the same article.
167. The details of this dispute may be found in Hashimoto, "Chūsei ni okeru cha no seisan to ryūtsū," in Nishimura Keiko, *Nihon kinsei kokka no shosō* (Tokyo dō, 1999), p. 187.
168. This paragraph condenses a complex story covering well over a century. For a detailed account, see Kumakura Isao and Wakita Haruko, "Chagyō to shōhin ryūtsū no hatten," *Uji shi shi* 2 *Chūsei no rekishi to keikan* (Uji: Uji shiyakusho, 1974), pp. 431–460; and Kumakura Isao and Kanbayashi Shutarō, "Chagyō no hatten to chashi," *Uji shi shi* 2 *Chūsei no rekishi to keikan* (Uji: Uji shiyakusho, 1974), pp. 626–717.
169. Michael Cooper, comp. and annot., *They Came to Japan* (Berkeley: University of California Press, 1965), p. 198. It should be noted that incremental improvements were made to the stone grinder around the same time, making for an even finer and sweeter tea. See Sawamura, "Chūsei izen no matcha no ryūdo to aji," pp. 39–45.
170. Hashimoto Motoko, "Nihon chūsei ni okeru Uji cha no rekishi," *Rokucha to kenkō* (Kyoto: Kyoto fu chagyō kai gisho, 2008), pp. 68–71. Also see Sawamura Shin'ichi, "Chūsei izen no matcha no ryūdo to aji," *Nihon chōri kagaku kaishi* 44 (2011): 39–45.
171. Sawamura also notes the refinement of striations in stone grinders by the late 1500s, which presumably produced a tastier powdered tea. The remains of a sixteenth-century stone grinder have been retrieved from the Asakura warrior family's castle at Ichijōdani, suggesting a possible military use for pulverizing gunpowder. See Sawamura, "Chusei izen no matcha," pp. 41–44; Sawamura, "Rikyū jidai izen no matcha," pp. 30–31.

## *Chapter Three: Tea Triumphs during the Edo Period, 1600–1868*

1. Tsuruga shi shi hensan iinkai, *Tsuruga shi shi: Tsūshi hen* (Tsuruga: Tsuruga shiyakusho, 1985), 1:468.
2. A *hon* is a unit of measurement that varied according to the productivity of the land. Usually it netted from twelve to thirteen *kan* to fourteen to fifteen *kan*. This includes the bag that was about .5 to one *kan*. One *kan* was equal to 3.75 kg.

3. *Tsuruga shi shi: Tsūshi hen,* 1:471–476.

4. Ibid., p. 469.

5. Ibid., pp. 492–495.

6. Ihara Saikaku, *The Japanese Family Storehouse,* trans. G. W. Sargent (Cambridge: Cambridge University Press, 1959), p. 93. For the Japanese, see *Nihon no koten* 52 *Nihon eitaigura* (Shōgakkan, 1983), pp. 113–114.

7. *Nihon eitaigura,* pp. 114–115.

8. Obama shi shi hensan iinkai, ed., *Obama shi shi: Tsūshi hen* (Obama: Obama shiyakusho, 1992), 1:829–830.

9. Ōishi, *Chagyō hattatsu shi,* p. 279, speculates that the tea was *bancha* or some other simple "steeped something."

10. *Tsuruga shi shi: Tsūshi hen,* 1:470.

11. Ibid.

12. Ibid., p. 279.

13. Ibid., p. 280.

14. Ibid., pp. 280–281.

15. Ibid., p. 282.

16. Ibid., p. 283. This manner of processing was a combination of methods brought in from different regions: steaming, adding the remaining boiling water from the pot, stir-roasting in a cook pot, loosening the bunched leaves by hand, and drying in the shade. The method for drying in the shade, where the cheap steeped tea (*bancha*) there was steamed, rolled on a mat, and then dried, shows influence from Mino. The particular method of rolling the tea leaves was unique to Etchū and other parts of the north. Peasants in the Tohoku were creating new brands of tea, revealing their ingenuity.

17. Were some Tohoku domains practicing mercantilist policies? On these policies in Tosa, see the work of Luke Roberts, *Mercantilism in a Japanese Domain: The Merchant Origins of Economic Nationalism in Eighteenth-Century Tosa* (Cambridge: Cambridge University Press, 1998).

18. Ibid., p. 283.

19. Another agricultural treatise about the north country is Muramatsu Hyōzaemon's *Muramatsu Family Lessons* (*Muramatsu kakun*), which summed up several decades of farming experience on a large piece of land with twenty servants and over ten head of cattle in Noto Province. For details, see ibid., p. 281.

20. The exact wording of the text is as follows: "Take the seeds of tea during the tenth month and plant them right away. But, since this is a time when there is no free time, bury them in the ground for storage. Then during the first or second month of the next year plant the seeds." Later "Ten persons' labor is needed for stir-roasted tea (*chaaburi*). Even though one includes the gathering of firewood and other tasks, we do not note work done during the off-season [of farming]. But in addition, even though the labor used in tea plucking is great, as most can be offset by cash taken in [from selling the tea] to hire daily laborers, it is not included in our calculation." See *Nihon nōsho zenshū* 10 *Seiryōki* (Nōsangyoson bunka kyōkai), pp. 20, 31, 41, 83–84, and 118. Interestingly enough, João Rodrigues noted around 1600 that the tea bush could be grown from transplanted branches.

21. *Hyakushō denki,* vol. 1, annotated by Furushima Toshio (Iwanami shoten, 2001), pp. 96–97. Dutch visitors to Japan noted that small tea plots were situated on the boundaries of rice paddies. See Engelbert Kaempfer (1651–1719), a German physician with a position in the Dutch East India Company; *Kaempfer's Japan,* ed., trans., and annot. Beatrice M. Bodart-Bailey (Honolulu: University of Hawai'i Press, 1999), pp. 65 and 293. Also note Carl Peter Thunberg (1743–1828), a Swedish botanist who enrolled as a physician in the Dutch East India Company, arriving in Nagasaki in 1775; *Japan Extolled and Decried,* annotated and introduced by Timon Screech (New York: Routledge, 2005), p. 213.

22. Ōishi, *Chagyō hattatsu shi*, pp. 264–265. Also note *Local Rumors* (*Chihō kikigaki*), written by Ōhata Saizō from Kii Province during the early 1700s, in which the author advocates planting tea in mountain dry fields, uncultivated land, the edges of river valleys, and empty land at the foot of mountains. The land referred to in this passage included many "mountain tea patches" (*yamacha*) and suggests the profitability of these lands for local farmers.

23. Hitomi Hitsudai, *Honchō shokkan*, annotated by Shimada Isao (Heibonsha, 1977), pp. 116–118. For planting, the author advises "In general, you plant one of these every one foot (*shaku*) five or six inches (*sun*) in square area; the distance between each planting should be three feet." Rodrigues called the best grade of leaves for powdered tea "falcon's claws" because when the leaves were new and heated uniformly in a way to prevent burning, the leaves all rolled up like the claws of a falcon (Ōishi, *Chagyō hattatsu shi*, p. 239). Philipp Franz von Siebold, *Manners and Customs of the Japanese* (Tokyo: Charles E. Tuttle Company, 1973), p. 232, discussed manuring with various substances.

24. Hitomi, *Honchō shokkan*, p. 119. Rodrigues also had a low opinion of steeped tea in which the leaves were merely immersed in hot water. See Michael Cooper, "The Early Europeans and Tea," in Paul Varley and Kumakura Isao, eds., *Tea in Japan* (Honolulu: University of Hawai'i Press, 1989), p. 123. As Patricia Graham has pointed out, Rodrigues resided in Nagasaki, home to a sizable immigrant Chinese population in the 1500s. There he witnessed firsthand the Chinese consuming the type of tea that was then popular in China, steeped tea (*sencha*). See Patricia Graham, *Tea of the Sages: The Art of Sencha* (Honolulu: University of Hawai'i Press, 1998), pp. 19–20.

25. Hitomi, *Honchō shokkan*, pp. 120–121. Hitomi went into great detail as to how exactly the boiling process was to be conducted: "First, make a ring with straw and set it on top of the mouth of an iron kettle (*kama*). Above this straw ring place a bamboo sieve and use it as a colander. The size of the hole in the bamboo sieve should be about the same as a rice sieve. Put the plucked tea shoots into the sieve without allowing the shoots to overlap and steam them with the boiling water of the iron pot. Whenever the fire under the pot dies down the tea shoots will scorch if you do not boil water in the pot. Whenever the fire is too hot, the hot water in the pot will boil away and this also is bad. The hot water in the pot simply must boil without dissipating and the fire under the pot should burn without being too hot—those are the best conditions. Measure the time with a clock when you are boiling; or measure by counting things."

Hitomi also suggested the proper wood for the flames: "Generally speaking, avoid pine firewood for [heating] the kettle. If you use pinewood, sap enters the steam and the shoots will smell bad. The best firewood is from oak (*kunugi*). Place an iron ring in the center of the fireplace, measure the amount of firewood, put it in the iron ring and light it. Wait for the fire to go past half the firewood and you will steam high-grade shoots. For steaming the rest, the amount of firewood does not matter." Rodrigues also described the method of preservation. Kaempfer believed that the proper storage method could rejuvenate bad tea (*Kaempfer's Journal*, p. 114). Kaempfer also described the "miserable" appearance of tea bushes that had been plucked bare and wrote in detail about the sorting of different grades of tea (see p. 434). Siebold also discussed leaf sorting (p. 232). On plucking, see also Carl Peter Thunberg, *Japan Extolled and Decried*, p. 213.

26. Ōishi, *Chagyō hattatsu shi*, p. 270.

27. Ibid. p. 119.

28. Ibid., pp. 270–271.

29. Miyazaki Yasusada, *Nihon nōsho zenshū* 13 *Nōgyō zensho* (Nōsan gyoson bunka kyōkai, 1978), pp. 79–80.

30. Miyazaki, *Nōgyō zensho*, pp. 80–81. On planting and shrub growth, note Thunberg, *Japan Extolled and Decried*, p. 213, and Siebold, *Manners and Customs of the Japanese*, p. 232.

31. Miyazaki, *Nōgyō zensho,* pp. 81–83. Ōishi's comment is on p. 272 of his *Chagyō hattatsu shi.*

32. These four methods are clearly described by Kōzu, *Chanoyu no rekishi,* pp. 244–245.

33. Miyazaki, *Nōgyō zensho,* pp. 84–85.

34. Ibid., p. 86.

35. Ōishi, *Chagyō hattatsu shi,* p. 273.

36. Miyazaki, *Nōgyō zensho,* p. 87. Thunberg described a "brown decoction" that may have been partially oxidized steeped tea. Siebold, *Manners and Customs of the Japanese,* pp. 232–233, described a "dry" and "wet" method. In the dry method Siebold suggests tilting the iron pan. He seems to have been referring to stir-roasted and steamed, steeped leaf teas, respectively. See also Ōishi, *Chagyō hattatsu shi,* pp. 255–260.

37. Miyazaki, *Nōgyō zensho,* pp. 87–88. Kaempfer described a processing method that fell somewhere between stir-roasting and steeped leaf tea; see *Kaempfer's Journal,* pp. 269–270. Note that the translation into English by Bodart-Bailey differs in important respects from that available in Ōishi, *Chagyō hattatsu shi,* p. 247. Thunberg also detailed a process that was close to stir-roasting (p. 213).

38. Miyazaki, *Nōgyō zensho,* p. 88.

39. Ibid., p. 89.

40. Ōishi, *Chagyō hattatsu shi,* pp. 275–278. In the years after Miyazaki's monumental work, several authors wrote books that touched on tea. The well-known Confucian scholar and expert on medicinal plants Kaibara Ekken (1630–1714) brushed *Basic Medicinal Plants of Japan* (*Yamato honzō*) in 1708, in which he dubbed tea the "open-your-eyes" plant. In 1713, Terashima Ryōan edited the first encyclopedia in Japan named *Illustrated Encyclopedia of the Three Realms in China and Japan* (*Wakan sansai zue*). His book was by its very nature general in its coverage, but Terashima noted that tea was an aid to the poor and served as a tax for the government. He also wrote: "Powdered tea comes from Uji in Yamashiro and the best steeped tea from Toganoo in Yamashiro and Ashikubo village in Abe District in Suruga Province. Tea made of a mixture of leaves and stalks from Hyūga and Tanba is also good. Mandokoro in Ōmi, Shimoichi in Yamato, and Fudōbō in Iyo Province are above average." The other remarkable notation was of a tea made in China by fermentation in a closed-off bamboo stick (*catechu*), supposedly used to cure infants of various poxes (*shosō*). Finally, Miyake Yarai wrote a book on commerce titled *The Bag for Myriad Money in Commerce* (*Bankin sugihai bukuro*) in 1732. This work is of interest primarily because the author devoted equal space to powdered and steeped tea and suggested that the origins of the popularity of steeped tea lay in between 1690 and 1700.

41. Ōishi, *Chagyō hattatsu shi,* pp. 284–286. Also note Kōzu, *Chanoyu no rekishi,* p. 245.

42. See Kōzu, *Chanoyu no rekishi,* pp. 245–247, and the excellent treatment by Patricia Graham, *Tea of the Sages,* pp. 20–22; 28–38; 48–75.

43. Quotation is drawn from Ōishi, *Chagyō hattatsu shi,* p. 286. For more on Ōeda and the cultural milieu of steeped tea, see Graham, *Tea of the Sages,* pp. 20–135.

44. See Ōishi, *Chagyō hattatsu shi,* pp. 265–267, for a claim for steamed steeped tea in early eighteenth-century Shizuoka, and pp. 285–286 for a late fourteenth-century claim for Uji. Ōishi rightly regards both with suspicion.

45. Quotation drawn from ibid., p. 286.

46. Ibid., pp. 288–289, relates these and other stories concerning the origin of the ever-popular *gyokuro.* Besides the three stories in the text, Ōishi relates a tale about origins in Ashikubo village in Shizuoka around 1788. Ashikubo figures in the Bunsei Tea Incident of 1824.

47. For more on *gyokuro,* see Graham, *Tea of the Sages,* pp. 2, 139, 156, 184.

48. David Howell, "Hard Times in the Kanto: Economic Change and Village Life in Late Tokugawa Japan," *Modern Asian Studies* 23 (1989): 363.

49. Ōishi, *Chagyō hattatsu shi,* p. 287. Ueda concludes: "If you store up purple-black tea for a long time, it will turn black. Tea roasted for too long may have good taste but lacks the pure fragrance. Also, if the tea is not processed [properly] it may remain green, but its plant essence will remain and there will be no sweet taste."

50. Ibid., pp. 289–290.

51. Ōkura Nagatsune, *Nihon nōsho zenshū* 14 *Kōeki kokusan kō* (Nōsangyoson bunka kyōkai, 1978), p. 309.

52. Ibid., p. 310.

53. Ibid.

54. Ibid., p. 312.

55. Ibid.

56. Ibid.

57. Ibid., pp. 317–318. Although Ōkura makes no mention of the uses to which his stir-roasted tea might be put, it seems likely to the author that such "good" tea was bound for the market.

58. Ōishi, *Chagyō hattatsu shi,* p. 292.

59. This section owes much to ibid., pp. 293–311.

60. As might be imagined, there are numerous sources on Uji tea in the Tokugawa period. Although my discussion relies primarily on Ōishi, *Chagyō hattatsu shi,* pp. 298–300, I have also consulted Hayashiya Tatsusaburō and Fujioka Kenjirō, eds., *Uji shishi* 2 *Chūsei no rekishi to keikan* (Uji: Uji shiyakusho, 1974); Yoshimura Tōru, *Uji cha no bunka shi* (Uji: Uji shi kyōiku iinkai, 1993); Tsubunouchi Junji, "Uji chashi to Owari han," in Kishino Toshihiko, ed., *Owari han shakai no sōgō kenkyū* (Osaka: Seibun dō, 2007), 3:339–356; and Tsubunouchi Junji, "Nagoya no Uji seihikicha hanbai o meguru shinkō chashōnin to Uji chashi," in Kishino Toshihiko, ed., *Owari han shakai no sōgō kenkyū* (Osaka: Seibun dō, 2009), 4:318–335.

Among Europeans who visited Japan, Uji tea was well known. Apparently Rodrigues paid especially close attention to it, because he knew the surname of the managers there (by the time of his visit, the Kanbayashi) and that they numbered about fifteen to twenty persons. He was also familiar with the merchants who acted on behalf of the imperial house, counting eleven people. Engelbert Kaempfer also called Uji tea the best in Japan (*Kaempfer's Japan,* p. 318).

61. For two excellent studies of mountain tea in southern Kyushu, see Ōga Ikuo, *Kinsei sanson shakai kōzō no kenkyū* (Azekura shobō, 2005), pp. 15–134, on Takachiho village located in Usuki district in Hyūga Province, and pp. 165–314 on the mountain Shiiba, situated in Hitoyoshi Domain in Higo Province. Both places are located in Miyazaki today.

62. Quotation is drawn from Ōishi, *Chagyō hattatsu shi,* p. 296.

63. Ibid., p. 300.

64. Ibid., pp. 300–301. For mountain tea in the Nara region, also see Komeie Taisaku, *Chū kinsei sanson no keikan to kōzō* (Azekura shobō, 2002), for his excellent study of Ido village located in the mountains of Yoshino.

65. Quotation from Ōishi, *Chagyō hattatsu shi,* p. 303. To be sure, the origin from Hiyoshi Shrine is of doubtful provenance.

66. Quotation is drawn from ibid., p. 303.

67. Quotation comes from ibid., p. 304.

68. Wigen, *The Making of a Japanese Periphery,* p. 57.

69. See *Taiyaku Saikaku zenshū* 17 *Irozato mitokoro zetai. Ukiyo eiga ichidai otoko,* trans. Fuji Akio (Meiji shoin, 2007), pp. 70–71.

70. Ōishi, *Chagyō hattatsu shi,* p. 308.

71. For Osaka, see Komatsu Kazuo, "Kinsei Osaka ni okeru seicha ryūtsū no henshitsu katei," *Shakai keizai shigaku* 36 (1970): 23; for Sunpu, see Ōishi, *Chagyō hattatsu shi,* p. 313.

72. On this transition, see especially Komatsu, "Kinsei Osaka ni okeru seicha ryūtsū no henshitsu katei," pp. 20–43; Aoki Hideki, "Owari han Ōshū chakata shihainin no katsudō to Mino cha no hattatsu," *Jōestsu shakai kenkyū* 7 (October 1992): 25–34; Miyamoto Tsutomu, "Shun'en cha ikken no rekishiteki tokushitsu," in Honda Takashige, ed., *Kinsei Shizuoka no kenkyū* (Osaka: Seibun dō, 1991), pp. 381–419; Wakabayashi Atsushi, "Bunsei cha ikken no kōzō," *Shizuoka daigaku kyōiku gakubu kenkyū hōkoku* 10 (1959): 55–79; and Kamishiraishi Minoru, "Bunsei cha ikken," *Chihō shi kenkyū* 277 (February 1999): 18–35.

73. Articles on the pleasure districts of the major cities are legion. For starters, see Donald H. Shively, "Sumptuary Regulation and Status in Early Tokugawa Japan," *Harvard Journal of Asiatic Studies* 25 (1964–1965): 123–164; Donald H. Shively, "The Social Environment of Tokugawa Kabuki," in Nancy G. Hume, ed., *Japanese Aesthetics and Culture* (Albany: State University of New York, 1995), pp. 193–245; Donald H. Shively, "Popular Culture," in John Hall and James McClain, eds., *The Cambridge History of Japan: Early Modern Japan* (Cambridge: Cambridge University Press, 1991), pp. 706–770. The economic argument about the rise of consumer society during the Edo period owes much to Penelope Francks, *The Japanese Consumer: An Alternative Economic History of Modern Japan* (Cambridge: Cambridge University Press, 2009), pp. 11–46.

74. For this general description, I rely on Kitagawa Morisada, *Morisada mankō*, ed. Asakura Haruhiko and Kashikawa Shūichi (Tokyodō, 1992), 1:137–138; 143–145; 154; and 158. This work was composed in the mid-nineteenth century. On Tokugawa tea shops, see also Merry White, *Coffee Life in Japan* (Berkeley and Los Angeles: University of California Press, 2012), pp. 13–14. N.B.: White's terminology differs from mine in some respects.

75. Kitagawa, *Morisada mankō*, 4:127–128.

76. Siebold, *Manners and Customs of the Japanese*, p. 232; Ōishi, *Chagyō hattatsu shi*, pp. 252–253. On his way back from Edo to Kyoto, Siebold stopped at a tea shop for a drink and some rice cakes. His party stopped yet one more time for tea during the journey from Osaka to Nagasaki. Siebold's travels showed that tea shops dotted the roads throughout central and western Japan. Also note that Ōishi includes a short section on the observations of Robert Fortune, an Englishman who came to Japan in 1860; see Ōishi, *Chagyō hattatsu shi*, pp. 260–261. Fortune's comments duplicate many of the previous comments. On Fortune and his involvement with tea, see Sarah Rose, *For All the Tea in China* (New York: Viking Press, 2010).

77. Kitagawa, *Morisada mankō*, 3:189. Also on these types of "tea shops" see Tsukada Takashi, *Kinsei Osaka no toshi shakai* (Yoshikawa kōbunkan, 2006), pp. 84–156; Katō Seiji, "Tenpō kaikaku ni okeru 'kagema chaya' no haishi," *Fūzoku shigaku* 23 (March 2003): 80–95.

78. Shively, "The Social Environment of Tokugawa Kabuki," p. 214.

79. "Yari no Gonza kasane katahira," *Chikamatsu zenshū* (Iwanami shoten, 1989), 10:129–198.

80. I am grateful to Rebecca Corbett for this idea. See her fine article, "Learning to Be Graceful: Tea in Early Modern Guides for Women's Education," *Japanese Studies* 29 (2009): 81–94.

81. Yamada Shin'ichi, *Edo no ocha—haikai cha no saijiki* (Yasaka shobō, 2007), pp. 14–15.

82. Ibid., p. 73.

83. Yamada Shin'ichi, *Hana tachibana mo cha no kaori* (Shizuoka shinbun sha, 2008), p. 20.

84. Tsunoyama Sakae et al., eds., *Nihon no ocha 3 Ocha to bunka* (Gyōsei, 1988), p. 213.

85. Ibid., p. 214.

86. Watanabe Shinichirō, *Edo no onnatachi no gurume jijō* (Toto Books, 1994), p. 13.

87. Watanabe Shinichirō, *Edo no shomin ga hiraita shoku bunka* (Mitsuki shobō, 1996), p. 109.

88. Tsunoyama et al., *Ocha to bunka*, p. 217.

89. Ibid., pp. 162–165.

90. Hayashi Hideo and Aoki Michio, eds., *Banzuke de yomu Edo jidai* (Kashiwa shobō, 2003), pp. 28–29.

91. Ibid., pp. 172–173. For a more complete collection of advertisements, including those already noted, see Aoki Michio, ed., *Kettei ban banzuke shūsei* (Kashiwa shobō, 2009), pp. 64–65; 86–91; 110–117; 122–123; 126–129; 186–187; 236–237; and 322–323.

92. The prints are available in *Ocha to ukiyo-e: egakareta Edo no ocha jijō* (Gyōsei, 1997), printed as a catalogue for an exhibition at the Iruma Municipal Museum. The prints may be found on pp. 5, 29, and 43.

93. Francks, *The Japanese Consumer,* p. 92.

94. Kaempfer, *Kaempfer's Japan,* p. 65.

95. Ibid., pp. 269–270.

96. Thunberg, *Japan Extolled and Decried,* p. 212.

97. Siebold, *Manners and Customs of the Japanese,* p. 232. Once again, the accuracy of the translation in matters of tea terminology is open to doubt according to Ōishi. Siebold (1796–1866) was a German who journeyed to Japan in 1832 at the age of twenty-seven.

98. Siebold, *Manners and Customs of the Japanese,* p. 133.

99. There are several notable articles on this conflict. See Wakabayashi Atsushi, "Bunsei cha ikken no kōzō," *Shizuoka daigaku kyōiku gakubu kenkyū hōkoku* 10 (1959): 55–79; and Kamishiraishi Minoru, "Bunsei cha ikken," *Chihō shi kenkyū* 277 (February 1999): 18–35; Kamishiraishi Minoru, "Kinsei chūki Kawane cha no kōshō kiroku," *Tōyō daigaku daigakuin kiyō* 34 (1997): 657–673; Miyamoto Tsutomu, "Sun'en cha ikken no rekishiteki tokushitsu," in Honda Takashige, ed., *Kinsei Shizuoka no kenkyū* (Osaka: Seibun dō, 1991), pp. 381–419; Sasagawa Hiroshi, "Hokuen chihō ni okeru Bunsei cha ikken no tenkai to kōzō," *Shikan* 20 (March 1988): 61–75; Sasagawa Hiroshi, "Kinsei kōki hokuen chihō ni okeru sonraku kōzō," *Shikan* 17 (December 1981): 1–18; "Sankan sonraku no shiteki kenkyū," *Shikan* 14 (1978): 1–194; and Okamura Tatsuo, "Kinsei kōki Suruga no kuni Abe gun ni okeru cha ryūtsū no hen'yō," *Komazawa daigaku daigakuin shigaku ronshū* 40 (May 2010): 64–78. There is also a summary of events in Shizuoka shiyakusho, ed., *Shizuoka shishi: kinsei* (Shizuoka: Shizuoka shiyakusho, 1979), pp. 804–813.

100. The following discussion of the 1824 farmers' petition is based on the original document printed in Shizuoka shiyakusho, ed., *Shizuoka shishi: Kinsei shiryō II* (Shizuoka: Shizuoka shiyakusho, 1975), pp. 646–658. A duplicate of the same complaint may be found on pp. 792–802.

101. Wakabayashi, "Bunsei cha ikken no kōzō," pp. 78–79; Miyamoto, "Sun'en cha ikken no rekishiteki tokushitsu," pp. 381–419.

102. Sasagawa, "Bunsei cha ikken no tenkai to kōzō," pp. 64–73.

103. Kamishiraishi, "Bunsei cha ikken," pp. 32–33.

104. *Shizuoka shishi: Kinsei,* p. 808.

105. *Shizuoka shishi: Kinsei shiryō II,* pp. 806–813 (to Sunpu); and pp. 813–817 (to Edo). Also note the copies of petitions on pp. 802–806, which appear to have summarized the complaints. These documents, addressed to the Sunpu official (*bugyō*), notified him of the problems and stated that the plaintiffs were taking up the issue in Edo. Also see related documents in *Shizuoka shishi: Kinsei shiryō I,* pp. 736–774 and 912–918.

106. *Shizuoka shishi: Kinsei shiryō II,* pp. 824–833.

107. Ibid., pp. 658–666. For scholarly commentary on the "gathering places," see Miyamoto, "Sun'en cha ikken no rekishiteki tokushitsu," pp. 398–414; and Okamura, "Kinsei kōki Suruga no kuni Abe gun ni okeru cha ryūtsū no hen'yō," pp. 64–78.

108. The contents of this third suit have been reconstructed using *Shizuoka shishi: Kinsei shiryō I,* pp. 775–777, *Shizuoka shishi: Kinsei shiryō II,* pp. 835–842, and *Shizuoka shishi: Kinsei,* p. 810.

109. For the documents of this period, see *Shizuoka shishi: Kinsei shiryō I,* pp. 777–799; 810–825.

110. *Shizuoka shishi: Kinsei shiryō II,* p. 841.

111. Ibid., pp. 833–835.

112. *Shizuoka shishi: Kinsei,* pp. 811–812. For the original document, see *Shizuoka shishi: Kinsei shiryō I,* pp. 799–802. Also see related documents on pp. 802–810.

113. Cited in Markman Ellis, Richard Coulton, and Matthew Mauger, *Empire of Tea: The Asian Leaf that Conquered the World* (London: Reaktion Books, 2015), p. 98.

114. Ōishi, *Chagyō hattatsu shi,* p. 245.

## *Chapter Four: Modern Tea*

1. Two essential references are Ōishi, *Chagyō hattatsu shi,* pp. 314–438, and Teramoto Yasuhide, *Senzen ki Nihon chagyō shi kenkyū* (Yūhikaku, 1999).

2. Shinya Sugiyama, *Japan's Industrialization in the World Economy, 1859–1899* (London and Atlantic Highlands, NJ: The Athlone Press, 1988), pp. 14–76.

3. Ibid., pp. 52–55. Sugiyama provides no indication of the number of tea firms, but overall the Euro-Americans had 440 firms in East Asia in 1869.

4. Robert Hellyer is currently writing an essay on the export trade with the United States, and interested readers should refer to his work.

5. Ōishi, *Chagyō hattatsu shi,* pp. 316–318.

6. Ibid., pp. 320–321.

7. Ōishi Sadao, *Shizuoka ken chasanchi shi* (Nōsangyoson bunka kyōkai, 2004), pp. 21–327.

8. Ōishi, *Chagyō hattatsu shi,* p. 326.

9. Ibid., p. 327.

10. Ibid., pp. 330–331.

11. Ibid., pp. 386–388.

12. *Seicha zukai,* in *Nihon nōsho zenshū* 47 (Nōsangyoson bunka kyōkai, 1997), pp. 199–243. The discussion in this paragraph refers to pp. 213–227 and related illustrations.

13. Ōishi, *Chagyō hattatsu shi,* p. 345.

14. Ibid., pp. 355–357.

15. Ibid., pp. 358–360.

16. Ibid., p. 362.

17. Tsunoyama Sakae et al., eds., *Nihon no ocha* 3 *Ocha to bunka* (Gyōsei, 1988), p. 220.

18. Ibid.

19. Ibid., p. 223.

20. *Seicha zukai,* pp. 199–213.

21. Ōishi, *Chagyō hattatsu shi,* pp. 373–379.

22. On homemade tea, see Tanisaka Chikako, *Jikayō cha no minzoku* (Ōkawa shobō, 2004).

23. The following brief and general discussion comes from Yamamoto Shōzō, *Chagyō chiiki no kenkyū* (Daimeido, 1973), pp. 112–122.

24. Isamu Mitsuzono, "Mail-Order Retailing in Pre-War Japan: A Pathway of Consumption before the Emergence of the Mass Market," in Penelope Francks and Janet Hunter, eds., *The Historical Consumer: Consumption and Everyday Life in Japan, 1850–2000* (New York: Palgrave Macmillan, 2012), pp. 259–283.

25. Ibid., p. 277.

26. Ibid.

27. Hashima Tomoyuki, ed., *Shinbun kōkoku bijutsu taikei: Meiji hen* 2 *inshoku shikōhin* (Ōzora sha, 1999); Hashima Tomoyuki, ed., *Shinbun kōkoku bijutsu taikei: Taishō hen* 7 *inshoku shikōhin* (Ōzora sha, 2003).

28. Seijō daigaku minzokugaku kenkyū jo, ed., *Nihon no shoku bunka* (Iwasaki bijutsu sha, 1990); Seijō daigaku minzokugaku kenkyū jo, ed., *Nihon no shoku bunka: Hoi hen* (Iwasaki bijutsu sha, 1995).

29. White, *Coffee Life in Japan*, pp. 7–11. Smil and Kobayashi, *Japan's Dietary Transition and Its Impacts* (Cambridge, MA: MIT Press, 2012), p. 63, give the date for Japan's first coffeehouse as 1897.

30. White, *Coffee Life in Japan*, pp. 47–62.

31. Natsume Soseki, *And Then* (University of Tokyo Press, 1978), p. 11.

32. Natsume Soseki, *The Wayfarer* (Rutland, VT: Charles E. Tuttle Company, 1967), p. 163.

33. Natsume Soseki, *Botchan* (Kodansha, 1972), pp. 37–38.

34. Tanizaki Jūnichirō, *Some Prefer Nettles* (New York: Alfred A. Knopf, 1955), p. 133.

35. For these following thoughts on the adoption of cuttings instead of seeds for planting, as well as fertilizers, pesticides, and mechanized plucking, I rely on Ōishi, *Chagyō hattatsu shi*, pp. 413–425.

36. Ibid., pp. 397–406.

37. Ibid., pp. 406–412.

38. On mechanization, see ibid., pp. 425–438.

39. Ibid., pp. 437–438.

40. See Smil and Kobayashi, *Japan's Dietary Transition and Its Impacts*, pp. 7–10; 21.

41. Yamamoto, *Chagyō chiiki no kenkyū*, pp. 115–122. Note the map on p. 117 and the chart on p. 120, both of which show the increasing regionalization of Shizuoka's tea market and producers.

42. Hashima, *Shinbun kōkoku bijutsu taikei: Shōwa senjika hen* 15 *inshoku shikōhin iryōhin zakka* (Ōzora sha, 2007), p. 244.

43. Ibid.

44. Samuel Yamashita, *Leaves from an Autumn of Emergencies* (Honolulu: University of Hawai'i Press, 2005), p. 91.

45. See *Kanagawa ken kessen shoku seikatsu kufūshū* (Osaka: Sangyō keizai shinbun sha, 1944), pp. 75–76. I am indebted to Eric Rath for this point.

46. Yamashita, *Leaves from an Autumn of Emergencies*, p. 100.

47. Smil and Kobayashi, *Japan's Dietary Transition*, p. 65.

48. White discusses coffee in Japan in all its social and cultural contexts in *Coffee Life in Japan*, pp. 66–118; 122–172.

49. Hayashi Eiichi, ed., *Nihon no ocha:* 2 *Ocha to seikatsu* (Gyōsei, 1988), pp. 178–197.

50. *ACC/CM nenkan '68*, p. 146.

51. *ACC/CM nenkan 80*, p. 232.

52. The information from the preceding two paragraphs comes from Fujimoto Yoshihira, ed., *Nihon no shoku seikatsu zenshū*, 47 vols. (Nōsangyoson bunka kyōkai, 1988–1992).

53. Tanizaki Jūnichirō, *The Makioka Sisters* (Charles E. Tuttle Company, 1957), p. 47.

54. Kawabata Yasunari, *The Sound of the Mountain* (Charles E. Tuttle, 1970), p. 28.

55. Howard Hibbett, ed., *Contemporary Japanese Literature* (New York: Alfred A. Knopf, 1977), p. 149.

56. Informal conversation held at *Kokusai Nihon bunka kenkyū sentaa* in Kyoto during June/July 2014. The name of the scholar escapes me. For the record, he may have been waxing a bit nostalgic.

57. *Cha kankei shiryō*, p. 82.

58. White, *Coffee Life in Japan*, p. 117. Later, on pp. 118–122, the author asks "why did tea leave the public space?" But has green tea really "left the public space" or, as I am arguing, is it simply in the process of redefining itself? When the author writes that "Japanese green tea is the world standard for green teas" and that "[c]offee and tea are nonoverlapping beverages," I find myself in greater agreement with her assessment.

59. All Japan Radio & Television Commercial Confederation, *ACC/CM 2007*, pp. 36–37.

60. I found this information at https://yunomi.us/12209/41st-auction-kanto-region-tea-competition (accessed March 18, 2016).

61. My thanks go to Sawamura Shin'ichi of Itoen for this information on the retail market for tea as well as a guided tour of Itoen's facilities in Shizuoka.

62. I am grateful to Tanikawa Kenji of Waseda University for sharing materials with me. I should also note the appeal of movies about Sen Rikyū. See Tim Cross, "Rikyū Has Left the Tea Room: National Cinema Interrogates the Anecdotal Legend," in Morgan Pitelka, ed., *Japanese Tea Culture* (London: RoutledgeCurzon, 2003), pp. 151–183.

## *Conclusion*

1. See Ethan Segal, *Coins, Trade, and the State* (Cambridge, MA: Harvard University Press, 2011), pp. 140–147. This insight presents a new perspective for analyzing economic relations during the ages of the Nara and Heian courts.

2. The allusion to the tea ceremony raises the question of tea's cultural role and brings another comparative dimension of the beverage to the fore. Wherever tea has traveled in the world, it always seems to have had strong associations with ceremony, poetry, and the solitary life. Certainly, that has been true in Japan, where *chanoyu* has been turned into an art for the masses in modern times, but the same generalization holds for China, where the art of steeped tea was highly ritualized. In Korea, tea was frequently associated with ceremony, even as early as the Silla dynasty. Of course, the British have their own way of tea. In all four societies, the drinking of tea—and perhaps even the fragrance of roasting tea—led savants to break into poetry. Often these poets were hermits who led a solitary existence. To be sure, tea also has connotations of hospitality and sociability. Is there something about the chemical composition of *Camellia sinensis* that leads inevitably to these human behaviors? It is an interesting question that I leave for others to ponder. On the art of steeped tea in China, see Graham, *Tea of the Sages*, pp. 9–22. For Korea, see Suk, "History and Philosophy of Korean Tea Art," pp. 4–11. For Great Britain, see Ellis, Coulton, and Mauger, *Empire of Tea*, pp. 139–160.

3. Hayami Akira, *Japan's Industrious Revolution: Economic and Social Transformations in the Early Modern Period* (London and Tokyo: Springer, 2015). Jan de Vries, *The Industrious Revolution: Consumer Behavior and the Household Economy, 1650 to the Present* (New York: Cambridge University Press, 2008).

4. See my *Japan's Medieval Population: Famine, Fertility, and Warfare during a Transformative Era* (Honolulu: University of Hawai'i Press, 2006).

5. See Gregory Clark and Ysbrand van der Werf, "Work in Progress? The Industrious Revolution," *Journal of Economic History* 58 (1998): 830–843; and Merry Wiesner-Hanks, *Early Modern Europe, 1450–1789* (New York: Cambridge University Press, 2006). Of course, this point differentiates Japanese tea from other current consumer commodities in Japan such as chocolate, coffee, tobacco, and beer. In this respect, Japanese tea as a consumer item is probably much like Japanese rice wine, bean paste, soy sauce, and silk.

6. This is, of course, a considerable oversimplification of what occurred in Edo society and economy. See Thomas Smith, "Pre-Modern Economic Growth: Japan and the West," *Past and Present* 60, no. 1 (1973): 127–160; Susan Hanley and Kozo Yamamura, *Economic and Demographic Change in Preindustrial Japan, 1600–1868* (Princeton, NJ: Princeton University Press, 1977); and Conrad Totman, *Early Modern Japan* (Berkeley and Los Angeles: University of California Press, 1993). Hanley and Yamamura stress the marked growth of the Tokugawa economy throughout the period, while Totman emphasizes the ecological limits of growth after 1700. Smith's article is notable for several reasons, but for this discussion, the de-urbanization that he described for the advanced regions of Japan (the Kinai and

Kanto), coupled with the increased vigor of peripheral Japan, remain basic insights applicable to the story of tea.

7. Ellis, Coulton, and Markman, *Empire of Tea*, pp. 73 and 179.

8. In *The Great Divergence* (Princeton, NJ: Princeton University Press, 2000), pp. 281–282, Kenneth Pomeranz has written: "For one thing, tobacco, sugar, coffee, and tea were all somewhat addictive, easy to prepare and consume quickly, and provided short bursts of energy. This made them perfect for punctuating long work days, especially away from home: these characteristics became more important as home and workplace were separated, especially in the factory age. . . . *Moreover, these new "everyday luxuries" were all (except for tobacco) commodities that did not grow in Europe and thus could never be made within the household; consequently, they could only be obtained through producing for the market. . . . Consequently, the exotic commodities that became parts of many people's ordinary lives in this period may have contributed in important though unquantifiable ways to the reallocation of labor time from production for home use to production for the market, which in turn was crucial to Europe's "internally generated" gains from increased division of labor"* (emphasis added). To what extent was Great Britain's earlier and broader development of the market and consumerism merely a reflection of the fact that the British could not grow tea, whereas the Japanese had been doing so for a millennium by the time Japan met the Euro-Americans?

# List of Characters

*aburicha* アフリ茶
*akichi* 明地
*akutō* 悪党
*aozamurai* 青侍
*aracha* 荒茶
*asacha* 朝茶
Awa cha 阿波茶
*aze* 畔; 畦; あぜ

Baizan shucha furyaku
  梅山種茶譜略
*bakufu* 幕府
*bancha* 番茶
*banji* 万事
Bankin sugihai bukuro 万金産業袋
*batabatacha* バタバタ茶
*bu* 歩
*bugyō* 奉行
Buzen no kuni Usa Hachimangū
  massha wakan ukidono kedai
  ichi no zu 豊前国宇佐八幡宮末社
  和間浮殿境内市図

*cha aburi* 茶あぶり
*chabako* 茶箱
*chabatake bugyō* 茶畑 奉行
*chagai* 茶がい
*chagashi* 茶菓子
*chagayu* 茶がゆ
Chagyō kumiai 茶業組合
Chagyō shūdan kai 茶業 集談会
*chahan* 茶飯
Chajing 茶経
*chajom* 茶店
*chakai* 茶会
*cha kaisho* 茶 会所
*chakouri* 茶小売り
*chamachi* 茶町
*cha mise* 茶見世
*chamomi fu* 茶揉み 婦
*cha nakagai shō* 茶仲買商
*cha no ha* 茶の葉
*chanoyu* 茶の湯
*cha o senzu beshi* 茶ヲ煎ス へし
*chasei* 茶精
*chashi* 茶師
*cha suai* 茶仲
*chatō* 茶桶
*cha ton'ya* 茶 問屋
*chatsubo dōchū* 茶壺 道中

*chausu* 茶臼
*chaya* 茶屋
*chaza* 茶座
*chazuke* 茶漬
*chazumifu* 茶摘み婦
Chihō kikigaki 地方 聞書
*chinpi* 陳皮
*chō* 町
*chūbatake* 中畠
*chūjūki* 中揉機

Daibiroshana jōbutsu kyō-so 大毘盧遮那成仏経疎
(*dai*)*chawan* 大茶碗; 大茶垸
*daigokuden* 大極殿
Daihannya-kyō 大般若経
Daijōin jisha zōjiki 大乗院寺社雑事記
*daikan*(*sho*) 代官所
Daikan shingi 大鑑清規
*daikokuten* 大黒天
*daikyō* 大饗
*dancha* 団茶
*dan'ochi* 檀越
*dashicha* 出し茶
*deai chaya* 出会い茶屋
*dōbōshū* 同朋衆

Eihei shingi 永平清規
Eishō nenchūki 永正年中記
Engi 延喜

*fukucha* 福茶
*furiuri* 振り売り
Fusō ryakki 扶桑 略記

*gagaku* 雅楽
*gebatake* 下畑
*gehin* 下品
Genkyū shi utaai 元久詩歌合
Gion ōmandokoro ezu 祇園大政所絵図
Gion sha shake kiroku 祇園社 社家記録
Gion sha shamu shikkō Hōjuin kenshin shojō 祇園社社務執行宝寿院顕詮書状
*gō* 合
*gobancha* 五番茶
Go Hokōkōin zatsuji yōroku 後法興院雑事要録
*goku* 極
*gokusōin* 穀倉院
*goku tsume* 極結
*goku zorae* 極揃
Gonki 権記
*gon no sōjō* 権僧正
*gōnō* 豪農
*gosho* 御所
*goyōcha* 御用茶
*gun* 郡
*gyakushū* 逆修
*gyokuro* 玉露
Gyokuyō 玉葉

*hacha* 葉茶
Haedong jegukugi 海東諸国記
*hako* 箱
*hamaokuri* 浜送り
Harutomi sukune no ki 晴富宿禰記
*hassaku* 八朔
*heicha* 餅茶
*hetsui* へつい
*hiki* 疋
*hikutsu* ひくつ
*hikuzu* 籔屑; ひくず
*hishaku* 柄杓
*hitashicha* 淹し茶
*hoiro* 焙爐; 焙炉
*hōjō-e* 放生会
*hokuto goshūhō* 北斗御修法
Hōkyōji monjo 宝鏡寺 文書
*hon* 本

*honbatake* 本畑
Honchō hokke genki 本朝法華験記
Honchō monzui 本朝文粋
Honchō mudai shi 本朝無題詩
Honchō shokkan 本朝食鑑
Honchō zoku monzui 本朝続文粋
Honzō wamyō 本草和名
*hyakushō* 百姓
Hyakushō denki 百姓伝記

*ibiricha* いびり茶
*ichibancha* 一番茶
*Ikiru* 生きる
*ikkoku* 一石
Ima jinmei 今 神名
*imo cha* 芋茶
*inaka cha* ゐ中ちゃ
*inshu* 院主
Irozato mitokoro zetai 色里御所世帯
Isei teikin ōrai 異制庭訓往来
Ishinpō 医心法

*jian* 寺庵
*jikayō cha* 自家用茶
*jitō* 地頭
Jizō bosatsu reigenki-e 地蔵菩薩霊験記絵
*jōbatake* 上畑
*jōcha* 上茶
Jōshōji nenchū aiorichō 成勝寺年中相折帖
*jotan* 助炭
*jūnenki* 揉捻機

*kabu* 下部
*kabuki* 歌舞伎
*kabu nakama* 株 仲間
*kabusecha* かぶせ茶
*kago chaya* 鹿子茶屋
*kaisho* 会所
*kaiten momi* 回転揉み
*kake chaya* 掛茶屋
*kama* 釜
*kamado* 竈
*kamairicha* 釜炒り茶
Kanezawa bunko 金沢文庫
*kanjin* 勧進
*kanjō bugyō* 勘定奉行
Kankinshū 閑吟集
*kankyō* 乾薑
*kan(me)* 貫（目）
Kanmon gyoki 看聞御記
Kanrin shū 旱霖集
Kantō ōgenki 関東往還記
*karamono* 唐物
*kashiya* 貸屋
Katsuhara monjo 葛原 文書
Katsuragawa myōōin shiryō 葛川明王院史料
*katsuyū tenmoku* 褐釉天目
*keihan chaen* 畔畦 茶園
Kennai ki 建内記
*kin* 斤
*ki no midokkyō* 季の御読経
Kissa yōjōki 喫茶 養生記
*kitakuni* 北国
Kiyomizudera monjo 清水寺文書
Kōeki kokusan kō 広益国産考
*kōgei nōsakubutsu* 工芸 農作物
Kōka shunjū 耕稼春秋
*kokeicha* 固形茶
*koku* 石
*kokubunji* 国分寺
*kokubun niji* 國分尼寺
*kokucha* 黒茶
*Konjaku monogatari* 今昔 物語
*kōrokan* 鴻臚館
*kuji* 公事
*kukicha* 茎茶
*kunugi* 挙
*kurashiki* 蔵敷
*kuro* クロ

*kurōdo*(*shiki*) 蔵人（職）
*kurōdodokoro* 蔵人所
*kuronicha* 黒尼茶
*kusen* 口銭
Kyōgaku shiyōshō 経覚私要抄
*kyōgen* 狂言
Kyōgen kyōki 教言卿記
Kyōō Gokokuji monjo 教王護国寺文書

*maegashira* 前頭
*mama* ママ
*mame cha* 豆茶
*mappō* 末法
*matcha* 抹茶
*matsudai* 末代
*mieiku* 御影供
*mimono* 御物
*mise uri* 見せ売り
*miso* 味噌
*mitate banzuke* 見立て 番付
*miyagomori* 宮籠
*miya no tsukai* 宮の仕い
*momikiri* 揉み切り
*momu* 揉む
*monme* 匁
moromori ki 師守記
*mujō* 無上
Muramatsu kakun 村松 家訓
*myōgakin* 冥加金

*nabe* 鍋; なべ
*nagamochi* 長持
Narazuke 奈良付け
*nashicha* なし茶; 梨茶
*nen* ねん
*nezashi* 根ざし
*nibancha* 二番茶
Nihon keizai shinbun 日本経済新聞
Nihon ōjō gokuraku ki 日本往生極楽記

Nōji yuisho 農事遺書
Nōmukyoku seicha shikensho 農務局製茶試験所
Nōrin shō chagyō shiken jo 農林省茶業 試験 所
Nōshōmushō seicha shiken sho 農商務省 製茶 試験 所

Ōae zōji 大饗雑事
*ōban* 大番
*obon* (*odori*) お盆（踊り）
*ōchamori* 大茶盛
*ōishita saibai* 覆い下栽培
*ōryō deiri* 横領 出入り

*racha* 羅茶
*rakugo* 落語
*ren* 連
*ri* 里
*rincha* 林茶
*rōjicha* 臘茶
Rokudō chinnōji sankei manjara 六道珍皇寺参詣曼荼羅
*rokuto* 六斗
*rōnō* 老農
*roppō shū* 六法衆
*ryō* 両
*ryōri chaya* 料理 茶屋
*Ryōunshū* 凌雲集

*sadō* 茶道
*saikanki* 再乾機
Saikyūki 西宮記
*saji* 匙
Sakeiki 左經記
*sanbancha* 三番茶
Sanbō ekotoba 三宝絵詞
*sancha* 散茶
*sashiki* さし木
*Satsuma no kami* 薩摩守
*segaki* 施餓鬼

*seicha* 製茶
Seicha ichiran 製茶 一覧
Seicha kyōshin kai 製茶共進会
*seicha massatsuki* 製茶 摩擦器
Seicha shinsetsu 製茶 新説
Seicha zukai 製茶 図解
Seifū sagen 清風瑣言
*seijūki* 精揉機
Seiwan chawa 青湾茶話
Sekiso ōrai 尺素 往来
*sen* 銭
*sencha* 煎茶
*senjicha* 煎じ茶
*senjimono* 煎じ物
*senryū* 川柳
*sen'yaku* 仙薬
*setsubun kai* 節分 会
*setsucha* 節茶
*settai sho* 接待 所
*shaku* 尺
*shamu shikkō* 社務執行
*shibachairi kuji* 柴茶入公事
Shichijū ichiban shokunin utaawase 七十一番職人歌合
Shika nōgyō dan 私家農業談
*shikōhin* 嗜好品
*shincha* 新茶
Shinmin kangetsu shū 新民観月集
Shinsen rōeishū 新撰朗詠集
Shinshūki 信秋記
*shō* 升
*shōen* 荘園; 庄園
*shōgan* 賞翫
*shosō* 諸瘡
*shotō* 所当
*shugo daimyo* 守護 大名
*sō* 惣
*sojūki* 粗揉機
*sōron* 相論
*sotoni* 外荷
*Suda Hachiman gūsha rensho mōshijō an* 須田八幡宮社連署申し状 案
*sumō* 相撲
*sun* 寸
*suricha* すりちゃ
Suruga zasshi 駿河雑誌
(o)*sutecha* （お）捨て茶
Sūzenji monjo 崇禅寺 文書

Takao kan pūzu byōbu 高雄観楓図屏風
*tan* 段; 反
Tansan monjo 談山 神社 文書
*tarecha* 浸茶
*temae* 点前
*tenguri* 天繰り; テングリ
*tenjin chaya* 天神茶屋
*tenmoku* 天目
*tenryō* 天領
*ten'yaku-ryō* 典薬寮
*tōcha* 闘茶
*tōcha* 唐茶
*tōgama* 唐釜
Tōji hyakugō monjo-ke 東寺百合文書 け
Tōji monjo 東寺 文書
Tōki shū 東帰集
*ton'ya* 問屋
*tōricha* 通り茶
*toriki* 取り木
*tsubo* 壺; 坪
*tsugiki* 接ぎ木
*tsuizen kuyō* 追善供養
*tsutsumi* つつみ; 袋; 裹
*t'u* 荼

Uesugi bon rakuchū rakugai zu byōbu 上杉本 洛中洛外 図 屏風
*ukiyo-e* 浮世絵
*umeboshi* 梅干し

Ungakuonkin 雲壑猿吟
*unkyaku* 雲脚
*urabon* 盂蘭盆
*uricha* 売り茶
*usu* 臼

*waka* 和歌
Wakan sansai zue 和漢三才図絵
Wamyō ruiju shō 和名類聚抄
*waranbe* わらんべ
*waroki cha* わろき ちや

*yabukita* やぶきた
*yakken* 薬研
*yamabatake* 山畠
*yamacha* 山茶
Yamashina ke raiki 山科 家 礼記
Yamato honzō 大和 本草
Yamato kokoro 大和 心
Yari no Gonza kasane katabira 遣の権三重帷子
*yasechi* 痩地; やせ地
Yonera monjo 米良 文書
*yorikiri* ヨリキリ
*yotsugashira charei* 四頭茶礼
*yubikucha* 湯びく茶
*yudecha* ゆで茶
Yūgaku ōrai 遊学往来
*yūsaku shō* 優作 賞

*zaikata shōnin* 在方 商人
*zatcha* 雑茶
*zauri* 座売り
*zazen* 座禅
*Zen Nihon chashō kurabu* 全日本茶商 クラブ

# Bibliography

Unless otherwise indicated the city of publication is Tokyo.

## Primary Sources


All Japan Radio & Television Commercial Confederation. *ACC/CM nenkan*. Vols. 1968, 1979–1982, 1997–2013.

*Azuma kagami*. In *Shintei zōho kokushi taikei*, vols. 32–33. Yoshikawa kōbunkan, 1964.

*Cha kankei shiryō*. Nihon chagyō chūō kai, 2010.

*Chanoyu kaiga shiryō shūsei*. Heibonsha, 1992.

*Chikamatsu zenshū*, vol. 10. Iwanami shoten, 1989.

Hitomi Hitsudai. *Honchō shokkan*. Annotated by Shimada Isao. Heibonsha, 1977.

*Hyakushō denki*, vol. 1. Annotated by Furushima Toshio. Iwanami shoten, 2001.

Ihara Saikaku. *Nihon no koten* 52 *Nihon eitaigura*. Shōgakkan, 1983.

———. *Taiyaku Saikaku zenshū* 17 *Irozato mitokoro zetai. Ukiyo eiga ichidai otoko*. Translated by Fuji Akio. Meiji shoin, 2007.

Ikeda Yoshinobu, ed., *Chūsei nōmin no seikatsu*. Kyoto: Kōraku dō, 1992.

*Kamakura ibun*, vols. 1–44. Tokyo dō, 1973–1997.

*Kanezawa bunko komonjo*, vols. 1–12. Yokohama: Kanagawa kenritsu Kanezawa bunko, 1964.

Kitagawa Morisada. *Morisada mankō*. Edited by Asakura Haruhiko and Kashikawa Shūichi. 5 vols. Tokyodō, 1992.

*Konjaku monogatari shū*. In *Shin Nihon koten bungaku taikei*, edited by Komine Kazuaki. Vol. 36. Iwanami shoten, 1994.

Miyazaki Yasusada. *Nihon nōsho zenshū* 13 *Nōgyō zensho*. Nōsan gyoson bunka kyōkai, 1978.

*Nihon no shoku seikatsu zenshū*. Edited by Fujimoto Yoshihira. 47 vols. Nōsangyoson bunka kyōkai, 1988–1992.

*Nihon nōsho zenshū* 10 *Seiryōki*. Nōsangyoson bunka kyōkai, 1980.

Ōkura Nagatsune. *Nihon nōsho zenshū* 14 *Kōeki kokusan kō*. Nōsangyoson bunka kyōkai, 1978.

*Saidaiji kōmyō Shingon-e no chōsa hōkokusho.* Nara: Gangōji bunka zai kenkyūjo, 1982.
*Seicha zukai* in *Nihon nōsho zenshū* 47. Nōsangyoson bunka kyōkai, 1997.
Seijō daigaku minzokugaku kenkyūjo, ed. *Nihon no shoku bunka.* Iwasaki bijutsu sha, 1990.
———, ed. *Nihon no shoku bunka: Hoi hen.* Iwasaki bijutsu sha, 1995.
Sen Sōshitsu et al., eds. *Sadō koten zenshū.* Vol. 2, *Kissa yōjōki.* Kyoto: Tankō sha, 1956.
Shizuoka shiyakusho, ed. *Shizuoka shishi: Kinsei shiryō I and II.* Shizuoka: Shizuoka shiyakusho, 1974–1975.
Shōkai. *Kantō ōgenki.* Edited by Hosokawa Ryōichi. Heibon sha Tōyō bunko, 2011.
*Shoku Nihongi.* In *Shintei zōho kokushi taikei.* Yoshikawa kōbunkan, 1976.
*Shōyūki.* In *Dai Nihon kokiroku.* 11 vols. Iwanami shoten, 1959–1992.
Sŏng Hui-gyŏng. *Nongsangdang Ilbon hangnok.* Annotated by Murai Shōsuke. Iwanami shoten, 1987.
Tsuruga shi shi hensan iinikai, ed. *Tsuruga shi shi: Shiryō hen.* Vol. 5. Tsuruga: Tsuruga shiyakusho, 1979.
*Yamanashi ken shi minzoku chōsa hōkokusho* 2 *Fukushi no minzoku,* pp. 157–168. Kōfu: Yamanashi ken, 1995.

**Secondary Sources**

Aida Nirō. *Chūsei no sekisho.* Yoshikawa kōbunkan, 1943.
Aoki Hideki. "Owari han Ōshū chakata shihainin no katsudō to Mino cha no hattatsu." *Jōestsu shakai kenkyū* 7 (October 1992): 25–34.
Aoki Michio, ed. *Kettei ban banzuke shūsei.* Kashiwa shobō, 2009.
Aoki Michio and Hayashi Hideo, eds. *Banzuke de yomu Edo jidai.* Kashiwa shobō, 2003.
Benedict, Carol. *Golden-Silk Smoke: A History of Tobacco in China, 1550–2010.* Los Angeles and Berkeley: University of California Press, 2011.
Benn, James. *Tea in China: A Religious and Cultural History.* Honolulu: University of Hawai'i Press, 2015.
Chiba Noritaka. "Honganji to chanoyu." In *Rekishi to bukkyō no ronshū,* pp. 15–28. Kyoto: Jishōsha, 2000.
Clark, Gregory, and Ysbrand van der Werf. "Work in Progress? The Industrious Revolution." *Journal of Economic History* 58 (1998): 830–843.
Cooper, Michael. "The Early Europeans and Tea." In Paul Varley and Kumakura Isao, eds., *Tea in Japan,* pp. 101–134. Honolulu: University of Hawai'i Press, 1989.
———, comp. and annot. *They Came to Japan.* Berkeley: University of California Press, 1965.
Corbett, Rebecca. "Learning to be Graceful: Tea in Early Modern Guides for Women's Education." *Japanese Studies* 29 (2009): 81–94.
Cort, Louise. *Shigaraki: Potter's Valley.* New York: Kodan sha, 1979.
De Visser, M. W. *Ancient Buddhism in Japan.* Leiden: E. J. Brill, 1935.
De Vries, Jan. *The Industrious Revolution: Consumer Behavior and the Household Economy, 1650 to the Present.* New York: Cambridge University Press, 2008.
Ellis, Markman, Richard Coulton, and Matthew Mauger. *Empire of Tea: The Asian Leaf That Conquered the World.* London: Reaktion Books, 2015.
Farris, William Wayne. *Japan's Medieval Population: Famine, Fertility, and Warfare in a Transformative Age.* Honolulu: University of Hawai'i Press, 2006.
———. "Shipbuilding and Nautical Technology in Japanese Maritime History: Origins to 1600." *The Mariner's Mirror* 95 (August 2009): 260–284.

"Feature: Commodities in History," with contributions by Tariq Ali, Alison Frank, Daniel Smail, Josh Specht, and Jeremy Zallen. www.hcs.harvard.edu/tempus/Book_Reviews_files/xii_2_feature.pdf (accessed during 2012–2013).

Francks, Penelope. *The Japanese Consumer: An Alternative Economic History of Modern Japan.* Cambridge: Cambridge University Press, 2009.

———. "Rural Industry, Growth Linkages, and Economic Development in Nineteenth-Century Japan." *The Journal of Asian Studies* 61 (February 2002): 33–55.

Fujiwara Shigeo. "Kaya shōkō." In *Emaki ni chūsei o yomu,* pp. 101–145. Yoshikawa kōbunkan, 1995.

Fukuchi Shōsuke. *Heian jidai no cha.* Kadokawa shoten, 2006.

Fukushima Kaneharu. "Kamakura kōki no Kamakura Kyoto no kōryū." In *Kamakura jidai no kissa bunka,* pp. 117–129. Kyoto: Sadō shiryōkan, 2008.

———. "Kamakura to tōgoku no cha." In *Kamakura jidai no cha,* pp. 36–39. Yokohama: Kanagawa kenritsu Kanezawa bunko, 1998.

———. *Kanezawa Hōjō shi to Shōmyōji.* Yoshikawa kōbunkan, 1997.

Futaki Ken'ichi. *Chūsei buke shakai no sahō.* Yoshikawa kōbunkan, 1999.

Goble, Andrew. *Confluences of Medicine in Medieval Japan.* Honolulu: University of Hawai'i Press, 2011.

Gorai Shigeru. *Shomin shingyō no shosō.* Kadokawa shoten, 1995.

Graham, Patricia. *Tea of the Sages: The Art of Senchi.* Honolulu: University of Hawai'i Press, 1998.

Hanley, Susan, and Kozo Yamamura. *Economic and Demographic Change in Preindustrial Japan.* Princeton, NJ: Princeton University Press, 1977.

Hasegawa Yoshikazu. "Hiyoshi sannō matsuri no gokū kennō." *Kikan Kokoku to bunka* 87 (June 1999): 102–103.

Hashima Tomoyuki, ed. *Shinbun kōkoku bijutsu taikei: Meiji hen 2 inshoku shikōhin.* Ōzora sha, 1999.

———, ed. *Shinbun kōkoku bijutsu taikei: Shōwa senjika hen 15 inshoku shikōhin iryōhin zakka.* Ōzora sha, 2007.

———, ed. *Shinbun kōkoku bijutsu taikei: Taishō hen 7 inshoku shokōhin.* Ōzora sha, 2003.

Hashimoto Motoko. "Chūsei chaen ni tsuite." *Nenpō chūsei shi kenkyū* 31 (2006): 159–182.

———. "Chūsei kōki sōsai girei ni okeru kissa bunka ni tsuite." *Nara shien* 55 (2010): 1–16.

———. "Chūsei ni okeru cha no seisan ni tsuite."*Cha no bunka* 9 (2010): 70–79.

———. "Chūsei ni okeru cha no seisan to ryūtsū." In Nishimura Keiko, ed., *Nihon kinsei kokka no shosō,* pp. 177–198.

———. "Chūsei no chaya ni tsuite." *Rakuhoku shigaku* 11 (2009): 1–19.

———. "Heian Kamakura no kissa bunka." In *Kōza Nihon chanoyu zenshi,* pp. 25–51. Kyoto: Shibunkaku shuppan, 2013.

———. "Kamakura jidai ni okeru Sōshiki kissa bunka no juyō to tenkai ni tsuite." *Nara shien* 46 (March 2001): 18–35.

———. ""Muromachi jidai nōson ni okeru Sōshiki kissa bunka no juyō ni tsuite." *Nenpō chūsei shi kenkyū* 27 (2002): 101–124.

———. "Nihon chūsei ni okeru Uji cha no rekishi." *Rokucha to kenkō,* pp. 59–76. Kyoto: Kyoto fu chagyō kai gisho, 2008.

———. "Shimo Kawabe no shō ni okeru kissa bunka." *Kanezawa Hōjō shi Shimōsa no kuni Shimo Kawabe no shō no sōgōteki kenkyū,* pp. 46–52. Yokohama: Kanagawa kenritsu Kanezawa bunko, 2010.

Hayami, Akira. *Japan's Industrious Revolution: Economic and Social Transformations in the Early Modern Period.* London and Tokyo: Springer, 2015.
Hayashi Eiichi, ed. *Nihon no ocha 2 ocha to seikatsu.* Gyōsei, 1988.
Hayashiya Tatsusaburō and Fujioka Kenjirō, eds. *Uji shishi 2 Chūsei no rekishi to keikan.* Uji: Uji shiyakusho, 1974.
Hibbett, Howard, ed. *Contemporary Japanese Literature.* New York: Alfred A. Knopf, 1977.
Hinsch, Bret. *The Rise of Tea Culture in China.* Lanham, Boulder, New York, and London: Rowman and Littlefield, 2016.
Horimoto Kazushige. "Chanoyu kara mita Hakata." In Tanihashi Akio, ed., *Sadō gaku taikei 2 Sadō no rekishi,* pp. 297–327. Kyoto: Tankō sha, 2000.
Howell, David. *Capitalism from Within.* Berkeley and Los Angeles: University of California Press, 1995.
———. "Hard Times in the Kantō: Economic Change and Village Life in Late Tokugawa Japan." *Modern Asian Studies* 23 (1989): 349–371.
Iezuka Tomoko. "Chūsei chaya kō." *Ritsumeikan bungaku* 605 (March 2008): 44–58.
Ihara Saikaku. *The Japanese Family Storehouse.* Translated by G. W. Sargent. Cambridge: Cambridge University Press, 1959.
Imatani Akira. *Kyoto 1547 nen.* Heibon sha, 1988.
Inagaki Hiroaki. "Chūsei kuge no cha." In Tanihashi Akio, ed., *Sadō gaku taikei* 2 *Sadōgaku no rekishi,* pp. 53–90. Kyoto: Tankō sha, 1999.
Ishibashi Kentarō. "Tōcha to monkō." *Kusado sengen* 235 (December 1996): 5–7.
Ishida Masahiko. "'*Kantō ōgenki*' ni iu 'chocha' ni tsuite." *Chatō* 17 (1981): 13–30.
Itō Tadamasa. "Imabori jūzenshi sha no dōan to miyaza." In Nakamura Ken, ed., *Yōkaichi shishi 2 Chūsei,* pp. 546–592. Yōkaichi: Yōkaichi shiyakusho, 1983.
Itō Toshikazu. "Chūsei kōki ni okeru Tōdaiji ryō Yamato no kuni Kawakami no shō no yakibata keiei to cha saibai." *Nihon joshi daigaku bungaku bu kiyō* 48 (1999): 29–47.
Iwama Machiko. *Cha no iyaku shi.* Kyoto: Shibunkaku, 2009.
Kaempfer, Engelbert. *Kaempfer's Japan.* Edited, translated, and annotated by Beatrice M. Bodart-Bailey. Honolulu: University of Hawai'i Press, 1999.
Kamishiraishi Minoru. "Bunsei cha ikken." *Chihō shi kenkyū* 277 (February 1999): 18–35.
———. "Kinsei chūki Kawane cha no kōshō kiroku." *Tōyō daigaku daigakuin kiyō* 34 (1997): 657–673.
Kam Sung-hi. *Hanguk cha saenghwol jangsho.* Seoul: Hanguk cha saeng hwal mun hwayon, 1994.
Kanagawa ken. *Kessen shoku seikatsu kufū shū.* Osaka: Sangyō keizai shinbun sha, 1944.
Katō Seiji. "Tenpō kaikaku ni okeru 'kagema chaya' no haishi." *Fūzoku shigaku* 23 (March 2003): 80–95.
Kawabata Yasunari. *The Sound of the Mountain.* Charles E. Tuttle Company, 1970.
Kawashima Masao. "Chaten kō." *Tankō* (October 1975), pp. 33–37.
Kawazoe Shōji. "Kamakura chūki no taigai kankei to Hakata." *Kyushu shigaku* 88–90 (1988): 131–156.
———. "Yōsai to Imazu Seiganji." *Nihon rekishi* 332 (January 1976): 10–25.
Kida Taiichi. "Science of Tea—Part II." *Chanoyu Quarterly* (Autumn 1970), pp. 51–59.
Kim Pa Mang. "Kōrai Richō no kissa bunka to rekishi." In Takahashi Tadahiko, ed., *Sadō gaku taikei 7 Tōyō no cha,* pp. 183–224. Kyoto: Tankō sha, 2000.
Kokuritsu rekishi minzoku hakubutsukan, "Kodai chūsei toshi seikatsu shi (bukka)." http://www.rekihaku.ac.jp/up-cgi/searchrd.pl (accessed June 15, 2011).

Komatsu Kazuo. "Kinsei Osaka ni okeru seicha ryūtsū no henshitsu katei." *Shakai keizai shigaku* 36 (1970): 20–43.

Komeie Taisaku. *Chū kinsei sanson no keikan to kōzō.* Azekura shobō, 2002.

*The Konjaku Tales Japanese Section* (II) *from a Medieval Japanese Collection.* Translated, annotated, and introduced by Yoshiko Dykstra. Osaka: Kansai Gaidai University, 2001.

Koyama Kyōko. "Chūsei Kyoto ni okeru shomin no chaya." *Rakuhoku shigaku* 6 (2004): 102–117.

Kōzu Asao. *Chanoyu no rekishi.* Kadokawa sensho, 2009.

Kumahara Masao. *Kamakura no cha.* Kawahara shoten, 1948.

Kumakura Isao. *Chanoyu no rekishi—Sen Rikyū made.* Asahi sensho, 1990.

Kumakura Isao and Kanbayashi Shutarō. "Chagyō no hatten to chashi." *Uji shi shi* 2 *Chūsei no rekishi to keikan,* pp. 626–717. Uji: Uji shiyaku sho, 1974.

Kumakura Isao and Wakita Haruko. "Chagyō no shōhin ryūtsū hatten." *Uji shi shi* 2 *Chūsei no rekishi to keikan,* pp. 431–460. Uji: Uji shiyakusho, 1974.

Kumakura Isao et al., eds. *Yōsai 'Kissa yōjōki' no kenkyū.* Kyoto: Kyūtai shuppan sha, 2014.

Kurabayashi Masatsugu. *Kyōen no kenkyū:saiji sakuin hen.* Ōfū sha, 1980.

Mair, Victor, and Ehrling Hoh. *The True History of Tea.* London: Thames and Hudson, 2009.

McNeill, William. "The Historical Significance of the Way of Tea." In Paul Varley and Kumakura Isao, eds., *Tea in Japan,* pp. 255–264. Honolulu: University of Hawai'i Press, 1989.

Meeks, Lori. *Hokkeji and the Reemergence of Female Monastic Orders in Premodern Japan.* Honolulu: University of Hawai'i Press, 2010.

Mintz, Sidney. *Sweetness and Power.* New York: Penguin Books, 1985.

Mitsuzono, Isamu. "Mail-Order Retailing in Pre-War Japan: A Pathway of Consumption before the Emergence of the Mass Market." In Penelope Francks and Janet Hunter, eds., *The Historical Consumer: Consumption and Everyday Life in Japan, 1850–2000,* pp. 259–283. New York: Palgrave Macmillan, 2012.

Miwa Shigeo. *Mono to ningen no bunka shi* 25 *Usu.* Hōsei daigaku shuppan kyoku, 1978.

Miyamoto Tsutomu. "Sun'en cha ikken no rekishiteki tokushitsu." In Honda Takashige, ed., *Kinsei Shizuoka no kenkyū,* pp. 381–419. Osaka: Seibun dō, 1991.

Miyazaki Enjun. *Chūsei bukkyō to shomin seikatsu.* Kyoto: Nagata bunshō dō, 1987.

Moriya Atsushi and Nakamura Yasuo. "Uji sarugaku no katsudō." *Uji shi shi:* 2 *Chūsei no rekishi to keikan,* pp. 710–717. Uji: Uji shiyaku sho, 1974.

Murai Yasuhiko. *Cha no bunka shi.* Iwanami shinsho, 1979.

Nagai Susumu. "Chūsei tōgoku no ritsuin no cha." *Kamakura* 107 (2009): 27–41.

———. *Kanezawa Hōjō shi no kenkyū.* Yagi shoten, 2006.

———. *Kanezawa Sadaaki.* Yoshikawa kōbunkan, 2003.

———. "Sōron: Buke no miyako Kamakura no cha." In *Kikaku ten: Buke no miyako Kamakura no cha,* pp. 5–10. Yokohama: Kanezawa bunko, 2010.

Nagashima Fukutarō. "Yōsai zenshi to nanto no cha." *Nanto bukkyō* 16 (1965): 41–50.

Nagata Naoki. "Kokiroku ni miru Muromachi jidai no charei ni tsuite." *Geinōshi kenkyū* 134 (May 1996): 17–37.

Nakamura Shūya. "Yōsai izen no cha." In Tanihashi Akio, ed., *Sadō gaku taikei 2 Sadō no rekishi,* pp. 331–378. Kyoto: Tankō sha, 2000.

Nakamura Yōichirō. *Bancha to Nihonjin.* Yoshikawa kōbunkan, 1998.

———. *Cha no minzokugaku.* Meicho shuppan, 1992.

Nakano Yasuhide. *Shūgi, kissho, jufu.* Yoshikawa kōbunkan, 1988.
Nanbada Tetsu. "Kaiga ni miru shomin no incha fūzoku—shaji sankei manjara zu o chūshin ni." *Sadō shukin 2 Chanoyu no seiritsu,* pp. 24–33. Shōgakkan, 1984.
Natsume Soseki. *And Then.* University of Tokyo, 1978.
———. *Botchan.* Kodansha, 1972.
———. *The Wayfarer.* Rutland, VT: Charles E. Tuttle Company, 1967.
Nezu Munenobu. "*Daikan shingi* to gozan bungaku ni okeru kissa no shokeitai." *Nagano kenritsu rekishikan kenkyū kiyō* 9 (March 2003): 30–45.
Niigaki Tsutomu. "Okinawa ni okeru chanoyu no fukyū to sono eikyō." *Nantō kōko* 26 (2007): 209–220.
Nishimura Masaru. *Seichi no sōzōryoku.* Hōzōkan, 1998.
Nyūnoya Tetsukazu. "Ippuku issen cha shōkō." *Ritsumeikan bungaku* 509 (December 1988): 207–212.
Obama shi shi hensan iinkai, ed. *Obama shi shi: Tsūshi hen.* Vol. 1. Obama: Obama shiyakusho, 1992.
*Ocha to ukiyo-e: Egakareta Edo no ocha jijō.* Gyōsei, 1997.
Ōga Ikuo. *Kinsei sanson shakai kōzō no kenkyū.* Azekura shobō, 2005.
Ōhashi Toshio. "Chūsei Kamakura no chaen." *Sadō geppō* 471 (October 1951): 8–10.
Ōishi Sadao. *Nihon chagyō hattatsu shi.* Nōsangyoson bunka kyōkai, 2004.
———. *Shizuoka ken chasanchi shi.* Nōsangyoson bunka kyōkai, 2004.
Okamura Tatsuo. "Kinsei kōki Suruga no kuni Abe gun ni okeru cha ryūtsū no hen'yō." *Komazawa daigaku daigakuin shigaku ronshū* 40 (May 2010): 64–78.
Ono Yoshihiro. "Saga chō no Owari ni okeru rokuyū tōki seisan to sono haikei." *Kodai bunka* 54 (October 2002): 27–36.
Ōtsuki Yōko. "Ki no midokkyō no hikicha." *Kodaishi no kenkyū* 13 (December 2006): 17–27.
———. "Kyūseiki shotō no Tōfū bunka to cha." *Shoku Nihongi kenkyū* 363 (August 2008): 16–32.
———. "Tōsō Gikū ni tsuite no shohoteki kōsatsu." *Higashi Ajia bunka kōshō kenkyū* 1 (2010): 129–140.
Pitelka, Morgan. *Handmade Culture: Raku Potters, Patrons, and Tea Practitioners.* Honolulu: University of Hawai'i Press, 2005.
———, ed. *Japanese Tea Culture: Art, History, and Practice.* London: Routledge Curzon, 2003.
———. *Spectacular Accumulation: Material Culture, Tokugawa Ieyasu, and Samurai Sociability.* Honolulu: University of Hawai'i Press, 2015.
Pomeranz, Kenneth. *The Great Divergence: China, Europe, and the Making of the Modern World Economy.* Princeton, NJ: Princeton University Press, 2000.
"Remember to Drink Your Tea." *Tufts University Health & Nutrition Letter* 22 (January 2005): 6.
Roberts, Luke. *Mercantilism in a Japanese Domain: The Merchant Origins of Economic Nationalism in Eighteenth-century Tosa.* Cambridge: Cambridge University Press, 1998.
Rose, Sarah. *For All the Tea in China.* New York: Viking Press, 2010.
Rupp, Katherine. *Gift-Giving in Japan.* Stanford, CA: Stanford University Press, 2003.
Sakurai Eiji. "Ichi ni toshi o miru." *Asahi hyakka Nihon no rekishi bessatsu 7 Rekishi o yominaosu: Chūsei no tate to toshi,* pp. 60–69. Asahi shinbun sha, 1994.
"Sankan sonraku no shiteki kenkyū." *Shikan* 14 (1978): 1–194.
Sasagawa Hiroshi. "Hokuen chihō ni okeru Bunsei cha ikken no tenkai to kōzō." *Shikan* 20 (March 1988): 61–75.

———. "Kinsei kōki hokuen chihō ni okeru sonraku kōzō." *Shikan* 17 (December 1981): 1–18.
Sawamura Shin'ichi. "Chūsei izen no matcha no ryūdo to aji." *Nihon chōri kagakkai shi* 44 (March 2011): 39–45.
———. "Rikyū jidai izen no matcha no ryūdo ni kansuru kōsatsu." *Chanoyu bunkagaku* 17 (February 2010): 26–39.
Segal, Ethan. *Coins, Markets, and the State: Economic Growth in Early Medieval Japan.* Cambridge, MA: Harvard University Press, 2011.
Sen Sōshitsu XV. *The Japanese Way of Tea.* Honolulu: University of Hawai'i Press, 1998.
Shively, Donald. "Popular Culture." In John Hall and James McClain, eds., *The Cambridge History of Japan: Early Modern Japan,* pp. 706–770. Cambridge: Cambridge University Press, 1991.
———. "The Social Environment of Tokugawa Kabuki." In Nancy G. Hume, ed., *Japanese Aesthetics and Culture,* pp. 193–245. Albany: State University of New York, 1995.
———. "Sumptuary Regulation and Status in Early Tokugawa Japan." *Harvard Journal of Asiatic Studies* 25 (1964–1965): 123–164.
Shizuoka shiyakusho, ed. *Shizuoka shishi; kinsei.* Shizuoka: Shizuoka shiyakusho, 1979.
Smil, Vaclav, and Kazuhiko Kobayashi. *Japan's Dietary Transition and Its Impacts.* Cambridge, MA: MIT Press, 2012.
Smith, Thomas. "Pre-Modern Economic Growth: Japan and the West." *Past and Present* 60, no. 1 (1973): 127–160.
Sōma Noriko. "Ki no midokkyō ni okeru hikicha ni tsuite." *Geinōshi kenkyū* 169 (April 2005): 1–15.
Sugiyama, Shinya. *Japan's Industrialization in the World Economy, 1859–1899.* London and Atlantic Highlands, NJ: The Athlone Press, 1988.
Suk Yong-un. "History and Philosophy of the Korean Tea Art." *Koreana: Korean Art and Culture: Tea and Tea Culture* 11 (Winter 1997): 4–11.
Surak, Kristen. *Making Tea, Making Japan.* Stanford, CA: Stanford University Press, 2013.
Takagi Shingen. "Tōsō Gikū no raichō o meguru shomondai." *Kōyasan daigaku ronsō* 16 (February 1981): 55–90.
Takahashi Akihito. "Shiki chawan kubote yōki kō." *Kokuritsu rekishi minzoku hakubutsu kan kenkyū hōkoku* 71 (March 1997): 531–587.
Takahashi Shūei. "Kamakura jidai no mikkyōsho ni miru cha." *Kanezawa bunko kenkyū* 315 (October 2005): 1–9.
———. "Kanezawa bunko shiryō ni miru Kamakura jidai no cha." In Ōsumi Kazuo, ed., *Chūsei bukkyō to sono shūhen,* pp. 150–163. Yoshikawa kōbunkan, 2000.
Takahashi Yasuo. "Chaya: machishū bunka no ichidanmen." *Nihon toshi shi nyūmon* 3 *Hito,* pp. 238–239. Tokyo daigaku shuppan kai, 1990.
———. *Rakuchū rakugai.* Heibonsha, 1988.
Takemoto Chizu. "Sadō shi ni miru 'rinkan chanoyu' no ichizuke." In Futaki Ken'ichi, ed., *Sengoku shokuhō ki no shakai to girei,* pp. 417–435. Yoshikawa kōbunkan, 2006.
Tamamuro Taijō. "Sōshiki to butsuji." In Takeda Chōshū, ed., *Sōsō bosei kenkyū shūsei* 3 *Senzo kuyō,* pp. 66–92. Meicho shuppan, 1979.
Tanaka Fumio. "Tōjin no taiNichi kōeki." *Keizai kei* 229 (October 2006): 11–23.
Tanaka Minoru. *Chūsei shiryō ronkō.* Yoshikawa kōbunkan, 1994.
Tanihashi Akio. "Kaisho no cha to ippuku issen no cha." *Tankō* (May 1993), pp. 90–99.
Tanisaka, Chikako. *Jikayō cha.* Ōkawa shobō, 2004.

Tanizaki Jūnichirō. *The Makioka Sisters.* Charles E. Tuttle Company, 1957.

———. *Some Prefer Nettles.* New York: Alfred A. Knopf, 1955.

Terada Takashige. "Nara ken ni okeru shoki chagyō no tenkai ni tsuite." *Nara gaku kenkyū* 7 (March 2004): 17–25.

Teramoto Yasuhide. *Senzenki Nihon chagyō shi kenkyū.* Yūhikaku, 1999.

Thunberg, Carl Peter. *Japan Extolled and Decried.* Annotated and introduced by Timon Screech. New York: Routledge, 2005.

Totman, Conrad. *Early Modern Japan.* Berkeley and Los Angeles: University of California Press, 1993.

Tsubunouchi Junji. "Nagoya no Uji seihikicha hanbai o meguru shinkō chashōnin to Uji chashi." In Kishino Toshihiko, ed., *Owari han shakai no sōgō kenkyū,* 4:318–335. Osaka: Seibun dō, 2009.

———. "Uji chashi to Owari han." In Kishino Toshihiko, ed., *Owari han shakai no sōgō kenkyū,* 3:339–356. Osaka: Seibun dō, 2007.

Tsuji Nobuo. "Kazari to furo to cha." In *Kazari to Nihon bunka,* pp. 146–167. Kadokawa shoten, 1998.

Tsukada Takashi. *Kinsei Osaka no toshi shakai.* Yoshikawa kōbunkan, 2006.

Tsunoyama Sakae et al., eds. *Nihon no ocha 3 Ocha to bunka.* Gyosei, 1988.

Tsuruga shi shi hensan iinkai. *Tsuruga shi shi: Tsūshi hen.* Vol. 1. Tsuruga: Tsuruga shiyakusho, 1985.

Tsutsui Kōichi. "Dōjō kara shichū no sankyo e." *Rekishi kōron* 3 (September 1977): 80–88.

Varley, Paul, and Kumakura Isao, eds. *Tea in Japan: Essays on the History of Chanoyu.* Honolulu: University of Hawai'i Press, 1989.

von Siebold, Phillipp, Franz. *Manners and Customs of the Japanese.* Charles E. Tuttle Company, 1973.

Wakabayashi Atsushi. "Bunsei cha ikken no kōzō." *Shizuoka daigaku kyōiku gakubu kenkyū hōkoku* 10 (1959): 55–79.

Watanabe Shin'ichirō. *Edo no onnatachi no gurume jijō.* Toto Books, 1994.

———. *Edo no shomin ga hiraita shoku bunka.* Mitsuki shobō, 1996.

White, Merry. *Coffee Life in Japan.* Berkeley and Los Angeles: University of California Press, 2012.

Wiesner-Hanks, Merry. *Early Modern Europe, 1450–1789.* New York: Cambridge University Press, 2006.

Wigen, Kären. *The Making of a Japanese Periphery, 1750–1920.* Berkeley and Los Angeles: University of California Press, 1995.

Yamada Shin'ichi. *Edo no ocha—haikai cha no saijiki.* Yasaka shobō, 2007.

———. *Hana tachibana mo cha no kaori.* Shizuoka shinbun sha, 2008.

Yamada Tetsuya. "'Shōgetsu shōnin ate Kōben shojō' ni tsuite." *Chanoyu bunkagaku* 3 (March 1996): 67–72.

Yamagishi Tsuneto. "Hōe no hensen to 'ba' no yakuwari." In *Girei ni miru Nihon no bukkyō,* pp. 199–241. Kyoto: Hōzōkan, 2001.

Yamaguchi Satoshi. "Identeki tayōsei kara mita Nihon rokucha no kigen ni tsuite." *Cha no bunka* 5 (2004): 104–110.

Yamamoto, Shōzō. *Chagyō chiiki no kenkyū.* Daimeidō, 1973.

Yamashita, Samuel. *Leaves from an Autumn of Emergencies.* Honolulu: University of Hawai'i Press, 2003.

Yasuda Motohisa. *Nihon no rekishi 7 Insei to Heishi.* Yoshikawa kōbunkan, 1974.

Yoneda Mariko. "Chaso Yōsai zō no saikentō." *Geinōshi kenkyū* 177 (April 2007): 1–16.

Yoshimura Tōru. "Chatō ni miru mō hitotsu no cha bunka kenkyū: Sōgōteki na chabunka shi kenkyū o motomete." *Kyoto bunka tanki daigaku kiyō* 31/32 (1999): 3–12.
———. "Chūsei no cha: Chōsei to chagyō." *Kyoto bunka tanki daigaku kiyō* 3 (January 1985): 109–210.
———. "'Ippuku issen to monzen no chaya." *Chūsei chiiki shakai no rekishi zō,* pp. 273–290. Aun sha, 1997.
———. "Nitchū chazoku no hikaku shakai shi kenkyū." In *Sadō bunka gakujutsu josei kenkyū,* pp. 7–14. Santoku an, 2001.
———. "Nitchū chazoku no hikaku shakai shi kenkyū." In *Sadō bunka gakujutsu josei kenkyū,* pp. 1–8. Santoku an, 2002.
———. "San'iku sōsō girei ni miru Nitchū chazoku no hikaku kenkyū." *Hikaku Nihon bunka kenkyū* 8 (2004): 35–61.
———. *Uji bunko* 4 *Uji cha no bunka shi.* Uji: Uji shi kyōiku iinkai, 1993.
Yunomi Tea Shop, "The 41st Auction of Kanto Region Tea Competition." https://yunomi.us/12209/41st-auction-kanto-region-tea-competition (accessed March 18, 2016).
Zhang Jian-li. "Heian jidai kara Kamakura jidai ni okeru seicha." *Geinōshi kenkyū* 155 (2001): 1–19.
———. "Muromachi jidai ni okeru chaen to seicha." *Ritsumeikan bungaku* 574 (March 2002): 1–62.
———. *Sadō to chanoyu.* Kyoto: Tankō sha, 2004.

# Index

**Bold** page numbers refer to illustrations or tables.

Abe Masanobu, *The Suruga Journal* (*Suruga zasshi*), 95
advertising: in Edo period, 108, 111–112, **112**; newspaper, 143–145, **144**, 157; television commercials, 159, 163
agriculture: in Edo period, 73, 74, 123; productivity increases, 3, 34, 173; rice, 54–55, 56, 192n21; treatises, 83–87, 88–91, 97, 173, 192n19. *See also* tea farming
Akiba Yasukichi, 140
All-Japan Tea Merchants' Club (ZenNihon chashō kurabu), 158
Anrakuji, 21, 180n52
Anshōji, 14
Aozora Tea, 157
art: scroll paintings, 82; wood-block prints (*ukiyo-e*), 108, 112
Ashikaga Yoshimasa, 69, 84
Ashikaga Yoshinori, 57

Baisaō (Shibayama Kikusen), 93
*bancha*. *See* coarse steeped tea
Bitchū Province, 22, 59
black tea: exports, 132, 141–142, 151; Japanese production, 151–152; oxidized (*kuronicha*), 49, 186n80; processing methods, 5; production in modern era, 131, 133
botanical developments, 149–152
bottled tea, 127, 162–163, 164, 166, 174
"bowl for a coin" phrase, 3, 61, 63
brands, tea, 94–95, 98, 100–102, 129, 137, 151. *See also* Toganoo tea; Uji tea
brick tea, 16–17, 37
Britain: tea drinking, 175, 200n2, 201n8; tea imports, 124, 129
Buddhism: cultural impact, 34–35; rituals, 27, 29, 42, 57, 64–65. *See also* temples
Buddhist monks: in China, 8, 12–14, 20–21, 22, 53–54, 181n57; gifts of tea, 10, 12; in Japan, 7, 8; myths, 9–10, 21, 28, 182n76; sutra recitation, 15–16, 18, 27; tea cultivation, 9, 14, 21, 29, 30, 37–38, 41, 43, 46, 48, 53–54; tea shops, 60–61; Zen, 13, 50–51, 53–54, 182n80
Buddhist monks, tea consumption: in ancient times, 9–10; in China, 9–10, 12–14, 20–21, 23–24; in Kamakura era, 42–43; medicinal value, 17; in medieval era, 27–28, 29; ritual associations, 15, 27, 178n6 (ch. 1); Zen monks, 51, 187n89
Buddhist sects: Kegon, 28–29; Ritsu, 27, 36, 41; Shingon, 9–10, 23, 25, 27, 28, 180n36, 188n66; Tendai, 9–10, 13, 21, 22, 23. *See also* Zen Buddhism
Bunsei Tea Incident, 105, 114–122

caffeine, 5, 6, 171
catechins, 5
Chang-ya, 14
*chanoyu*. *See* tea ceremony
*chatsubo dōchū* (tea-jar journey), 98–100
China: immigrants from, 14, 23–24, 67, 93, 100, 193n24; merchants, 13, 14, 21; Ming dynasty, 53, 67, 92; ship captains, 23, 181n57; Song dynasty, 20–21, 22, 23–24, 25–26; Tang dynasty, 9–10, 12–13, 167; tea bowls, 9, 38, 63–64; tea consumption, 8, 9, 200n2; tea cultivation, 5, 8; tea drinking by monks, 9–10, 12–14, 20–21, 23–24; tea grinders, 38–39, 184n23; tea plants, 5, 53; trade with Japan, 13, 14, 23, 38, 43
Chōgen, 22, 23
Chōsokabe family, 101–102
coarse steeped tea (*bancha*): in contemporary Japan, 161; drinkers, 86, 145; harvesting, 80; in modern era, 131, 132, 137; processing methods, 95, 96, 101; from Shizuoka, 104; from Tosa, 101, **101**; vendors, 63
coffee: caffeine, 5, 171; competition with tea, 127, 133–134, 156, 157–158, 159, 161, 166, 170, 174; vending machines, 162
coffee culture, 146, 165
*Collection of Monthly Agrarian Instructions for a New People, A* (*Shinmin kangetsu shū*), 83
comedic skits, 63, 82, 111, 189n140, 190n142
commercial organizations. *See* merchant organizations
consumer society: dietary transformation and, 156; as economic development driver, 4; in Edo period, 74, 97–98, 108, 114, 123–124; negative impacts, 175; role of tea consumption, 4, 173–175, **174**. *See also* advertising
consumption of tea: in ancient times, 7–9, 10–11, 12–19, 32, 167; with bath, 65; in China, 8, 9–10, 200n2; by commoners, 63–65, 72, 81, 86–87; in contemporary Japan, 4, 32, 127, 160–164, 166; daily, 123, 126, 145; demand, 4, 18, 30, 53; in Edo period, 3, 86–88, 94, 96, 97–98, 107, 108–109, 113–114, 123–124; by elites, 7–9, 11, 12, 13, 14–16, 17–19, 24, 32, 40, 42, 43–44, 69–70, 71; at festivals, 109; in fifteenth and sixteenth centuries, 52, 82; future of, 175–176; in Korea, 57, 180n48, 200n2; measuring, 98; by military troops, 46; in modern era, 113, 126–127, 134, 143–145, 156–160, 166, **174**; in northern Japan, 75, 81, 160; by peasants, 4, 96, 107; with rice, 103, 109, 160; by samurai, 24, 29–31, 35–36, 41; spread, 3, 4, 18, 31–32, 35, 64–65, 145, 173–174; stimulative effects, 3, 5, 66, 87, 123, 171; surveys, 145, 159–160; in wartime, 157. *See also* Buddhist monks, tea consumption; rituals; tea gatherings
"country tea" (*inaka cha*), 38
culture, Japanese: comedic skits, 63, 82, 111, 189n140, 190n142; in Edo period, 73, 108; films, 160; functions of tea, 2, 71; kabuki plays and actors, 109–110, 111; literature, 146–147, 160; popular, 165; scroll paintings, 82; traditional, 163, 165; wood-block prints (*ukiyo-e*), 108, 112. *See also* poetry

Daianji, Nara, 9, 11, 14, 15
Daigo, tea fields, 88, 91
Daigoji, 27, 45
Daijiji, 27
*Daijōin jisha zōjiki*, 65
Daitokuji, 69
Dazaifu, 13, 14, 21
De Vries, Jan, 172
dietary transformation, 156, 157–158, 174
Dōji, 9
druggist's mortars (*yakken*), 16–17, **16**, 26, 27, 179n30
Dutch East India Company, 109, 122, 146
Dutch traders, 34, 73, 109, 113–114, 124, 192n21

Echigo Province, 57, 77, 79, 81, 93
economic development: drivers, 3–4; in Edo period, 73–74, 87, 95–96, 97–98; industrious revolution, 66, 74, 81, 87, 90, 123, 171–173; in medieval era, 34; in Meiji period, 125; role of tea, 4, 66, 72, 87, 123, 171–173; in twentieth century, 126, 156; virtuous circle, 66, 87, 171–172
Edo: festivals, 109; growth, 73; merchant organizations, 115–121; restaurants, 103, 108; sex shops, 109; tea consumption, 86–87; tea shops, 103, 108; tea trade, 107
Edo period: advertising, 108, 111–112, **112**; agriculture, 73, 74, 123; consumer society, 74, 97–98, 108, 114, 123–124; economic

development, 73–74, 87, 95–96, 97–98; politics, 73–74; tea consumption, 3, 86–88, 94, 96, 97–98, 107, 108–109, 113–114, 123–124; tea farming, 74, 79–82, 83–85, 88–89, 96, 98, 102–107, 123, 172; tea industry, 94–98, 100–108, 122–124, 129, 175; tea markets, 81–82, 87, 90, 91, 94, 105, 121–122, 129, 172; tea processing, 86, 89–91, 92–97, 193n25, 194nn36–37; tea shops, 105, 108, 196n76; trade, 107–108, 141
Eisai. *See* Yōsai
Eison, 27, 29–30, 182n76
Enchin, 14
Enni, 181n57
Ennin, 13–14
Enryakuji, 14, 20, 21, 22, 23, 47
entertainment districts. *See* "floating world"
esoteric Buddhism, 9–10, 25, 27–28, 29
Etchū Province, 80, 192n16
Europe, tea imports, 124, 127–129, 141–142. *See also* Dutch traders; Jesuits
Experimental Laboratory for Tea Processing of the Agricultural Office (*Nōmukyoku seicha shikensho*), 135, 149
exports, 126, 127. *See also* trade
exports, tea: black tea, 132, 141–142, 151; to Europe, 124, 127–129; marketing structures, 143; new markets, 134; raw tea, 133; to United States, 127, 129, 130, 132, 133–134, 142, 162; volumes, 133–134, **133**, 147, 152, 156, 161–162, **162**

farming. *See* agriculture; tea farming
films, 160
Five Mountains Poetry, 51–52
"floating world," 108, 109
foods: dietary transformation, 156, 157–158, 174; dishes including tea, 16, 103, 109, 145, 160. *See also* restaurants; rice
Francks, Penelope, 66, 87, 171–172
Frois, Luis, 63
Fujiwara family, Byōdōin estate, 180n37
Fujiwara no Fuyutsugu, 11, 19
Fujiwara no Michinaga, 17
Fujiwara no Sanesuke, 17, 18
Fujiwara no Tadachika, 19
Fujiwara no Tsunefusa, 19
Fujiwara Tadazane, 18–19, 180n37
Fujiwara Tamefusa, 19
Fujiwara Yorinaga, 19, 180n37
Fujiwara Yukinari, 18
Fukujuen, 163
Fukuoka, Haraguchien, 159
Fukuoka tea, 100
Fukushima earthquake and tsunami, 126, 165
Furuta Oribe, 165

gift giving: by court officials, 50; by elites, 40, 42, 57; in fifteenth and sixteenth centuries, 52, 56–57; in fourteenth century, 49–50; among monks, 30, 42–43, 49; among samurai, 57; of tea, 7–8, 10, 12, 13, 21, 30, 31, 32, 38
Gion Shrine, 47–48, 49, 61, 62–63, 64
GoDaigo, retired emperor, 44, 46
GoIchijō, retired emperor, 18
GoSaga, retired emperor, 27
GoToba, retired emperor, 27, 28, 35
Graham, Patricia, 193n24
green tea: consumption in Japan, 4, 32, 174; exports, 133, 134, 142, 162, 164–165; health benefits, 4, 143, 145, 163; Japanese production, 160–161; worldwide appeal, 1, 4, 142. *See also* tea
grinders, 17, 18, 23–24, 38–39, **39**. *See also* stone grinders
*gyokuro*. *See* "jeweled dew" tea

Hakata, 22, 23–24, 181n57
Haraguchien, 159
harvesting (plucking) tea: laborers, 56, 103, 136–137, 139; mechanization, 152, 155; modern techniques and tools, 136–137; multiple pickings, 37, 80; timing, 56, 79–80, 81
Hashimoto Kanbenosuke, 60
Hayami Akira, 171, 172
health. *See* medicinal value of tea
Heian, 10, 13, 14
Heian period, 12, 13, 18–21
Hiei, Mount, 12, 14, 22. *See also* Enryakuji
Hirohashi Morimitsu, 57
Hitomi Hitsudai, *Food Mirror for This Dynasty* (*Honchō shokkan*), 83, 84–87, 88, 89, 103, 105, 193n23, 193n25
Hiyoshi Shrine, 103, 188n115
Hōjō family, 22, 35, 36
Hōjō Masako, 22, 24
Hōjō Takatoki, 42
Hong Lin-min, 67

Honshu, 44, 53, 68, 75, 80–81, 129, 130
hospitality stations (*settai sho*), 60–61
Hyōgo, 59, 65, 102

Ibaraki tea, 105–106, 107, 138
Iga Province, 41, 50
Ihara Saikaku, 77–78; *Irozato mitokoro zetai* (Households from Three Places in the Red-Light District), 105
Ikeda Shūji, 158
*Illustrated Explanation of Tea Processing, An* (*Seicha zukai*), 137, 141
Inaba Province, 52, 53
India: Assam tea, 142, 151; tea plants, 5, 151; tea production, 133, 141, 142, 150
Indonesia, tea production, 133, 141, 150
industrialization, 3–4. *See also* economic development
industrious revolution, 66, 74, 81, 87, 90, 123, 171–173
insecticides, 135, 148–149
Ippodō Tea Shop, 158–159
Irobe family, 57
Ise Shrine, 54, 55
Ise tea, 45, 75, 103, 134, 139
Itoen, 17, 162, 164, 179n30
Izumi Province, 38, 45, 46

Japanese society: in ancient times, 7; commoners, 7, 35, 63–65, 72, 81, 86–87; in Edo period, 73–74; future changes, 175–176; in medieval era, 53; rural villages, 34, 56, 64; in twentieth century, 126. *See also* consumer society; culture; peasants; samurai
Jesuits, 34, 63, 70, 195n60
"jeweled dew" (*gyokuro*) tea, 93–94, 100–101, 131–132, 136, 161, 162, 194n46
Jianzhen (Ganjin), 9
*Jizō bosatsu reigenki-e*, 60–61
Jōjin, 20–21
Jōkei, 27
Jōshōji, 21

kabuki plays and actors, 109–110, 111
*kabusecha*, 131, 161
Kaempfer, Engelbert, 122, 193n25, 194n37, 195n60
Kaga domain, 79
Kagoshima tea, 100–101, 134, 150, 151
Kaibara Ekken, 77, 194n40

*kamairicha*. *See* stir-roasted tea
Kamakura, 29–32, 35, 43, 59
Kamakura period, 21–27, 35–44
Kamakura shogunate, 22–23, 24, 29, 35–44
Kamisaka Seiichi, 93
Kanbayashi family, 59, 70, 84, 99, 102, 195n60
Kanezawa, 43, 59
Kanezawa Akitoki, 36, 42
Kanezawa Hōjō, 36–38, 40, 42, 43
Kanezawa Sadaaki, 36–38, 39, 40–41, 42, 43–44
Kano Koshiro, *An Agricultural Testament* (*Nōji yuisho*), 79–80
Kanto: tea production, 38, 105–106; temples, 41. *See also* Kamakura
Katsumi Shinsaku, 152
Kawabata Yasunari, *The Sound of the Mountain*, 160
Kawaji Toshiakira, 120–121
Ken'a, 38, 39, 41, 42–43
Kenninji, 23, 30, 51, 61
Kii Province, 28, 45, 48, 52, 53, 54, 59, 84, 95
Kinai, 10, 14, 29, 41, 45, 52–53, 57, 77
Kitagawa Utamaro, *A Collection of Six Famous Beauties (Okita of Nanbaya)*, **113**
Kitano Shrine, 61, 64
Kobashi Risuke, 77–78
Kobe, 127–128
Kōfukuji, 9, 21, 56, 58, 60, 64
Korea: ambassadors, 57; Chosŏn dynasty, 57, 67; elites, 8; Koryŏ dynasty, 180n48; Silla, 13, 178n6 (ch. 1), 200n2; spread of tea to, 8; tea consumption, 57, 180n48, 200n2; tea grinders, 184n23
Kōya, Mount, 21, 27, 46
Kōzanji, 28–29, 41–42, 69
Kujō Kanezane, 19
Kūkai, 9–10, 11, 12–13, 14, 27
Kurosawa Akira, *Ikiru*, 160
Kusado Sengen, 65
Kyoto: festivals, 109; imperial court, 35; Rokuhara Office, 35, 36, 41, 43; tea consumption, 41, 64–65; tea shops, 60, 61, 64, 108, 158–159, 163; tea trade, 59, 107; temples, 20, 21, 23, 30, 36, 51, 61
Kyushu: battles, 44; Chinese immigrants, 14, 23–24, 67, 100; tea fields, 23, 50; tea production, 14, 67, 68, 100–101, 130, 154; temples, 21, 27; trade, 13, 14; Ureshino, 67–69, 91, 145

laborers: rice farming, 56; tea consumption, 3, 66, 87, 123, 171; tea farming, 47–49, 56, 134, 136, 152; tea harvesting, 56, 103, 136–137, 139; tea processing, 47–49, 74, 122, 134, 137–139, 155; women, 134, 136, 138–139
land values, 46, 48
leaf tea (*hacha*), 37, 183n4
literature, references to tea, 146–147, 160. *See also* poetry
*Lotus Sutra*, 41, 42, 55
Lu Yu, *The Classic of Tea* (*Chajing*), 8, 16–17, 25, 26

Machidaen honten, 158
Makinohara, Shizuoka, 131, 134–135, 140
Mandokoro tea, 103–104
marketing, 163, 165. *See also* advertising; bottled tea
markets: auctions, 164; in Edo period, 81–82, 87, 90, 91, 94, 105, 172; in fifteenth and sixteenth centuries, 58–60; mail order, 143; in Meiji period, 142–143; in modern era, 157–159; retailers, 163–164. *See also* merchants; prices; tea shops
Marukyū Koyamaen, 164
*matcha*. *See* powdered tea
Matsumoto Machines, 152
Matsuo Bashō, 110
medicinal value of tea: antioxidants, 6; from boiled water, 3, 65–66, 123, 172; evidence of, 180n52; of green tea, 4, 143, 145, 163; for hangovers, 17, 24, 25, 87; health benefits, 3, 6, 7, 14–16, 17–18, 25, 63, 87, 166; in Kamakura period, 42; in medieval era, 30; vitamin C, 143, 145; Yōsai on, 24–25
medieval era: economic development, 34; Japanese society, 53; tea consumption, 27–32, 37, 49, 57, 63; tea markets, 37, 46–47, 48
Meiji period, 125, 129–131, 134–135, 141–143. *See also* modern era
Meiji Tea, 157
merchant organizations, 59–60, 62, 76, 78, 105, 107–108, 118. *See also* Bunsei Tea Incident
merchants: Chinese, 13, 14, 21; in Edo period, 94, 107; foreign, 34, 73, 109, 113–114, 124, 128, 192n21; middlemen, 76, **77**, 78, 116, 117, 143; in modern era, 157, 158; in northern Japan, 76–78; tea drinking, 65. *See also* Dutch traders; teahouses; tea industry
Mibu family, 55, 56
Mie tea, 106, 131, 138, 150, 151
Minamoto no Sanetomo, 23, 24
Minamoto Tsuneyori, 18
Ministry for Agriculture, Forestry, and Fisheries, 161
Ministry of Agriculture and Commerce, 139, 150
Ministry of Agriculture and Forestry, 149, 151, 152
Mino Province, 45, 49, 53, 75, 77, 78, 129, 192n16
Miyagi prefecture, 106
Miyake Yarai, 194n40
Miyamoto Shōun, *Discussions of Household Agriculture* (*Shika nōgyō dan*), 80–82
Miyazaki tea, 100, 134, 150
Miyazaki Yasusada, 80, 83, 140, 172; *Complete Works on Agriculture*, 88–91, 97
Mizuno Tadakuni, 118
Mochizuki Hatsutarō, 140
modern era: tea consumption, 113, 126–127, 134, 143–145, 156–160, 166, **174**; tea farming, 134–137, 141, 142, 147–152, 155, 165–166; tea industry, 126–127, 131–134, **132**, 139–145, 147, 155–156, 158–160, 165–166, **174**; tea processing, 137–141, 142, 152–155; tea shops, 158–159, 164; technology, 125
Motoori Norinaga, 103
mountain tea: environmental conditions, 5, 79, 88–89; in Kamakura, 37–38; locations, 31, 45, 54, 100, 101, 102, 103–105; in north, 79; use of term, 38. *See also* Toganoo
Murata Jukō, 70, 71
Muromachi shogunate, 44, 53, 55, 57, 64, 67, 69
Mutsu Province, 76, 77, 86
Myōe, 28–29, 41, 69
Myōkōen, 159
Myōrakuji, 57

Nagai Kafū, 146, 147
Nagasaki, 73, 93, 100, 109, 127–128, 193n24
Nagatani Yoshihiro, 91–93, 98
Nakahara Hirotoshi, 19
Nakahara Moromori, 49–50, 186n81
Nakashima Masahisa, 76–77

Nara: Daianji, 9, 11, 14, 15; tea consumption, 87; tea farming, 30–31, 102–103; tea merchants, 60; tea shops, 60, 61; tea transactions, 59; temples, 36. *See also* Kōfukuji
Nara period, 9, 10, 12
Nara tea, 87, 150, 189n88
Natsume Soseki, 146
Ninnaji, 20, 21, 41, 46–47, 69
Ninshō, 41
northern Japan: merchants, 76–78; tea consumption, 75, 81, 160; tea farming, 74–75, 79–82, 106–107, 129, 130; tea processing, 79, 81, 91, 192n16; trade, 75–78
nutrition. *See* foods

Obama, 75, 78, 107
Ōbayashi Yūya, 149, 150
Ōeda Ryūhō, *Tea Chats on an Azure Bay* (*Seiwan chawa*), 92
Ogawa Kashin, 93
Okinawa, 53, 100, 145
Ōkubo Toshimichi, 141–142
Ōkura Nagatsune, *A Consideration for Broadly Profiting the National Industry* (*Kōeki kokusan kō*), 95–97, 123, 135
Ōmi Province, 55, 56, 64, 103–104, 188n105
Ōnin War, 64
Onjōji, 20, 21, 36
*The Ordinances of Engi*, 9, 15
Organization for Progress in Tea Processing (Seicha kyōshin kai), 141
Osaka: festivals, 109; tea shops, 103, 108, 109; tea trade, 96, 100, 102, 107; traders, 76–77, 78
Ōtaka Zenbei, 94
Ōtomo family, 100
Ōtsuka Giichirō, 135
Owari domain, 99–100
Owari Province, 9, 77, 95, 104, 129

paintings, 82
parboiled tea (*yubiku cha*), 89–90
Parhae, 12, 13
peasants: Bunsei Tea Incident, 114–122; tea consumption, 4, 96, 107; tea farming, 35, 56, 79, 91, 115–117; villages, 34, 56, 64
*Peasant's Life, A* (*Hyakushō denki*), 83–84, 85
peddlers, 3, 62, **62**, 82, 109
Perry, Matthew, 74, 100, 114, 119, 120, 125
PET bottles, 127, 162–163, 164, 166, 174
plucking tea. *See* harvesting
poetry: Chinese, 43, 44; haiku, 108, 110; inspired by tea, 200n2; references to tea, 10, 14, 19–20, 21, 51–52, 110–111; by Zen monks, 51–52
population growth, 34, 53, 66, 72, 73, 107, 159
porcelain tea bowls, 9, 13, 61, 63–64
powdered tea (*matcha*): in contemporary Japan, 164; in Edo period, 84; elite demand for, 70; exports, 132; introduction to Japan, 21–22, 23–24; leaf-picking methods, 136; in medieval era, 37, 63; in Meiji period, 131; in modern era, 132, 154; processing methods, 154. *See also* Uji tea
prices, tea: auctions, 164; in Edo period, 105, 121–122, 129; in fifteenth and sixteenth centuries, 58–59; in medieval era, 37, 46–47, 48; in Meiji period, 139; in twentieth century, 152
*Pure Precepts of the Great Mirror* (*Daikan shingi*), 51

raw tea (*aracha*), 133, 164
*Record of a Journey to the Kanto and Back, The* (*Kantō ōgenki*), 29
*Record of the Western Palace, The* (*Saikyūki*), 15–16
restaurants, 1, 4, 103, 108, 162
rice: cultivation, 54–55, 56, 192n21; dishes, 103, 109, 160
rituals: associations with tea in different societies, 200n2; court, 15–16, 18, 19, 27, 180n41; family, 42, 65, 80; funerary, 27; New Year's, 57, 109, 111, 160; religious, 15–16, 27, 29, 42, 57, 64–65, 178n6 (ch. 1); of samurai, 57; of Tokugawa shogunate, 98–100
Rodrigues, João, 70, 192n20, 193n24, 195n60
Rokuhara Office, 35, 36, 41, 43
roof-over method, 42, 70, **71**, 85
Ryōgen, 20

Saga, Emperor, 10–11, 12, 102
Saichō, 9–10, 11, 12, 14, 21–22, 23
Saidaiji, 29, 41, 182n76
Saitama prefecture, 134, 138, 150, 151, 158
Sakai Jinshirō, 136

Sakamoto Tōkichi, 93
samurai: gift exchanges, 57; landlords, 35; political power, 34, 35; rituals, 57; tea consumption, 24, 29–31, 35–36, 41; tea farming, 134–135; tea merchants and, 60
Sanuki, 14, 53
Sasayama domain, 102
Sayama tea, 105, 134
Sen Rikyū, 70, 71
*sencha* (steeped tea): in contemporary Japan, 161, 162; development, 82–83, 91–93; drunk by Chinese immigrants, 193n24; exports, 132; in modern era, 132, 157; Nagatani's innovations, 92–93; popularity, 4, 82, 93, 97–98, 145; prices, 101; processing methods, 92, 94–95, 137; use of term, 178n5
Settsu Province, 45, 46, 52, 53
Shibayama Kikusen (Baisaō), 93
Shigaraki tea, 81, 94, 95, 104
Shikoku Province, 53, 68, 94, 101, 107, 129, 130, 131
Shimazu domain, 100–101
Shimōsa Province, 36, 41, 45, 53, 86, 106
Shizuoka: Ashikubo village, 104, 115, 194n40, 194n46; black tea produced, 152; Bunsei Tea Incident, 114–122; merchant organizations, 105; tea farming, 104, 110, 130, 131, 134, 135, 136, 151; tea market, 157, 164; tea processing, 137, 138, 143, 153, 154; trade routes, 104
Shōmyōji, 36, 37–38, 39, 40–41, 42–43, 47, 185n33, 186n71
Siebold, Philip Franz von, 109, 196n76
Silla, 13, 178n6 (ch. 1), 200n2
Sin Suk-ju, 61
"Something Steeped" (*senjimono*), 63
Son'ei, 30–31, 35–36, 183n88
Sŏng Hui-gyŏng, 57
*Sound of the Mountain, The*, 160
South African restaurants, 1, 162
Sri Lanka: tea plants, 151; tea production, 133, 141, 150
steeped tea: in China, 92; in early periods, 16; exports, 137; in modern era, 131, 132; popularity, 92, 93–94; preparation, 194n36; before *sencha* invention, 84, 86–87, 90; *senjicha*, 63, 82, 89, 90; use of term, 178n5. *See also* coarse steeped tea; *sencha*
stir-roasted tea (*kamairicha*): in medieval era, 49, 57; in modern era, 132; monks drinking, 187n89; processing methods, 90–91, 96–97, 153–154; "Tang tea" (*tōcha*), 67–69, 89, 97
stone grinders: in China, 38–39, 184n23; in Edo period, 84; introduction to Japan, 38–39; in modern era, 154; use of, 56, 63, 82, 191n169, 191n171
street tea peddlers (*furiuri*), 3, 62, **62**, 82, 109
Sūfukuji, 9, 10
Sugawara no Michizane, 14
Sugiyama Hikosaburō, 149, 150, 151
Sugiyama, Shinya, 127
Sunpu: castle, 104; merchant organizations, 105, 114, 115–121; tea trade, 105, 107
Suruga Province, 54, 115, 118, 120, 122
Suruga tea, 45, 84, 86, 90, 95, 104, 105, 129
*Sutra of Great Wisdom* (*Dai hannya-kyō*), 15, 18

Tachibana Kachiko, 13
Tada Motokichi, 142
Taihan, 10, 12
Taira no Nobunori, 19
Taishō period, 125–126. *See also* modern era
Taiwanese tea plants, 151
Takabayashi Kenzō, 139–140
Takamori meicha dō, 158
Takeno Jōō, 70, 71
Takezaki Yoshinori, 149–150
*Tales of Times Now Past* (*Konjaku monogatari*), 18
Tanba Province, 14, 45, 46, 53, 56, 78, 95, 99, 102
Tan'ei, 37, 38
"Tang tea" (*tōcha*), 67–69, 89, 97
Tanizaki Jūnichirō, 146–147, 160
tannin, 6, 136, 142
taxes: paid in tea, 57–58, 115; on tea bushes, 103; on tea production, 104; on tea shipments, 60; tribute, 10, 14, 31, 41
tea: brick, 16–17, 37; color and odor, 37, 39; containers, 40, 128, **128**; cultural references, 108; future in Japan, 175–176; introduction to Japan, 7, 8, 9–11, 21–22; leaf, 37, 183n4; taste change in thirteenth century, 38–40, 42, 44; as tribute item, 10, 14, 31, 41
tea bowls, 9, 13, 19, 24, 27, 38, 61, 63–64

tea bushes. *See* tea farming; tea plant
tea ceremony (*chanoyu*), 1–2, 84, 165, 200n2
tea fairs, 141
tea farming: in ancient times, 7, 10–12, 14, 32, 167; in Edo period, 74, 79–82, 83–85, 88–89, 96, 98, 102–107, 123, 172; environmental conditions, 5, 53, 79, 81, 88–89, 96; fertilizers, 79, 83, 85, 88, 89, 96, 134–135, 148, 173; fields, 46, 48, 59; on flat lands, 131, 134, 140; for home use, 54, 79, 81, 96, 107, 123, 142, 145, 157, 172; at Imperial Palace, 16; laborers, 47–49, 56, 134, 136, 152; mechanization, 141, 152; in Meiji period, 129–131, 134–135; in modern era, 134–137, 141, 142, 147–152, 155, 165–166; by monks, 9, 14, 21, 29, 30, 37–38, 41, 43, 46, 48, 53–54; in northern Japan, 79–82, 106–107, 129, 130; number of households, 161; by peasants, 35, 56, 79, 91, 115–117; planting, 83–84, 85, 88–89, 193n23; productivity, 37, 71–72, 130–131, 134–135, 148, 173; roof-over method, 42, 70, **71**, 85; in shady areas, 41–42, 54; spread, 31, 35, 38, 45, 52–54, 72, 74–75; swidden style, 38, 54, 105, 173; typology of fields, 54–55. *See also* harvesting; mountain tea
tea gatherings (*chakai*), 43–44
teahouses (*chaya*), 58, 60–64, 103. *See also* tea shops
tea industry: in contemporary Japan, 160–165, **161**; economic development role, 4, 66, 72, 87, 123, 171–173; in Edo period, 94–98, 100–108, 122–124, 129, 175; emergence, 45; in fifteenth and sixteenth centuries, 52–54, 56–66; in fourteenth century, 44–49, 52; geographical spread, 98, 106–107; historical evolution, 35, 71–72, 167–171; in modern era, 126–127, 129–134, **132**, 139–145, 147, 155–156, 158–160, 165–166, **174**. *See also* marketing; trade
Tea Industry Cooperative (Chagyō kumiai), 141
Tea Industry Symposium (Chagyō shūdan kai), 141
tea-jar journey (*chatsubo dōchū*), 98–100
tea merchants. *See* merchants
tea plant (*Camellia sinensis*): botanical developments, 149–151; description, 4–5; growth, 136; images in family crests, 108, 111; maturation period, 11; pests, 135, 148–149; pollination, 5, 12; propagation, 5, 12, 147–148, 149, 151; pruning, 89, 135, 136; seedlings, 147–148; strains, 150–151; varieties imported from China, 53–54. *See also* tea farming
tea processing: black tea, 5; braziers, 137; brick tea, 16–17; in China, 23–24, 25–26; in early periods, 7, 14–15, 16–17, 32, 167; in Edo period, 86, 89–91, 92–97, 193n25, 194nn36–37; on estates, 56; of green tea, 5; grinders, 17, 18, 23–24, 38–39, **39**, 184n23; laborers, 47–49, 74, 122, 134, 137–139, 155; mechanization, 126, 134, 139–140, 152–155, **153**; in modern era, 137–141, 142, 152–155; by monks, 21, 49; in northern Japan, 79, 81, 91, 192n16; of oxidized tea, 186n80; roasters, 49, **50**, 56, 89, 92; rolling by hand, 137, **138**; rotational crumbling, 138; of *sencha*, 92, 94–95, 137; standardization, 139, 140–141, 147; stir-roasting pots, 67–68, **68**, 90–91; in thirteenth century, 38–39; Yōsai on, 26–27. *See also* stone grinders
tea shops: in cities, 108, 163; comedic skits, 111; competition from coffee houses, 146; in Edo period, 105, 108, 196n76; modern companies, 158–159, 164; at temples, 61, 62–63, 64
tea utensils: bamboo containers, 38; in rituals, 42; scoops, 38; at temples, 27, 38, 51, 182n76; whisks, 26, 39–40, 44
tea vessels: ashes buried in, 19, 180n36; at temples, 27
temples: tea shops, 61, 62–63, 64; tea utensils, 27, 38, 51, 182n76; Zen, 51, 53, 57, 69. *See also* Buddhist monks; *and individual names*
Terashima Ryōan, 194n40
theater, kabuki plays and actors, 109–110, 111
toasted tea (*aburicha*), 49
Tōdaiji, 15, 21, 22, 23, 27, 28, 55, 57
Toganoo: Kōzanji, 28–29, 41–42, 69; tea fields, 29, 41–42, 54, 69, 88, 91
Toganoo tea, 29, 41–42, 44, 45, 57, 69, 93
Tohoku, 75, 79, 81, 129
Tōji, 13, 20, 21, 27, 61, 64, 65
Tōkaido, 99, 104
Tōkōji, 14, 104
Tokugawa Iemitsu, 98

Tokugawa Ieyasu, 34, 70, 73, 104
Tokugawa shogunate: Bunsei Tea Incident, 105, 114–122; economic development, 171, 172; establishment, 73; fall of, 125; tea-related rituals, 98–100; Uji tea fields, 70. *See also* Edo period
Tosa tea, 101–102, **101**
Tōtōmi Province, 52, 53, 57, 83, 115, 118
Toyotomi Hideyoshi, 34, 70
trade: with China, 13, 14, 23, 38, 43, 181n57; disruptions, 46; in Edo period, 107–108, 141; with Europe, 34, 73, 124, 127–129, 141; within Japan, 30, 31–33, 75–78; reforms, 118; regulations, 13; routes, 107, 119, 128; shipping boxes, 128, **128**; treaty ports, 127–128. *See also* exports; merchants
tribute tax, 10, 14, 31, 41
Tsuchiya Matasaburō, *Cultivating in Spring and Autumn* (*Kōka shunjū*), 79
*Tsukinami fūzoku zu*, **62**
Tsuruga, tea trade, 75–78, **76**, 107

Ueda Akinari, *Miscellaneous Comments on the Way of Pure Elegance* (*Seifū sagen*), 94–95, 104
*Uesugi bon rakuchū rakugai zu byōbu*, 64
Uji Saburōemon, 65
Uji Tawara village, 91–92, 94
Uji tea: comedic skits, 189n140; in Edo period, 98–100; exports, 150; fields, 59, 69, 70, 88; on Fujiwara estate, 180n37; marketing, 143; in medieval era, 186n62; popularity, 145; prices, 59; processing methods, 137–138; producers, 98, 99, 143, 164; reputation, 45, 69–70, 84, 91, 102, 112, 195n60; steeped tea methods, 93–94
United States: occupation of Japan, 157; tea imports, 127, 129, 130, 132, 133–134, 142, 162; tea served in restaurants, 1, 162; trade with, 127–129. *See also* Perry, Matthew
Urasenke, 164
Ureshino: Chinese immigrants, 67; tea, 67–69, 91, 95, 145, 163
Usui Kiichirō, 140

Wakasa Province, 53, 65, 75, 78, 107
Warring States period, 34, 56–57, 64, 65, 70
wood-block prints (*ukiyo-e*), 108, 112
World War II, 126, 130, 133, 148, 151, 157

Xu Gong-you, 13
Xu Gong-zhi, 13

Yamamoto Kihei, 93
Yamashina family, 58
Yamashiro Province, 9, 47, 53, 55, 56, 58, 59, 88, 91. *See also* Toganoo; Uji
Yamato Province, 10, 31, 44, 45, 46, 53, 54, 95
Yamauchi family, 101
*Yari no Gonza kasane katabira* (Pikeman Gonza), 109–110
Yi-kong, 13
Yin Yuan, 92
Yōchū, 10, 11, 12–13
Yokohama, 127–128, 143
Yonezaki, 106
Yōsai (Eisai), 21–27, 28, 182n66; *Drink Tea and Prolong Your Life* (*Kissa yōjō ki*), 24–26, 27, 182n64, 182n68
Yoshidaen, 164
Yoshino, 21, 44

Zen Buddhism: in China, 22, 23; monasteries, 51; monks, 13, 50–51, 53–54, 182n80; Ōbaku sect, 92; Rinzai, 21; tea associated with, 27, 51; temples, 51, 53, 57, 69. *See also* Buddhist monks
Zhang Guo-an, 23

# About the Author

William Wayne Farris is professor emeritus of Japanese history at the University of Hawai'i at Mānoa, where he served for twelve years as the Sen Sōshitsu XV Distinguished Chair of Traditional Japanese History and Culture and taught a course on "The Way of Tea" annually. He also held the Lindsay Young Chair in History at the University of Tennessee at Knoxville and was visiting professor at Harvard University in 1998. Farris is the author of numerous articles and seven books, including *Heavenly Warriors: The Evolution of Japan's Military, 500–1300; Sacred Texts and Buried Treasures: Essays in the Historical Archaeology of Ancient Japan;* and *Japan's Medieval Population: Famine, Fertility, and Warfare in a Transformative Age.*